Everyday Spelling

Authors

James Beers • Ronald L. Cramer • W. Dorsey Hammond

Scott Foresman
Addison Wesley

Editorial Offices: Glenview, Illinois • New York, New York
Sales Offices: Reading, Massachusetts • Duluth, Georgia • Glenview, Illinois
Carrollton, Texas • Menlo Park, California

1-800-552-2259
http://www.sf.aw.com

■ ACKNOWLEDGMENTS

TEXT

p. 133: Untitled haiku by Kikaku from *Word Works* by Cathryn Berger Kaye; illustrated by Martha Weston. Copyright © 1985 by the Yolla Bolly Press. By permission of Little, Brown and Company.

ILLUSTRATIONS

p. 11: Seitu Hayden; **pp. 12-33:** Susan Swan; **pp. 12, 38, 64, 81, 90, 116, 129, 132:** Marla Rubin; **pp. 23, 24, 28:** Linda Kinnamon; **pp. 38-59:** Mary Grand Pre; **pp. 40, 44, 47, 48, 51, 52, 55, 56, 59, 60:** John Manders; **pp. 60-62, 86-89, 112-115, 138-141, 164, 165, 167, 184-187, 189, 195, 197, 199, 201, 205-207, 210-213, 215, 219-221, 225-227:** Beth Herman Design Associates; **pp. 60, 63, 88, 210, 211:** Slug Signorino; **pp. 61, 89:** Patti Green; **pp. 62, 113, 166:** Fran Lee; **pp. 63, 86, 87, 89, 115, 139, 165, 204, 207-209, 220, 221:** B.J. Johnson; **pp. 64-85:** Kathy Petrauskas; **pp. 66, 69, 70, 73, 74, 77, 78, 81, 82, 85, 86:** Margaret Spengler; **pp. 87, 114, 140, 141, 202, 203:** Donna Reynolds; **pp. 90-111:** Marianne Wallace; **pp. 113-115, 139, 167, 184, 185, 222, 223:** Linda Kelen; **pp. 115, 138, 166, 192, 193, 214:** Carl Kock; **pp. 116-137:** Darryl Goudreau; **pp. 140, 193, 195, 209, 224, 225, 227:** Tom Herzberg; **pp. 142-163:** Linda Helton; **pp. 148, 152, 156, 164:** Joe Rogers; **pp. 189, 200, 201:** Leon Bishop; **pp. 190, 191:** David Uhl; **pp. 194, 195, 198, 199, 216, 217, 228, 229:** Jacque Auger; **p. 297:** Don Wilson; **p. 304:** Christine Mortensen

PHOTOGRAPHS

pp. 16, 42, 84, 162: Marilyn Meyerhofer; **pp. 77, 246B, 261T:** Hans Reinhard/Bruce Coleman, Inc.; **p. 77TR:** Michael & Patricia Fogden; **p. 77BL:** Belinda Wright/DRK Photo; **p. 109L:** Grant Heilman/Grant Heilman Photography, Inc.; **p. 109R:** Jane Grushow/Grant Heilman Photography, Inc.; **p. 131:** Connie Geocaris/Tony Stone Images; **pp. 153, 271T:** Lawrence Migdale; **pp. 167T, 256B:** Don & Pat Valenti; **p. 167C:** "Life on the Prairie, The Buffalo Hunt" by Currier & Ives, 1862, Library of Congress; **p. 182TR:** Steve McCutcheon; **p. 182TL:** Fred Bruemmer; **p. 182BL:** Francois Gohier/Photo Researchers; **pp. 182BR, 183TL, 183TC, 183TR:** Johnny Johnson/ AlaskaStock; **p. 183BR:** Chris Arend/AlaskaStock; **p. 201:** Dwight R. Kuhn/DRK Photo; **p. 203:** Library of Congress; **p. 210:** Vic Thomasson/Tony Stone Images; **p. 211:** Chris Haigh/Tony Stone Images; **p. 211:** Editions Houvet; **p. 213:** R. Maiman/Sygma; **p. 225L:** Ray Amati/Focus On Sports; **p. 225CL:** Focus on Sports; **p. 225CR:** J. Daniel/ ALLSPORT USA; **p. 225R:** Stephen Dunn/ALLSPORT USA; **p. 247:** Dr. Ralph Buchbaum/ Department of Zoology, University of Chicago; **pp. 248T, 274:** Courtesy NASA; **p. 250T:** James L. Ballard/ScottForesman & Co.; **p. 252T:** Robert B. Tolchin/ScottForesman & Co.; **p. 252B:** Michael & Patricia Fogden; **p. 256T:** J. Pickerell/The Image Works; **p. 260:** Miami Seaquarium; **p. 266B:** Cy Furlan; **p. 268B:** J.C. Stevenson/ Animals, Animals; **p. 270T:** Florida Division of Tourism; **p. 270B:** GemMedia; **p. 273T:** Belinda Wright/DRK Photo; **p. 277:** M. Austerman/Animals, Animals; **p. 278:** Raymond Schoder; **p. 280B:** Arizona State Museum, University of Arizona, Helga Teiwes, Photographer; **p. 284T:** Jurg Klages; **p. 284B:** Camermann International, Ltd.; **p. 286B:** Lorraine Rorke/The Image Works; **p. 287:** Geo. T. Hillman; **p. 290T:** Daniel L. Feicht; **p. 291:** Carmen Morrison/ScottForesman & Co.; **p. 292:** American Museum of Natural History, New York; **p. 293:** Michael Heron; **p. 299TL:** Robert Frerck/Odyssey/ Chicago; **p. 299TR:** Robert Frerck/Odyssey/Chicago; **p. 299B:** Marianne von Meerwall; **p. 300:** Dr. E. R. Degginger; **p. 306:** Jeff Foott; **p. 308:** The Kobal Collection.

Unless otherwise acknowledged all photographs are the property of Addison Wesley Educational Publishers, Inc.

■ CONTENTS

UNIT 3

■ CONTENTS

UNIT 5

■ CONTENTS

Cross-Curricular Lessons

■ CONTENTS

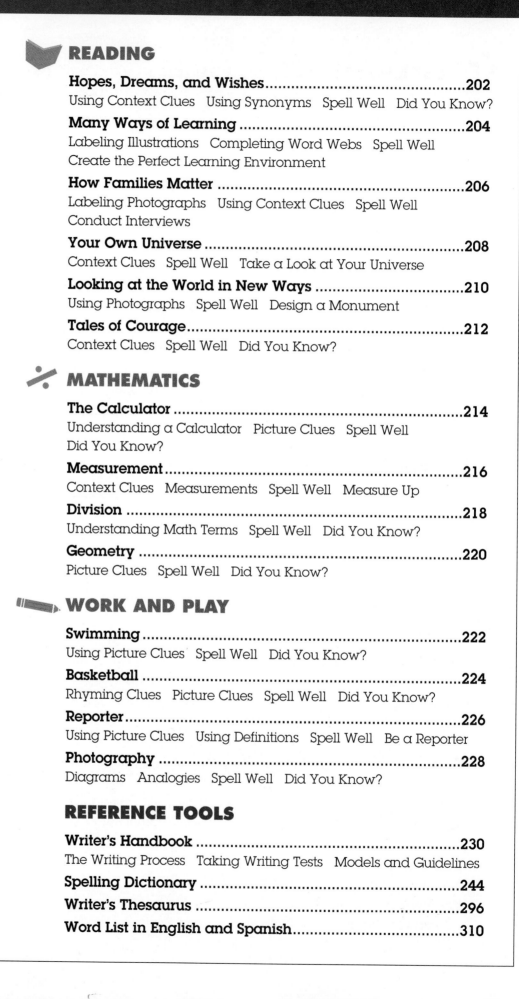

▼ READING

⠶ MATHEMATICS

✏ WORK AND PLAY

REFERENCE TOOLS

✳ FREQUENTLY MISSPELLED WORDS!

Lots of words on your spelling lists are marked with green asterisks ✳. These are the words that are misspelled the most by students your age.*

Pay special attention to these frequently misspelled words as you read, write, and practice your spelling words.

too	again	everybody	happened	would
a lot	they	off	heard	are
because	Christmas	through	I	enough
there	went	friends	whole	except
their	until	swimming	didn't	friend's
favorite	outside	want	first	probably
that's	said	you're	watch	upon
our	we're	another	people	vacation
when	sometimes	beautiful	always	brought
really	different	I'm	took	house
they're	where	let's	everyone	might
were	caught	then	morning	myself
it's	chocolate	believe	school	basketball
know	friend	cousin	something	hospital
finally	into	especially	with	opened

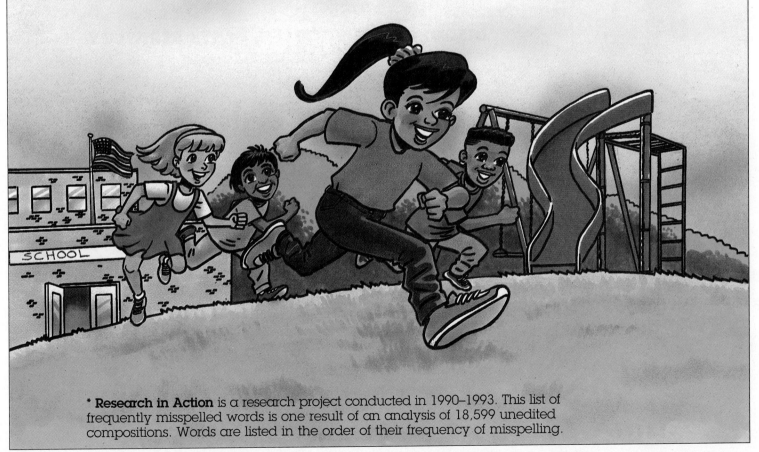

* **Research in Action** is a research project conducted in 1990–1993. This list of frequently misspelled words is one result of an analysis of 18,599 unedited compositions. Words are listed in the order of their frequency of misspelling.

Steps for Spelling Problem Parts

REVIEW THE STEPS FOR SPELLING   Here is the spelling strategy you should use when learning to spell a new word. Read it over step by step.

1. **Look** at the word. **Say** it and listen to the sounds.
2. **Spell** the word aloud.
3. **Think** about the spelling. Do you notice anything special that you need to remember?
4. **Picture** the word with your eyes shut.
5. **Look** at the word and **write** it.
6. **Cover** the word and picture it. **Write** the word again and **check** its spelling.

DISCOVER THE PROBLEM PARTS STRATEGY   If some words are still hard for you to spell, try the Problem-Parts Strategy.

Think.

Which part of the word gives me a problem?

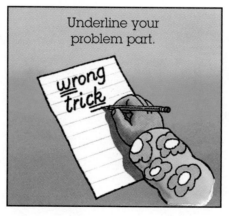

Underline your problem part.

wrong
trick

Picture the word.

"wrong" "trick"

TRY IT OUT   Practice the Problem-Parts Strategy with words that gave another writer problems. Follow the directions on the next page.

Work with a partner or group. Find the four misspelled words in the description below and write them correctly. Underline the part of each word that gave the writer problems. Use a dictionary if you need help.

1. _____

2. _____

3. _____

4. _____

I was down on one nee picking up mangoes when the squrrel saw me. It wiggled its nose at me. I bit into a mango and lafed. It turned and ran throgh the trees.

Now practice the Problem-Parts Strategy with your own personal words.

List four words you sometimes misspell. Be sure to spell them right. Underline the part of each word that gives you a problem. Picture the words. Focus on the problem parts.

Have a partner quiz you on your words. Then check the results. How did you do?

5. _____

6. _____

7. _____

8. _____

LOOK AHEAD Look at the next five lessons. Write four list words that look hard to spell. Underline the part of each word that you think might give you a problem.

1. _____

2. _____

3. _____

4. _____

Words with thr, scr, str, squ

Some words have consonant blends with three letters pronounced together: **thr**oat, **scr**een, **str**eet, **squ**are.

■ **STUDY** Say each word. Then read the sentence.

1. *throat* Her cold began with a sore **throat.**
2. *through* �֍ People strolled **through** the park.
3. *screen* The window **screen** has a hole.
4. *scratch* An itch will make you **scratch.**
5. *scream* Did I hear a **scream** for help?
6. *strange* The man wore a **strange** pink hat.
7. *street* She drove the car down the **street.**
8. *strike* The pitcher threw another **strike.**
9. *square* The bowl fits in a **square** box.
10. *squeeze* You **squeeze** a lemon to get juice.

11. *threat* All nations fear the **threat** of war.
12. *thrown* That ball was **thrown** too hard.
13. *thrill* Skydiving gives me a **thrill.**
14. *scrub* Use this pad to **scrub** the pan.
15. *skyscraper* The **skyscraper** has 62 stories.
16. *strawberry* The red fruit is a **strawberry.**
17. *strength* Gymnasts have great **strength.**
18. *squeal* I heard the **squeal** of a pig.
19. *squirm* The puppies **squirm** in their box.
20. *squirt* Water will **squirt** through a tube.

■ **PRACTICE** Sort the list words by writing
- five words with **thr**
- five words with **scr**
- five words with **str**
- five words with **squ**

■ **WRITE** Choose two sentences to write a riddle.

CHALLENGE!

arthritis
description
instrument
astronaut
squeezable

1.
2.
3.
4.
5.
6.
7.
8.
9.
10.
11.
12.
13.
14.
15.
16.
17.
18.
19.
20.

�֍ **WATCH OUT FOR FREQUENTLY MISSPELLED WORDS!**

DRAW YOUR OWN CONCLUSION   Write the list word
that matches each clue.

1. You might clear this when you begin to speak.
2. A piglet might make this sound if you chase it.
3. Never cross this without looking both ways.
4. A box often has this shape.
5. This is a delicious red fruit.
6. You do this to a match when starting a fire.
7. This is what you might call something odd or unusual.
8. An elevator is necessary if you live or work here.
9. Using soap, do this to get a floor clean.
10. If you have poison ivy, you'll feel the urge to do this.
11. Do this loudly if you are frightened and need help.
12. Sledding down a steep hill may give you this.
13. Little children may do this if they have to sit quietly.
14. An elephant might do this with the water in its trunk.
15. This keeps bugs from flying through an open window.

WORDS IN CONTEXT   Write the list word that is missing
from each animal's statement.

16. **Monkey:** I swing ___ the jungle from tree to tree.
17. **Zebra:** I was ___ to the ground by a lion, but I escaped.
18. **Gorilla:** I have the ___ of ten men.
19. **Boa:** I wrap around my prey and ___ very hard.
20. **Mongoose:** I'm so quick, even a cobra is no ___ to me.

1. _____
2. _____
3. _____
4. _____
5. _____
6. _____
7. _____
8. _____
9. _____
10. _____
11. _____
12. _____
13. _____
14. _____
15. _____
16. _____
17. _____
18. _____
19. _____
20. _____

Using the Problem Parts Strategy

Study the problem parts of words. Write two list words that
are hard for you. Underline the part of each word that gives
you the problem, and study it extra hard.

21. _____   22. _____

Take a Hint
This sentence may help you
remember the difference between
throne and *thrown.*
The king was thr**own**
from the throne he once **own**ed.

≡	Make a capital.
/	Make a small letter.
∧	Add something.
ℯ	Take out something.
⊙	Add a period.
¶	New paragraph

PROOFREAD A SIGN Find the misspelled word in the photograph below. Why do you think it is misspelled in this particular way? Write the word correctly.

PROOFREADING TIP
When you create a sign, watch for spelling errors. You don't want people laughing at your message.

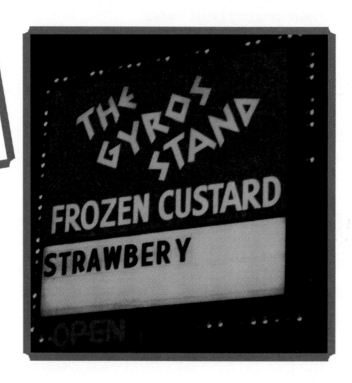

Word List

scrub	thrill
street	screen
threat	strength
skyscraper	squeeze
thrown	through
square	strike
scream	squirm
throat	scratch
strawberry	strange
squeal	squirt

Personal Words

1. _____

2. _____

CREATE A SIGN
Now it's your turn to try to get a message across. Imagine you own The Gyros Stand and want customers to try your exciting new dessert. Use list words to create a sign with a short, sweet message.

Review

PUZZLE IT OUT We are a collection of plans you will use for learning to spell new words. What are we? When you write the boxed words that match the definitions, the answer to the riddle will appear in the box.

throat	strange
through	street
screen	strike
scratch	square
scream	squeeze

1. rub to get rid of an itch
2. odd; unusual
3. a passage from the mouth to the stomach or the lungs
4. having four equal sides and four right angles
5. a road
6. press hard
7. from one side to the other
8. set on fire by rubbing
9. a loud cry for help
10. a glass surface on which information or pictures appear

1. ___ ___ ___ ___ ___ ___ ___
2. ___ ___ ___ ___ ___ ___
3. ___ ___ ___ ___ ___ ___
4. ___ ___ ___ ___ ___
5. ___ ___ ___ ___ ___ ___
6. ___ ___ ___ ___ ___
7. ___ ___ ___ ___ ___ ___
8. ___ ___ ___ ___ ___ ___
9. ___ ___ ___ ___ ___ ___
10. ___ ___ ___ ___ ___ ___

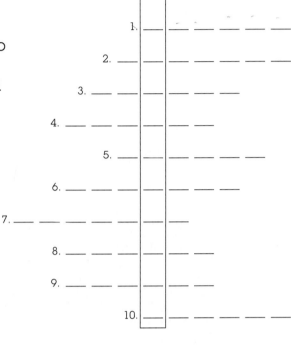

Using a *Dictionary*

GUIDE WORDS At the top of each dictionary page are two guide words in dark type. The first guide word is the first entry word on the page. The second guide word is the last entry word on the page. If the word you are looking for falls alphabetically between these two words, you are on the right page.

When words begin with the same letter, you must look at the second letter, third letter, and so on to alphabetize them. For example, look on page 284 in your Spelling Dictionary. Notice that the word *screen* follows *scream* and comes before *scrub*.

thought	
threat	
throat	
thrifty	
thresh	
spray	
squirt	
squeeze	
squeak	
squash	

Now, look at each pair of guide words to the right. Which of the boxed words fall between these guide words alphabetically? Write those words.

thrash/thrill	**square/squirm**
_____	_____
_____	_____
_____	_____

Words with kn, gn, wr, mb

SPELLING FOCUS

The underlined consonants stand for only one sound:
knot, si**gn**, **wr**ist, cli**mb**.

■ **STUDY** Say each word. Then read the sentence.

1. knot — I have a **knot** in my shoelace.
2. unknown — The book's author is **unknown.**
3. know ✳ — I **know** the answer to the question.
4. sign — The **sign** said "Big Sale Today."
5. design — The wallpaper has a striped **design.**
6. writing — She is **writing** a book about cats.
7. wrist — I wear a watch on my **wrist.**
8. wreck — The car is a rusty old **wreck.**
9. climb — Cats sometimes **climb** trees.
10. thumb — The baby sucks his **thumb.**

11. knit — Who **knit** that pretty sweater?
12. knob — The **knob** fell off the door.
13. kneel — My knees hurt when I **kneel.**
14. assign — She will **assign** homework later.
15. wreath — He hung a **wreath** on the door.
16. wrench — Use a **wrench** to tighten the bolts.
17. wren — A **wren** is a small, brown bird.
18. limb — A tree **limb** fell to the ground.
19. comb — I need to **comb** my hair.
20. lamb — Watch that frisky little **lamb.**

1.
2.
3.
4.
5.
6.
7.
8.
9.
10.
11.
12.
13.
14.
15.
16.
17.
18.
19.
20.

■ **PRACTICE** Sort the words by writing
- six words with **kn**
- six words with **wr**
- three words with **gn**
- five words with **mb**

■ **WRITE** Choose two sentences to include in
a paragraph.

CHALLENGE!

bologna
lasagna
align
cologne
wrestler

✳ **WATCH OUT FOR FREQUENTLY MISSPELLED WORDS!**

RHYME TIME   Write the list word that rhymes with each word below.

1. teeth
2. snow
3. biting
4. hum
5. rim
6. bench
7. list
8. clam
9. roam
10. peel
11. when
12. deck

DEFINING WORDS   Write the list word that means the same as the underlined words.

13. The explorers traveled to a land that was <u>not familiar</u> to them.
14. I like to <u>make clothing by looping yarn</u>.
15. We had to <u>use hands and feet to go over</u> the fence to get into our yard.
16. Please <u>tie the ends of</u> this rope tightly.
17. I caught my coat on the <u>handle on a door</u>.

1. _____
2. _____
3. _____
4. _____
5. _____
6. _____
7. _____
8. _____
9. _____
10. _____
11. _____
12. _____
13. _____
14. _____
15. _____
16. _____
17. _____

Seeing Meaning Connections

Write the list word that completes each sentence. The underlined word is a clue.

18. The <u>designer</u> will _____ a dress for her.

19. Please don't _____ another <u>assignment</u>.

20. Write the list word that both of the words you wrote above are related to: _____.

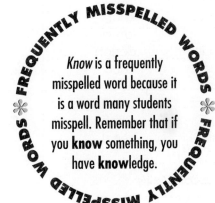

Know is a frequently misspelled word because it is a word many students misspell. Remember that if you **know** something, you have **know**ledge.

≡	Make a capital.
/	Make a small letter.
∧	Add something.
℮	Take out something.
⊙	Add a period.
¶	New paragraph

PROOFREAD A NOTE Read the thank-you note that Pat wrote her aunt. Find three misspelled words and three capitalization errors. Write them correctly.

PROOFREADING TIP

Pat is guilty of three "Capital Crimes"—mistakes with capital letters. Did you find them? If not, check the beginnings of sentences, the names of people, and the opening and closing of her note.

October 10, 20__

Dear aunt Sally,

Thank you for the sweater. I love the desine, especially the lamb on the pocket. did you knitt it yourself? I no I will wear it a lot.

love,

Pat

ANSWER THE NOTE Imagine that you are Pat's aunt. Answer the note above. Use some of your spelling words and personal words in your reply.

Word List

wrist	wreath
know	assign
thumb	knot
sign	lamb
unknown	design
wreck	knob
limb	wren
wrench	writing
knit	climb
comb	kneel

Personal Words

1. _____

2. _____

_____

_____

_____

_____

_____

_____

_____

Review

WORD ASSOCIATIONS Write the boxed word that you would associate with each situation described below.

1. a motorist stopping at an intersection
2. bystanders observing the scene of an automobile accident
3. a child making a birthday party list
4. a girl spotting her friend across a crowded room of strangers
5. a team of explorers hiking across a mountain range
6. a Boy Scout tying two pieces of rope together
7. a mother pulling her young son's hand from his mouth to keep him from sucking
8. astronauts exploring a strange planet
9. a jeweler measuring a customer for a new watch
10. an architect creating a floor plan for a new house

| knot |
| unknown |
| know |
| sign |
| design |
| writing |
| wrist |
| wreck |
| climb |
| thumb |

1. _____
2. _____
3. _____
4. _____
5. _____
6. _____
7. _____
8. _____
9. _____
10. _____

Word *Study*

HINK-PINKS Have you ever played the rhyming game called *Hink-Pink?* Now is your chance. First, you read a question. Then, you answer it with two rhyming words. Here's an example:

Q: What do you call damage done to a pack of playing cards?

A: a deck wreck

Now try to answer the questions below. Hint: One of the words is always a list word.

1. **Q:** What do you call an excellent drawing?

   A: a _____ _____

2. **Q:** What do you call a thin leg?

   A: a _____ _____

3. **Q:** What would you call a fastening made with rope that is lying on a heated stove?

   A: a _____ _____

Consonant Sounds /k/ and /f/

SPELLING FOCUS

Usually the sound /k/ is spelled **c, k,** or **ck: care, brake, track.** The sound /f/ can be spelled **ff, gh,** or **ph: stiff, laughed, photo.**

■ **STUDY** Say each word. Then read the sentence.

1. care   Parents **care** about their children.
2. because ✳   I fell asleep **because** I was tired.
3. brake   You use the **brake** to stop a car.
4. track   Runners often use this **track.**
5. pocket   Put the quarter in your **pocket.**
6. stiff   The leather boots are new and **stiff.**
7. enough ✳   Have you had **enough** to eat?
8. laughed   The audience **laughed** at the jokes.
9. photo   He took a **photo** of his family.
10. alphabet   The **alphabet** has 26 letters.

11. cover   Use a quilt to **cover** the bed.
12. record   I found an old phonograph **record.**
13. Kansas   **Kansas** is a state in the Midwest.
14. snack   An apple is my after-school **snack.**
15. attack   The enemy will **attack** at dawn.
16. muffin   She bought a blueberry **muffin.**
17. giraffe   A **giraffe** has a long neck.
18. rough   The road is **rough** and rocky.
19. dolphin   A **dolphin** is not a fish.
20. elephant   He rode on the big, gray **elephant.**

■ **PRACTICE** Sort the words by writing

- four words with **c**
- two words with **k**
- four words with **ck**
- four words with **ph**
- three words with **ff**
- three words with **gh**

■ **WRITE** Choose ten words to write in sentences.

CHALLENGE!

cuckoo clock
freckles
sheriff
autograph
headphones

1.
2.
3.
4.
5.
6.
7.
8.
9.
10.
11.
12.
13.
14.
15.
16.
17.
18.
19.
20.

✳ **WATCH OUT FOR FREQUENTLY MISSPELLED WORDS!**

POETRY IN MOTION   Complete the poem by writing list words.

Sitting by the TV eating a (1).
Watching a train smoking down the (2).
Energetic engineer pulling on the (3).
The gear is (4), so it doesn't take.
I (5) at his antics, sure enough.
Stopping that train was going to be (6).
Cow on the track without a (7).
Train finally stopped without a second to spare.

CLASSIFYING   Write the list word that fits in each group.

8. snapshot, picture, ___
9. Iowa, Nebraska, ___
10. pouch, clothes, ___
11. tape, CD, ___
12. letters, *a* to *z*, ___

13. set upon, fight, ___
14. roll, cupcake, ___
15. since, on account of, ___
16. plenty, full, ___

WHO AM I?   Write the list word naming each speaker.

17. "I love to swim and dive. I'm a _____."

18. "My sore throats are endless. I'm a _____."

19. "I fill my trunk with water. I'm an _____."

1. _____
2. _____
3. _____
4. _____
5. _____
6. _____
7. _____
8. _____
9. _____
10. _____
11. _____
12. _____
13. _____
14. _____
15. _____
16. _____

STRATEGIC SPELLING

Seeing Meaning Connections

recover
discover
coverlet

20. Write a list word that is related to the words in the box. _____

Write words from the box that fit the definitions.

Take a Hint
Is it *break* or *brake*?
Just remember to
brake at the lake.

21. to find out

22. to get back a lost item

23. a covering for a bed

_____ _____ _____

23

☰	Make a capital.
/	Make a small letter.
∧	Add something.
℮	Take out something.
⊙	Add a period.
¶	New paragraph

PROOFREAD A SELF-PORTRAIT

Julio's class is drawing self-portraits and writing short descriptions of them. Find four misspelled words and one incorrect pronoun in Julio's writing. Correct them.

PROOFREADING TIP

Would you ever say "Me go to the zoo"? Well, that's really what Julio did in his sentence. Drop "Mom and ..." to be sure the personal pronoun is correct.

Here I am at the zoo. Mom and me go a lot beacause we like the dofin show. An elefant and a girafe are behind me.

CREATE A SELF-PORTRAIT
Draw a picture of yourself doing something you enjoy. Write a description of where you are and what you're doing. Use some of your list words.

Word List

care	stiff
snack	dolphin
attack	rough
cover	elephant
pocket	muffin
Kansas	enough
brake	photo
track	laughed
because	alphabet
record	giraffe

Personal Words

1. _____

2. _____

Review

DEFINING WORDS   Write the boxed word that means the same as the underlined words.

care	stiff
because	enough
brake	laughed
track	photo
pocket	alphabet

1. After the accident, my neck was <u>hard to move</u>.
2. At age three, Mira can already recite the <u>letters of the English language arranged in their usual order</u>.
3. Many people <u>are concerned</u> about the future of our planet.
4. Do we have <u>a sufficient amount of</u> food for the party?
5. I went shopping <u>for the reason that</u> I needed new shoes.
6. My best <u>picture made with a camera</u> is the one of my dog.
7. I ran five laps around the race <u>course for running or racing</u>.
8. Della slammed on her <u>device for slowing down the motion of wheels or vehicles</u> pedal to avoid hitting the ducks.
9. Mr. Carter <u>made happy sounds and movements</u> when we explained what had happened on our way to school.
10. I put my lunch money into my <u>pouch sewed into clothing for carrying small items</u>, and now my money is gone.

1. _____
2. _____
3. _____
4. _____
5. _____
6. _____
7. _____
8. _____
9. _____
10. _____

Multicultural Connection

LANGUAGES   Julio saw these signs at the zoo. Each animal is named in English, Swahili, Spanish, and Japanese.

English	giraffe	lion	crocodile	spider
Swahili	twiga	simba dume	mamba	buibui
Spanish	jirafa	león	cocodrilo	araña
Japanese	kirin	raion	wani	kumo

Complete each sentence. Write the missing word in a different language each time.

1. Count the eight legs of the ___.
2. Can you tell the difference between an alligator and a ___?
3. The roaring of the ___ scared the baby.
4. The ___ can reach the treetop.

1. _____
2. _____
3. _____
4. _____

Adding -ed and -ing

SPELLING FOCUS

Here are four things to remember when adding **-ed** and **-ing**:

- Some base words are not changed: **happen, happened, happening.**
- In words that end with **consonant-e**, the **e** is dropped: **dance, danced, dancing.**
- In words that end in **y**, the **y** is changed to **i** when adding **-ed**, but kept when adding **-ing**: **study, studied, studying.**
- In one-syllable words that end with **consonant-vowel-consonant**, the final consonant is doubled: **stop, stopped, stopping.**

■ **STUDY** Look at each base word. Notice whether the spelling changes when **-ed** and **-ing** are added.

happen	1. *happened* ✳	2. *happening*
open	3. *opened* ✳	4. *opening*
dance	5. *danced*	6. *dancing*
study	7. *studied*	8. *studying*
stop	9. *stopped*	10. *stopping*

chase	11. *chased*	12. *chasing*
worry	13. *worried*	14. *worrying*
dry	15. *dried*	16. *drying*
rob	17. *robbed*	18. *robbing*
slip	19. *slipped*	20. *slipping*

■ **PRACTICE** Sort the list words by writing
- four words in which the final **e** is dropped
- seven words with no spelling changes
- six words in which the final consonant is doubled
- three words in which **y** changes to **i**

■ **WRITE** Choose three words to write a paragraph about a memorable event in your school or community.

1. _____
2. _____
3. _____
4. _____
5. _____
6. _____
7. _____
8. _____
9. _____
10. _____
11. _____
12. _____
13. _____
14. _____
15. _____
16. _____
17. _____
18. _____
19. _____
20. _____

CHALLENGE!

skied	skiing
argued	arguing
occurred	occurring

✳ **WATCH OUT FOR FREQUENTLY MISSPELLED WORDS!**

CONTEXT CLUES Use list words to finish the sentences.

1. The party-goers were _____ to the music.

2. The thief _____ the man of his wallet.

3. Is she _____ her present now?

4. Dad was very _____ when I was late.

5. The clown _____ on a banana peel.

6. We washed and _____ the dishes.

7. I was _____ for my history test all night.

8. The lion _____ the monkey up a tree.

9. What _____ to the injured ape?

10. We _____ talking to listen to the bird sing.

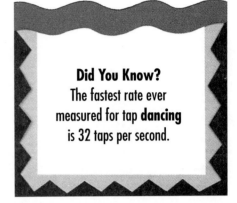

Did You Know?
The fastest rate ever measured for tap **dancing** is 32 taps per second.

ADD ENDINGS Complete each group with a list word.

11. worry, worried, ___
12. rob, robbed, ___
13. slip, slipped, ___
14. chase, chased, ___
15. open, ___, opening

16. study, ___, studying
17. dry, dried, ___
18. happen, happened, ___
19. stop, stopped, ___
20. dance, ___, dancing

11. _____
12. _____
13. _____
14. _____
15. _____
16. _____
17. _____
18. _____
19. _____
20. _____

STRATEGIC SPELLING

Building New Words

Use the rules you learned to complete the chart.

Base word	Add -ed	Add -ing
21. scrub	_____	_____
22. cause	_____	_____
23. cry	_____	_____

27

≡	Make a capital.
/	Make a small letter.
∧	Add something.
ℓ	Take out something.
⊙	Add a period.
¶	New paragraph

PROOFREAD A BLURB A **blurb** is a short, favorable description written on the jacket of a book or CD. The blurbs below were written about the book *Night of the Twisters.* Find four misspellings and two handwriting errors and write them correctly.

PROOFREADING TIP
Jodie knows how to spell the words, but her handwriting looks as though she doesn't. Not closing letters like **d** and **o** will really frustrate your reader.

"From the moment I opend this book I never stopt reading it!" – Jodie

"Frightening things kept hapeneng. I woried about Dan and Art." – Dana

WRITE A BLURB Write blurbs about two of the following: a favorite book, an enjoyable movie, or a good compact disc or tape. Try to use your list words.

Word List

opened	opening
happened	happening
chased	chasing
danced	dancing
worried	worrying
studied	studying
dried	drying
stopped	stopping
slipped	slipping
robbed	robbing

Personal Words

1. _____

2. _____

Review

WORDS IN CONTEXT Write the boxed words to complete Terry's story about a strange happening at a carnival.

happened	happening
opened	opening
danced	dancing
studied	studying
stopped	stopping

A strange event (1) on the night the carnival (2). After Darren and I bought our tickets, we couldn't help (3) to admire the bright lights, rides, exhibits, and games. Teenagers were (4) to rock music pouring from huge speakers. Children were eating the usual carnival treats. Suddenly, the carnival lights dimmed, the music (5), and the rides slowly came to a halt. "What's (6)?" Darren asked. I (7) his face and could see he was worried. "Look there!" a man shouted as he pointed at the sky. Darren and I peered upward through the (8) between two booths and saw a huge metallic object in the sky. We were (9) its unusual shape and lights that (10) in rhythmic patterns when the object took a sharp turn, shot upward, and disappeared. Then the lights shone brightly again, rides restarted, and everything was just as it had been before, except for one thing—the crowd had just witnessed the most amazing carnival act ever!

1. _____
2. _____
3. _____
4. _____
5. _____
6. _____
7. _____
8. _____
9. _____
10. _____

Using a *Thesaurus*

ENTRY WORDS Imagine that you are writing about the time you attended a game played by your favorite sports team. Your team won, and the game was the best you had ever seen. You want to express the excitement you felt, but the word *exciting* does not seem quite strong enough to you. You can look up *exciting* in a thesaurus to find synonyms, or other words with similar meanings.

A thesaurus provides a list of **entry words** in alphabetical order. The Writer's Thesaurus on pages 296–309 of your spelling book shows the entry words in larger type at the left of the columns.

Find the entry word *worried* in your Writer's Thesaurus. Notice the three synonyms for *worried*. Write the synonyms.

1. _____
2. _____
3. _____

Adding -er and -est

Here are four things to remember when adding **-er** and **-est:**

- Some base words do not change: **small, smaller, smallest.**
- In words that end with **consonant-e,** the **e** is dropped: **large, larger, largest.**
- In words that end in **y,** the **y** is changed to **i:** **happy, happier, happiest.**
- In one-syllable words that end with **consonant-vowel-consonant,** the final consonant is doubled: **hot, hotter, hottest.**

■ **STUDY** Look at each base word. Notice whether the spelling changes when **-er** and **-est** are added.

small	1. smaller	2. smallest
large	3. larger	4. largest
happy	5. happier	6. happiest
hot	7. hotter	8. hottest
sad	9. sadder	10. saddest

deep	11. deeper	12. deepest
close	13. closer	14. closest
scary	15. scarier	16. scariest
funny	17. funnier	18. funniest
fat	19. fatter	20. fattest

■ **PRACTICE** Sort the list words by writing
- four words in which the final **e** is dropped
- four words in which the base word does not change
- six words in which the final consonant is doubled
- six words in which **y** changes to **i**

■ **WRITE** Choose ten words to write in sentences.

1. _____
2. _____
3. _____
4. _____
5. _____
6. _____
7. _____
8. _____
9. _____
10. _____
11. _____
12. _____
13. _____
14. _____
15. _____
16. _____
17. _____
18. _____
19. _____
20. _____

CHALLENGE!

weirder	weirdest
gentler	gentlest
angrier	angriest

30

ANTONYM ALERT Write the list word that means the opposite of each word below.

1. larger
2. skinnier
3. smallest
4. colder
5. shallower
6. saddest
7. coldest
8. largest
9. farther
10. happiest
11. skinniest

HAPPY ENDINGS Add an ending to each word in parentheses to form a list word that completes the sentence.

12. (scary) This is the _____ thriller I've read.

13. (funny) Your skit was _____ than mine.

14. (deep) Pike Lake is the _____ lake around.

15. (close) Morgan is my very _____ friend.

16. (sad) Was *Sounder* _____ than *Old Yeller*?

17. (large) A gorilla is _____ than a gibbon.

18. (funny) Ribsy is the _____ dog of all time.

19. (happy) Al was _____ with the gift than Di.

20. (scary) I think snakes are _____ than lizards.

1. _____
2. _____
3. _____
4. _____
5. _____
6. _____
7. _____
8. _____
9. _____
10. _____
11. _____

STRATEGIC SPELLING

Building New Words

> **Did You Know?**
> The **smallest** horse ever recorded, Little Pumpkin, stood only fourteen inches tall and weighed twenty pounds.

Write the words that complete the chart. Remember what you learned.

Base word	Add -er	Add -est
21. busy	_____	_____
22. big	_____	_____
23. strange	_____	_____

≡	Make a capital.
/	Make a small letter.
∧	Add something.
℮	Take out something.
⊙	Add a period.
¶	New paragraph

PROOFREAD AN INVITATION Lizzy is having a party. Below is the first draft of her invitation. Correct three misspellings and one incorrect comparison.

PROOFREADING TIP

Remember to use **-er** when you compare two things. Use **-est** when comparing more than two.

COME TO A HALLOWEEN PARTY!!!

PLACE: Lizzy's house —202 Lake St.

TIME: October 31 from 3:00 to 6:00 P.M.

Wear your scaryest costume. We'll carve the fatest pumpkins and drink the hotest cider. I'll be the sadder ghoul in town unless you come!

WRITE AN INVITATION What kind of party would you like to give? Write an invitation for it. Use list words.

Word List

deeper	deepest
smaller	smallest
closer	closest
larger	largest
scarier	scariest
funnier	funniest
happier	happiest
hotter	hottest
fatter	fattest
sadder	saddest

Personal Words

1. _____

2. _____

COME TO A _____ PARTY!!!

PLACE: _____

TIME: _____

_____

_____

_____

_____

Review

ANALOGIES Write the boxed word that completes each analogy.

smaller	smallest
larger	largest
happier	happiest
hotter	hottest
sadder	saddest

1. Saddest is to unhappiest as merriest is to ___.
2. Smaller is to littler as bigger is to ___.
3. Loudest is to quietest as biggest is to ___.
4. Tightest is to loosest as happiest is to ___.
5. Nicest is to meanest as coldest is to ___.
6. Quicker is to faster as cheerier is to ___
7. Closer is to nearer as littler is to ___.
8. Thinner is to slimmer as unhappier is to ___.
9. Smallest is to biggest as littlest is to ___.
10. Cooler is to colder as warmer is to ___.

1. _____
2. _____
3. _____
4. _____
5. _____

6. _____
7. _____
8. _____
9. _____
10. _____

Word *Study*

EXAGGERATION Liz read a book in which a character "had eyes as large and brown as a coconut." She liked this exaggerated wording and was eager to try it out herself. Exaggeration is often used to emphasize, amuse, or surprise.

Liz practiced using exaggeration in her diary but left a few words out. Choose list words to finish the sentences.

October 31 My party was the (1) I've ever given— spilling over into five states. People came in costumes that were (2) than a barrel of comedians. One tiny kid dressed as a peanut and was (3) than one too! We drank cocoa that was (4) than an oven, and we ate so much that we felt (5) than an overweight elephant. Then we told stories that were (6) than a haunted hotel. It was the (7) time of my life!

1. _____
2. _____
3. _____
4. _____
5. _____
6. _____
7. _____

Review

Lesson 1: Words with thr, scr, str, squ

Lesson 2: Words with kn, gn, wr, mb

Lesson 3: Consonant Sounds /k/ and /f/

Lesson 4: Adding -ed and -ing

Lesson 5: Adding -er and -est

REVIEW WORD LIST

1. scratch	11. street	21. unknown	31. care	41. track
2. scream	12. thrill	22. wreath	32. cover	42. danced
3. screen	13. through	23. wreck	33. dolphin	43. dried
4. scrub	14. assign	24. wren	34. elephant	44. opening
5. skyscraper	15. climb	25. wrench	35. enough	45. stopping
6. square	16. design	26. writing	36. Kansas	46. studying
7. squeal	17. kneel	27. alphabet	37. photo	47. worried
8. squeeze	18. knit	28. attack	38. pocket	48. worrying
9. squirt	19. know	29. because	39. rough	49. scariest
10. strawberry	20. sign	30. brake	40. snack	50. smallest

BAKERY SPECIALS

Use the list words to complete the newspaper advertisement.

strawberry
scratch
snack
worrying
alphabet

1. _____

2. _____

3. _____

4. _____

5. _____

BELLA'S BAKERY

Every batch is made from (1).

SPECIALS OF THE WEEK:

Monday Fruit pies on sale today! Try (2) or apple.

Tuesday Stop (3) about your next party. Let Bella bake the cake.

Wednesday Children love chewing an initial with our (4) cookies.

Thursday Choose Bella's oatmeal bars for your after-school (5).

BICYCLES

get out and have fun

Where do you usually ride your bike? Do you ride all

_____ town or just on the _____ you

live on? Do you _____ hills or bounce along on

_____ trails? Maybe your town has a racing

_____. No matter where you ride, you should

remember these two tips. ❶ Always wear a helmet. ❷ Keep your bike

in good repair, especially the _____ system. Good

brakes make _____ safe. Take good

_____ of your bike, and it will take good care of you.

Bret writes articles about outdoor activities for the class news bulletin. Use each list word once to complete this article.

stopping   care   rough   brake   track   through   street   climb

Fairy Tales

Lindy doesn't like fairy tales, but she had to read one. Use the list words to complete her book review.

know	1. _____
scrub	2. _____
scariest	3. _____
danced	4. _____
wren	5. _____
scream	6. _____
kneel	7. _____
because	8. _____
knit	9. _____

The Sweetest Princess
A Book Review by Lindy Grach

This is another one of those stories about a sweet princess and the (1) old queen you could ever imagine. Every day, the princess has to (2) the hard marble floor until it shines. Not a day goes by that the queen doesn't (3) at the princess for some little thing, and the queen demands that the princess curtsey and (4) before her friends. The queen wants the princess to marry a neighboring king (5) he is rich. You probably (6) who the princess wants to marry. Right! A poor young man she (7) with at the fair. The only surprise in the book is that there is no fairy godmother, just a troll who asks the princess to (8) him a sweater from her golden hair. In return, he turns the queen into a (9), and the princess locks her safely in a bird cage. The princess marries the young man, and lives . . . well, you know the rest.

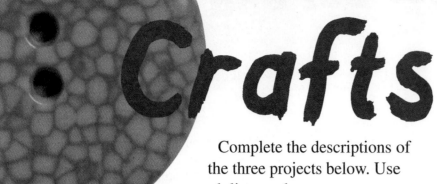

Crafts

Complete the descriptions of the three projects below. Use each list word once.

I. Make an outline picture of a city in winter. Cut squares and rectangles out of newspapers and make a (1) and other such buildings. Glue the buildings along the bottom of a piece of black construction paper. For snow, fill a spray bottle with water and white paint and (2) your paper. Then, (3) your name to your artwork.

II. Shape grapevines into a ring to make a festive (4) for your front door. Decorate it with bunches of (5) flowers.

III. Make a picture frame in the shape of a (6). Collect buttons of all sizes and colors. Make sure there are (7) buttons to cover the frame. Arrange them in an interesting (8) and then glue them on the frame.

sign
dried
design
square
squirt
skyscraper
wreath
enough

1. _____
2. _____
3. _____
4. _____
5. _____
6. _____
7. _____
8. _____

Pairing Things and Places

Write the list word that relates to each shape.

1. _____
2. _____
3. _____
4. _____
5. _____

Kansas   pocket   dolphin   wrench   elephant

1   2   3   4   5

WATER PARK

Complete the announcement below.
Use each list word once.

opening
squeal
cover
thrill
assign
worried
photo

1. _____
2. _____
3. _____
4. _____
5. _____
6. _____
7. _____

Hey Scouts!

Troop #116 is going to the grand (1) of Rocky Valley Water Park on Saturday, August 10. Imagine us as we holler and (2), sliding down the new water slide! Included will be a souvenir (3) of our group for us to take home. So, get ready for the (4) of your life! If you are (5) about how much the trip will cost, here's some good news. The park will (6) the cost for each scout who has earned a service badge. We plan to (7) seats on the bus, so tell Mr. Sato whom you'd like to sit with.

Science Fiction

Jason's writing group invented two plots for a science-fiction skit. Complete them using each list word once.

squeeze   studying   smallest   screen   writing   attack   wreck   unknown

The skit might be about alien creatures who come to Earth in a battered (1) of a spaceship plastered with bumper stickers.

They have come in the hopes of (2) the human sense of humor.

In one scene, the very (3) alien, measuring 2 feet, 6 inches, says, "Take me to your ladder!"

He uses it to climb up to the TV (4) so he can watch old Marx Brothers reruns.

The skit could be about time travel. Six students (5) into a small time machine and visit the year 2096.

Their Time-Travel Guide tells them that they will go to a distant place, but the exact location is (6).

In one scene, forces on Planet Circon prepare to (7) Mars with high-impact squirt guns.

When the kids return, they begin (8) a tell-all documentary of their amazing adventure.

1. _____
2. _____
3. _____
4. _____
5. _____
6. _____
7. _____
8. _____

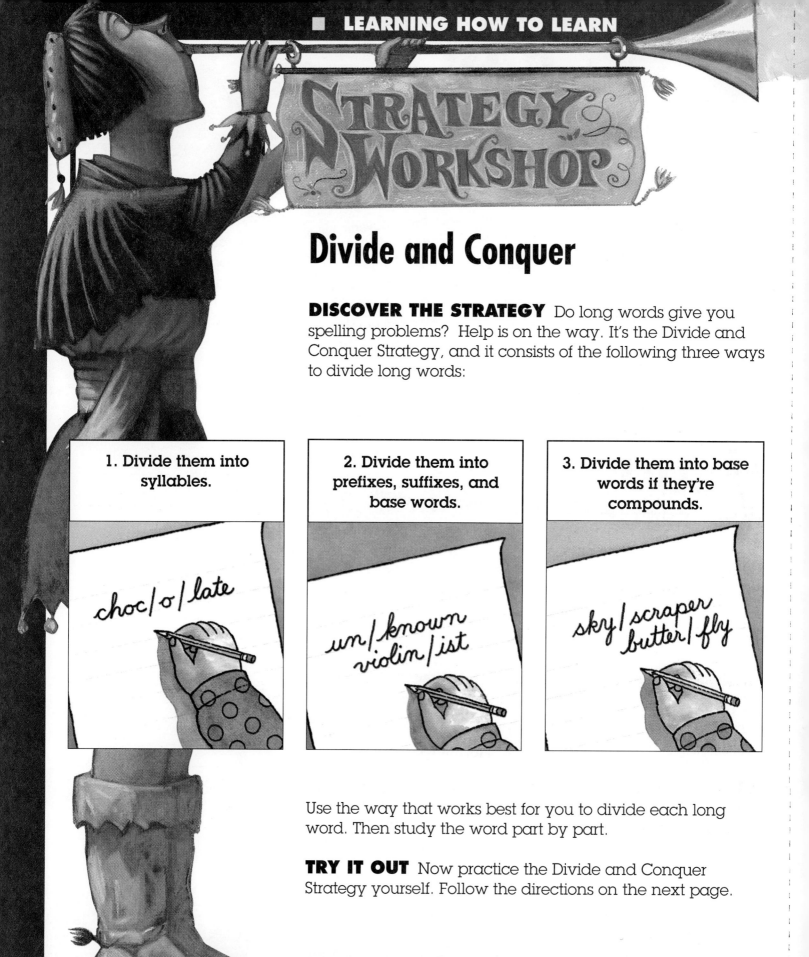

Divide and Conquer

DISCOVER THE STRATEGY Do long words give you spelling problems? Help is on the way. It's the Divide and Conquer Strategy, and it consists of the following three ways to divide long words:

1. Divide them into syllables.	2. Divide them into prefixes, suffixes, and base words.	3. Divide them into base words if they're compounds.
choc/o/late	un/known violin/ist	sky/scraper butter/fly

Use the way that works best for you to divide each long word. Then study the word part by part.

TRY IT OUT Now practice the Divide and Conquer Strategy yourself. Follow the directions on the next page.

1. Divide into Syllables Use this method with any long word. Remember: A syllable is a word or part of a word that you say as a unit: **(choc/o/late)**.

Write *America, alphabet,* and *elephant.* Listen for the syllables and draw lines between them. Check a dictionary for any words you're not sure of.

2. Divide Prefixes, Suffixes, and Base Words This method will help you see the parts of the word with a prefix or suffix. You will also see if adding a suffix changes the spelling of the base word.

Write *unhappy, beautiful,* and *rewrite.* Draw lines between each base word and any prefixes or suffixes.

Look back at the words you wrote. Underline the base word in which the spelling changed when the suffix was added.

3. Divide Compounds This method will show you that two words have been put together with no letters lost.

Write *everybody, afternoon,* and *something.* Draw a line between the two base words in each compound.

LOOK AHEAD Look ahead at the next five lessons. Write two list words that are long and look hard to spell. Divide each word to make it easier to study.

1. _____

2. _____

3. _____

4. _____

5. _____

6. _____

7. _____

8. _____

9. _____

1. _____   2. _____

Words with sh, ch, tch, wh

SPELLING FOCUS

Words can have two or three consonants together that are pronounced as one sound: **puni_sh_**, **_ch_apter**, **wa_tch_**, **_wh_enever**.

■ **STUDY**   Say each word. Then read the sentence.

1. *shown*   That movie was **shown** last week.
2. *short*   My aunt came for a **short** visit.
3. *punish*   They will **punish** the criminal.
4. *March*   Does winter end in **March?**
5. *chapter*   I read a **chapter** of the book.
6. *watch* ✳   Children **watch** the juggler.
7. *kitchen*   Who will clean the **kitchen?**
8. *whatever*   My sister does **whatever** I do.
9. *anywhere*   I can't find my shoe **anywhere.**
10. *whenever* Visit me **whenever** you can.

11. *shelter*   We found **shelter** in a barn.
12. *flashlight* Use a **flashlight** when it is dark.
13. *trash*   Don't put cans in the **trash.**
14. *chocolate* ✳ Dad made a **chocolate** cake.
15. *church*   The **church** bell rings on Sundays.
16. *pitcher*   He is a **pitcher** on a baseball team.
17. *catcher*   He threw the ball to the **catcher.**
18. *wheat*   Is that white or **wheat** bread?
19. *awhile*   Can you stay **awhile?**
20. *somewhere*   She is **somewhere** in the house.

■ **PRACTICE**   Sort the words by writing
- six words with **sh**
- four words with **tch**
- four words with **ch**
- six words with **wh**

■ **WRITE**   Choose two sentences to include in a paragraph.

CHALLENGE!

squash
champion
touchdown
crutches
wherever

✳ **WATCH OUT FOR FREQUENTLY MISSPELLED WORDS!**

1.
2.
3.
4.
5.
6.
7.
8.
9.
10.
11.
12.
13.
14.
15.
16.
17.
18.
19.
20.

BURIED WORDS Each word below is hidden in a list word. Write the list word.

1. eat
2. pitch
3. what
4. pun
5. arch

6. or
7. rash
8. own
9. chap
10. catch

MAKING ASSOCIATIONS Write the list word that you would associate with each word or phrase below.

11. protection ____
12. a short time ____
13. worship ____
14. clock ____
15. dark candy ____
16. cook's place ____

1. _____
2. _____
3. _____
4. _____
5. _____
6. _____
7. _____
8. _____
9. _____
10. _____
11. _____
12. _____
13. _____
14. _____
15. _____
16. _____

STRATEGIC SPELLING

The Divide and Conquer Strategy

Study long words piece by piece. Write *flashlight, somewhere, anywhere, whenever, chocolate,* and *pitcher.* Draw lines to break each word into smaller parts. Study the parts.

17. _____
18. _____
19. _____

20. _____
21. _____
22. _____

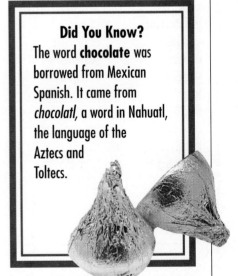

Did You Know?
The word **chocolate** was borrowed from Mexican Spanish. It came from *chocolatl,* a word in Nahuatl, the language of the Aztecs and Toltecs.

≡	Make a capital.
/	Make a small letter.
∧	Add something.
ℯ	Take out something.
⊙	Add a period.
⁋	New paragraph

PROOFREAD A SIGN A spelling error on a large outdoor sign really stands out. Find the two mistakes in the photograph below, and spell the words correctly.

PROOFREADING TIP
Watch out! Don't be caught making a big mistake. Keep a dictionary handy when you write signs.

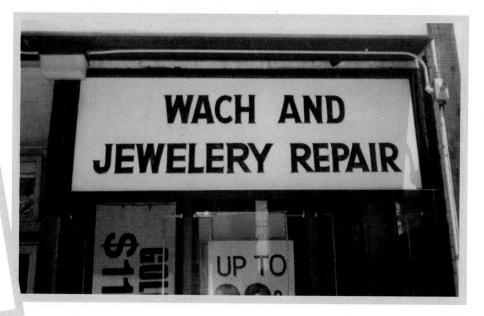

WACH AND JEWELERY REPAIR

CREATE A SIGN Think of one of your favorite stores. Create a sign for an item that is sold there. Try to use words from your spelling list. Check your sign for careless errors.

Word List

watch	somewhere
anywhere	short
punish	catcher
church	whatever
wheat	chapter
kitchen	whenever
shown	shelter
awhile	chocolate
pitcher	trash
flashlight	March

Personal Words

1. _____

2. _____

Review

RHYMES Write the boxed word that rhymes with the underlined word and makes sense in the sentence.

shown	watch
short	kitchen
punish	whatever
March	anywhere
chapter	whenever

1. Meet me at the <u>arch</u> on the last day in ___
2. The pilot was ___ where the plane had <u>flown</u>.
3. The <u>men</u> placed the groceries on the table in the ___.
4. The <u>librarian</u> said, "Choose ___ books you like, but <u>never</u> forget to return them."
5. My time visiting the old frontier <u>fort</u> was much too ___.
6. Did you see a <u>bear</u> ___ in Yellowstone National Park?
7. Just ___ me make this <u>blotch</u> disappear from your shirt sleeve.
8. In this ___, I learned that a bird of prey is called a <u>raptor</u>.
9. That <u>clever</u> comedian has his audiences howling with laughter ___ he performs.
10. Carl's parents won't ___ him for breaking the <u>dish</u> accidentally.

1. _____
2. _____
3. _____
4. _____
5. _____
6. _____
7. _____
8. _____
9. _____
10. _____

Using a *Thesaurus*

PARTS OF AN ENTRY To make your *Writer's Thesaurus* a useful resource, it is important to know all the parts of a thesaurus entry. Study the parts of the entry for the word *show*. Then answer the questions.

1. What part of speech is *show*?
2. Which synonym would you use to tell about a friend who showed you how to make a kite?
3. Which synonym would you use to tell about a boy who showed his kindness by helping an injured child?
4. What cross-references would lead you to other words with related meanings?
5. Write one antonym for *show*.

1. _____   4. _____
2. _____
3. _____   5. _____

Part of speech → | Definition →

Entry Word → **Show** v. to cause something to be seen. *Patrick wants to show his new shoes to Saburo.*

Synonyms → **Display** to show things in a way that gets attention. *Thalia yawned widely, displaying her braces.*
Exhibit to show something publicly. *Tara exhibited her paintings at the arts and crafts show.*
Demonstrate to show something in a way that helps people understand. *A company demonstrated its new milking machine at the county fair.*
Point out to show where something is or to call attention to something. *Manuel pointed out all the sights of Chicago.*
Cross-References → SEE *guide* and *turn up* for related words.

43

Words with Double Consonants

Sometimes double consonants stand for one sound. For example, you hear the sound /f/ one time in **different** and the sound /p/ one time in **supper.**

■ **STUDY**   Say each word. Then read the sentence.

1.	tomorrow	Her birthday is **tomorrow.**
2.	borrow	May I **borrow** your eraser?
3.	different ✳	Painters use **different** brushes.
4.	supper	We eat **supper** at 5:00.
5.	matter	It does not **matter** if he comes.
6.	written	You need **written** permission.
7.	bottle	Recycle that glass **bottle.**
8.	ridden	I have **ridden** a horse many times.
9.	odd	Elves wear **odd** shoes and hats.
10.	bubble	She blew a huge **bubble.**

11.	offer	I will **offer** to help them.
12.	suffer	Some people **suffer** from illness.
13.	slippers	She put on her robe and **slippers.**
14.	grasshopper	The **grasshopper** sat on a leaf.
15.	worry	They **worry** about our safety.
16.	current	We study **current** events.
17.	lettuce	He served a **lettuce** salad.
18.	paddle	Ducks **paddle** with their feet.
19.	shudder	Thunder makes me **shudder.**
20.	hobby	Model making is his **hobby.**

■ **PRACTICE**   First write the words in the list you think are easy to spell. Then write the words you think are difficult. Underline the double consonants in each word.

■ **WRITE**   Choose two sentences to write a rhyme.

1. _____
2. _____
3. _____
4. _____
5. _____
6. _____
7. _____
8. _____
9. _____
10. _____
11. _____
12. _____
13. _____
14. _____
15. _____
16. _____
17. _____
18. _____
19. _____
20. _____

CHALLENGE!

Mississippi
recess
impossible
antennas
allowance

✳ **WATCH OUT FOR FREQUENTLY MISSPELLED WORDS!**

ANTONYM ARGUMENT   Write the list word that is the opposite of the underlined word in each sentence.

1. Mo and Al are as <u>alike</u> as they can be.
2. At <u>breakfast</u> yesterday they didn't even eat.
3. "Why can't I <u>lend</u> your knit hat?" asked Mo.
4. "Because losing hats is a <u>job</u> with you," said Al.
5. "But I like its <u>ancient</u> style," responded Mo.
6. Mo agreed to a <u>spoken</u> contract before wearing the hat.
7. These <u>ordinary</u> fellows enjoy disagreeing.

WORDS IN CONTEXT   Write the list word that completes each sentence.

8. Both of my parents ___ from allergies.
9. Rabbits eat greens such as ___ and spinach.
10. I forgot to do it today, but I will be sure to do it ___.
11. I am learning how to ___ a canoe.
12. After her bath, she put on a robe and ___.
13. What is the ___ with that howling dog?
14. I bought this gum so I could blow a ___.
15. Do you buy apple juice in a can or a ___?
16. I had never ___ on a Ferris wheel before.
17. The ___ jumped from the leaf to the ground.

1. _____
2. _____
3. _____
4. _____
5. _____
6. _____
7. _____
8. _____
9. _____
10. _____
11. _____
12. _____
13. _____
14. _____
15. _____
16. _____
17. _____

STRATEGIC SPELLING

Building New Words

Write *worry, offer,* and *shudder.* Add **-ed** to complete the chart. Remember: Change the **y** to **i** before adding **-ed.**

Base word	Add-ed
18. _____	_____
19. _____	_____
20. _____	_____

FREQUENTLY MISSPELLED WORDS *FREQUENTLY MISSPELLED WORDS*

To spell **different** correctly, be sure to pronounce every syllable: **dif fer ent.**

☰	Make a capital.
/	Make a small letter.
∧	Add something.
ℓ	Take out something.
⊙	Add a period.
¶	New paragraph

PROOFREADING TIP

Lucas is careless with the same word twice. He repeats it in one place and leaves it out in another. These mistakes are easy to catch if you proofread.

PROOFREAD A MESSAGE Lucas read about someone finding an important message in a bottle. He wrote a message of his own. Find four spelling errors and two careless errors and correct them.

Dare to be diffrent!

If you padel your own canoe today, you you may captain the ship tommorow.

If your buble bursts, can blow another one.

WRITE A MESSAGE Pretend you are writing a message for a bottle. Tell someone what you think is important in life. Use list words and personal words.

Word List

different	written
offer	matter
suffer	bottle
slippers	lettuce
supper	ridden
grasshopper	paddle
tomorrow	shudder
worry	odd
current	bubble
borrow	hobby

Personal Words

1. _____

2. _____

Review

CONTEXT CLUES Use the context in each sentence to help you write the correct boxed word.

1. Whenever I ___ something, I try to return it as soon as possible.
2. Have you ___ on the new roller coaster at the amusement park?
3. A soap ___ floated up from the dishwater and hit me right in the eye.
4. What's the ___ with Tony? He seems upset about something.
5. My friend takes a ___ route to school than I do.
6. I thought it was ___ that the store was closed in the middle of the afternoon.
7. I would have ___ you a note, but I couldn't find a pencil.
8. I tipped over a ___ of juice and it spilled on the floor.
9. I'm busy today, but maybe we can go to a movie ___.
10. In our house, we must be ready to sit down for ___ promptly at 6:00.

tomorrow
borrow
different
supper
matter
written
bottle
ridden
odd
bubble

1. _____
2. _____
3. _____
4. _____
5. _____
6. _____
7. _____
8. _____
9. _____
10. _____

Word Study

ACROSTICS An **acrostic** is a way of connecting letters to spell different words, often about a particular subject. To make an acrostic, write a noun across or down the page. Then connect words that describe that noun. Try it with *grasshopper*. Use the words shown and add your own, or make up a new acrostic with a noun of your own.

grasshopper
green
leggy

47

Short e and Long e

SPELLING FOCUS

Short e is often spelled e: w<u>e</u>nt. Long e can be spelled
ea and ey: sp<u>ea</u>k, mon<u>ey</u>.

■ **STUDY** Say each word. Then read the sentence.

1. *them*   Let's share our food with **them.**
2. *went* ✳   Our class **went** to the museum.
3. *fence*   My father put up an iron **fence.**
4. *speak*   Actors must **speak** clearly.
5. *reason*   Dogs have a **reason** for barking.
6. *beat*   Use a whisk to **beat** the eggs.
7. *money*   You need **money** to buy food.
8. *valley*   Cows graze down in the **valley.**
9. *honey*   Bees make **honey.**
10. *monkey*   The **monkey** swung on a vine.

11. *credit*   She bought new clothes on **credit.**
12. *engine*   Can you fix the car **engine?**
13. *contest*   I won a prize in a poetry **contest.**
14. *least*   Which shirt is the **least** expensive?
15. *steal*   Thieves **steal** from others.
16. *treat*   I want to **treat** you to lunch.
17. *season*   Spring is my favorite **season.**
18. *hockey*   Ice **hockey** is popular in Canada.
19. *alley*   The trash cans are in the **alley.**
20. *donkey*   The gray **donkey** brayed loudly.

■ **PRACTICE** Sort the words by writing
▪ seven words with **long e** spelled **ea**
▪ seven words with **long e** spelled **ey**
▪ six words with **short e** spelled **e**

■ **WRITE** Choose two sentences to include in
a paragraph.

1. _____
2. _____
3. _____
4. _____
5. _____
6. _____
7. _____
8. _____
9. _____
10. _____
11. _____
12. _____
13. _____
14. _____
15. _____
16. _____
17. _____
18. _____
19. _____
20. _____

CHALLENGE!

escaped
celery
squeaked
bleachers
jersey

✳ **WATCH OUT FOR FREQUENTLY MISSPELLED WORDS!**

WORDS IN CONTEXT Write the list word that completes each sentence.

1. I can't hear you. Please ___ up.
2. Bees were in the hive making ___.
3. The necklace cost a great deal of ___.
4. Around the yard was a picket ___.
5. She had the most homework and I had the ___.
6. The king gave ___ all silver swords.
7. The child sat upon a long-eared ___.
8. The peasants farmed the fertile ___.
9. The cook ___ the eggs for the omelet.
10. She hid the gold so no one would ___ it.
11. The knight ___ riding off.

DEFINITIONS Answer each question with a list word.

12. Which list word is a sport?
13. What can you use to buy things if you have no cash?
14. What animal chatters and often lives in trees?
15. Which word means to think and understand?
16. Which names a narrow driveway behind a building?
17. What piece of machinery gives a car power?
18. Which word describes what winter is?
19. Which names something special that gives pleasure?

1. _____
2. _____
3. _____
4. _____
5. _____
6. _____
7. _____
8. _____
9. _____
10. _____
11. _____
12. _____
13. _____
14. _____
15. _____
16. _____
17. _____
18. _____
19. _____

STRATEGIC SPELLING

Seeing Meaning Connections

| contestant |
| uncontested |

Write the list word related in spelling and meaning to the boxed words.

20. _____

Complete the sentences using the words in the box.

Mai was a (21) on a new TV quiz show. All of her answers were correct, so her victory was (22) by her opponent.

21. _____   22. _____

Take a Hint
Do you have trouble remembering how to spell **beat** and **beet** ?
This riddle may help:
What do you do when you can't **beat the heat?** Eat a cool treat!

≡	Make a capital.
/	Make a small letter.
∧	Add something.
℮	Take out something.
⊙	Add a period.
¶	New paragraph

PROOFREAD A LETTER Find the four misspelled words in this letter to an advice columnist. Write them correctly and add the two missing punctuation marks.

PROOFREADING TIP
Don't forget what you know about the parts of a letter. What punctuation is needed at the end of the greeting and closing?

May 8, 20__

Dear Ms. Understanding

   Michelle and I have practiced all seson for the dance contist. We whent to the finals last year, but Michelle dropped out at the last second. We didn't speek for weeks! How can I help her?

   Yours truly

   Riana

Word List

credit	reason
speak	valley
alley	money
fence	engine
least	them
hockey	steal
went	monkey
contest	treat
beat	season
honey	donkey

Personal Words

1. _____

2. _____

ANSWER A LETTER Pretend you are Ms. Understanding. Answer Riana's letter. Use spelling words.

_____
_____
_____
_____
_____
_____
_____
_____

Review

CROSSWORD PUZZLE Fill in the crossword puzzle by writing the boxed word that matches each definition.

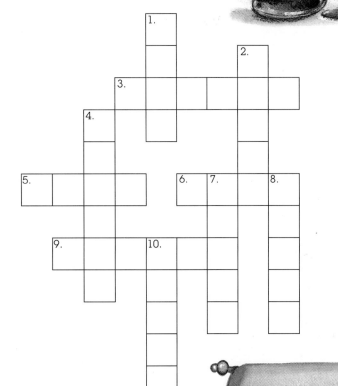

them
went
fence
speak
reason
beat
money
valley
honey
monkey

Across

3. low land between hills or mountains
5. past tense of go
6. the people being spoken about
9. explanation

Down

1. mix by stirring rapidly with a fork or spoon
2. a wall put around a yard
4. a mammal with a long tail; one of the most intelligent animals
7. a golden liquid that bees make out of nectar
8. coins
10. say with words; talk

Multicultural *Connection*

PROVERBS A **proverb** is a short, wise saying. People everywhere use proverbs to pass along common beliefs.

The Chinese proverb **Talk does not cook rice** is much like the English proverb **Actions speak louder than words.**

Write a proverb from the banner that has a similar meaning to these proverbs.

You can lead a horse to water, but you can't make it drink.

In unity there is strength.

Good things come to those who wait.

People from Thailand say:
  1. You don't force a buffalo to eat grass.

The Senegalese say:
  2. To catch a monkey requires patience.

The Iranians say:
  3. One finger cannot lift a pebble.

1. _____

2. _____

3. _____

51

Short Vowels a, i, o, u

Short **a** is usually spelled **a**: b**a**nd. Short **i** is usually spelled **i**: **i**nto. Short **o** is usually **o**: p**o**nd. Short **u** is usually spelled **u**, but it is also often spelled **ou**: tr**ou**ble.

■ **STUDY**   Say each word. Then read the sentence.

1. *band* — Do you like that rock **band?**
2. *cash* — She took the **cash** to the bank.
3. *into* ✳ — Come **into** the kitchen.
4. *river* — The **river** flows down to the sea.
5. *with* ✳ — Let's go **with** the hikers.
6. *pond* — Fish live in this **pond.**
7. *block* — He ran around the **block.**
8. *forgot* — Dad **forgot** to pack my lunch.
9. *trouble* — Does being late **trouble** you?
10. *young* — She is too **young** to see that movie.

11. *January* — A new year begins in **January.**
12. *blanket* — Put the wool **blanket** on the bed.
13. *backpack* — Her **backpack** is full of books.
14. *finger* — He pointed his **finger** at me.
15. *window* — I looked out the **window.**
16. *closet* — Coats hang in the **closet.**
17. *chop* — She will **chop** these carrots.
18. *cousin* ✳ — My aunt's son is my **cousin.**
19. *couple* — He will be gone a **couple** of days.
20. *tough* — An overcooked roast is **tough.**

■ **PRACTICE**   Sort the list words by writing
- five words with **short a** spelled **a**
- five words with **short u** spelled **ou**
- five words with **short o** spelled **o**
- five words with **short i** spelled **i**

■ **WRITE**   Use two sentences in an advertisement.

✳ **WATCH OUT FOR FREQUENTLY MISSPELLED WORDS!**

1.
2.
3.
4.
5.
6.
7.
8.
9.
10.
11.
12.
13.
14.
15.
16.
17.
18.
19.
20.

CHALLENGE!

package
Pilgrims
ignored
o'clock
southern

DEFINITIONS   Write the list word that fits each definition. Use the Spelling Dictionary if you need to.

1. the first month of the year
2. one of the five slender parts on a hand
3. to the inside of
4. water that flows into a lake or ocean
5. a small room for storing clothes or supplies
6. a group of musicians performing together
7. didn't remember
8. money in the form of coins and bills

VOWEL TRADE   Change the vowel in each word to make a list word with the **short o** sound.

9. black   10. chap   11. pend

BASE WORDS   Write the list words that are the base words for the words below.

12. coupled   15. cousins   18. untroubled
13. toughness   16. youngster   19. windowless
14. blanketed   17. backpacking

STRATEGIC SPELLING

Seeing Meaning Connections

withstand
withdraw
withhold

20. Write the list word that is related to the words in the box. _____

Then write the words from the box that fit the definitions.

21. to draw back or draw away _____

22. to refuse to give _____

23. to stand against or resist _____

1. _____
2. _____
3. _____
4. _____
5. _____
6. _____
7. _____
8. _____
9. _____
10. _____
11. _____
12. _____
13. _____
14. _____
15. _____
16. _____
17. _____
18. _____
19. _____

Did You Know?
The word **couple** comes from the Old French word *cople. Cople* came from the Latin word *copula,* meaning "bond." A married couple is thought to be bonded together.

53

	Make a capital.
/	Make a small letter.
∧	Add something.
ℓ	Take out something.
⊙	Add a period.
¶	New paragraph

PROOFREAD A MESSAGE Jane took a message for her cousin, Hiro, from his teacher, Ms. Cortez. Find four spelling errors and one handwriting error.

PROOFREADING TIP
Did Jane write "7279" or "1219"? When you take a phone message, be sure to write the phone number carefully.

You Have a Message!!!

To: _Hiro_   Date: _January 5_

Time: _4_ A.M. (P.M.)   From: _Ms. Cortez_

Phone #: _555-1219_   Taken by: _Jane_

Message

She has the bagpack you left at school. She will drop it off here tomarrow. It's no troble.

WRITE A MESSAGE Read the following telephone message. Write down only the important information.

"Hello, is Jane there? No? Well, this is Hiro, her cousin. I'm calling from a pay phone. Tell her I won't be there until 5:00. I'm at school, looking for my backpack."

Word List

cousin	chop
cash	finger
into	blanket
closet	forgot
with	band
couple	trouble
block	window
January	backpack
river	tough
young	pond

Personal Words

1. _____

2. _____

You Have a Message!!!

To: _____   Date: _____

Time: _4:15_ A.M. (P.M.)   From: _____

Phone #: _____   Taken by: _____

Message

_____

_____

_____

band	pond
cash	block
into	forgot
river	trouble
with	young

Review

CONTEXT CLUES Write the missing boxed words to complete the announcement below.

In case you (1), Fairview's summer festival will be held on July 2–4 at Merritime Park, just one (2) south of Lakeside Road and Briar Street. Here's just a sample of the wonderful entertainment at this year's festival.
- Afternoon and evening performances by the *Romper-Stompers* rock-and-roll (3).
- Lovely boat rides on the (4) that flows (5) our beautiful Lake Opeka.
- A fishing (6) with poles and prizes for (7) children.
- Food and game booths galore!

Bring your friends (8) you.

Admission is $5.00. Bring (9) only please.

Avoid (10) parking by driving directly to Lot 57.

1. _____
2. _____
3. _____
4. _____
5. _____
6. _____
7. _____
8. _____
9. _____
10. _____

Using a *Dictionary*

PRONUNCIATION Dictionaries include a **pronunciation key** on every other page in the book. It helps you pronounce the symbols in the dictionary. It might look like this: ———————→

a	hat	i	ice	u̇	put	ə stands for	
ā	age	o	not	ü	rule	a	in about
ä	far, calm	ō	open	ch	child	e	in taken
âr	care	ȯ	saw	ng	long	i	in pencil
e	let	ô	order	sh	she	o	in lemon
ē	equal	oi	oil	th	thin	u	in circus
ėr	term	ou	out	ᴛʜ	then		
i	it	u	cup	zh	measure		

Each word in the dictionary is followed by its **pronunciation** in parentheses. The entry for the word *window* might look like this: ———————→

→ **win•dow** (win′dō), an opening in an outer wall or roof of a building, or in a vehicle, that lets in air or light. It is usually a wooden or metal frame that surrounds panes of glass or plastic. *n.*

Using the pronunciation key, you see the **i** is pronounced like the **i** in *it*, and the **ow** is pronounced like the **o** in *open*.

The dot between **win** and **dow** tells you that *window* has two syllables. The **accent mark** (′) tells you to say the first syllable in *window* with more force than the second.

Read each pronunciation below. Write the word that each pronunciation stands for. In each two-syllable word, underline the syllable you would say with more force.

1. (tuf)   3. (fər got′)   5. (kuz′n)
2. (kloz′it)   4. (kash)   6. (trub′əl)

1. _____
2. _____
3. _____
4. _____
5. _____
6. _____

Long Vowels a, i, o

SPELLING FOCUS

Long vowels are often spelled with one letter: **station,** **wild.** They can also be spelled **vowel-consonant-e:** **whole, hide.**

■ **STUDY** Say each word. Then read the sentence.

1. station   Visitors arrive at the bus **station.**
2. danger   Dogs can sense **danger.**
3. April   **April** weather is often wet.
4. wild   Lions are **wild** cats.
5. behind   He is **behind** in his work.
6. whole ✳   I could eat that **whole** pie.
7. broke   The cat **broke** the glass vase.
8. drove   Our friends **drove** to Florida.
9. hide   Close your eyes and I'll **hide.**
10. decide   Did you **decide** to join us?

11. vacation ✳   They took a **vacation** by the sea.
12. cable   Wind tore down the power **cable.**
13. bacon   Dad cooked **bacon** and eggs.
14. pint   Will you buy me a **pint** of milk?
15. lion   A male **lion** has a mane.
16. smoke   They saw **smoke** from a campfire.
17. remote   She sailed to a **remote** island.
18. stole   A spy **stole** valuable papers.
19. invite   Let's **invite** them to dinner.
20. arrive   The plane will **arrive** at noon.

■ **PRACTICE** Sort the list words by writing
- six words with **long a**
- eight words with **long i**
- six words with **long o**

■ **WRITE** Choose ten words to write in sentences.

1.
2.
3.
4.
5.
6.
7.
8.
9.
10.
11.
12.
13.
14.
15.
16.
17.
18.
19.
20.

CHALLENGE!

operation
behavior
private
Rhode Island
apologize

✳ **WATCH OUT FOR FREQUENTLY MISSPELLED WORDS!**

COMPARE Write a list word that has the same first letter, last letter, and number of syllables as each word below.

1. lotion
2. beacon
3. stallion
4. Abdul

5. ramble
6. veteran
7. drier
8. divide

9. pant
10. wood
11. beyond
12. inside

VOWEL TRADE Change the vowel in each word to make a list word with the **long o** sound.

13. whale   14. brake   15. drive   16. stale

STRATEGIC SPELLING

Using the Rhyming Helper Strategy

A rhyming helper rhymes with a word and is spelled the same at the end. Write *hide, cable, arrive,* and *smoke.* Write a rhyming helper alongside each word. Underline the matching letters. Be sure your helper is spelled right.

List Word	Rhyming Helper
17.	
18.	
19.	
20.	

1. _____
2. _____
3. _____
4. _____
5. _____
6. _____
7. _____
8. _____
9. _____
10. _____
11. _____
12. _____
13. _____
14. _____
15. _____
16. _____

FREQUENTLY MISSPELLED WORDS ✳ **FREQUENTLY MISSPELLED WORDS** ✳

Can't remember when to use **whole** or **hole?** Remember this: A complete **whole** has a wide w, while **hole** has just an empty middle.

≡	Make a capital.
/	Make a small letter.
∧	Add something.
ℯ	Take out something.
⊙	Add a period.
¶	New paragraph

PROOFREAD A SUMMARY

Shanieka's class enjoyed a documentary film about Africa. Shanieka wrote a summary of what she saw. Correct four misspellings and one run-on sentence.

PROOFREADING TIP

Shanieka forgot this simple rule: To avoid a run-on sentence, use a comma and and.

Africa has deserts, jungles, and large cities. It is a place where willd animals roam and buildings touch the sky. A line roars loudly smock floats from a house. It would be a wonderful place to vacashun.

WRITE A SUMMARY
Think of an interesting film you saw lately. Write a summary of the film. Try to use some of your list words and personal words.

Word List

smoke	broke
cable	station
whole	stole
invite	arrive
April	danger
behind	drove
remote	hide
lion	bacon
vacation	wild
pint	decide

Personal Words

1. _____

2. _____

_____
_____
_____
_____
_____
_____
_____
_____
_____

Review

station	whole
danger	broke
April	drove
wild	hide
behind	decide

ANALOGIES   Write the boxed word that completes each analogy.

1. Rider is to rode as driver is to ___ .
2. Some is to all as part is to ___ .
3. Pardon is to blame as show is to ___ .
4. Ship is to port as bus is to ___ .
5. Study is to examine as determine is to ___ .
6. Wednesday is to Thursday as March is to ___ .
7. Here is to there as front is to ___ .
8. Kind is to cruel as calm is to ___ .
9. Swim is to swam as break is to ___ .
10. Rough is to bumpy as hazard is to ___ .

1. _____
2. _____
3. _____
4. _____
5. _____
6. _____
7. _____
8. _____
9. _____
10. _____

Word Study

IDIOMS   An **idiom** is a word picture that means something more than the words in it would suggest. One idiom has an interesting history.

Long ago in France, the people of Paris did not want Henry IV as their king. Henry decided to make war on them to "teach them a lesson." A wise counselor said to Henry, "If you destroy Paris, you will be king of a dead city. Would you chop off your nose to teach your face a lesson?" Henry spared Paris, became a popular king, and helped coin the idiom **cut off one's nose to spite one's face.**

praise oneself; boast
earn a living
have control over
get excited

Use the phrases in the box to help you write the meaning of each idiom below.

1. bring home the bacon

2. blow one's own horn

3. lose one's head

4. lead by the nose

1. _____
2. _____
3. _____
4. _____

Review

Lesson 7: Words with sh, ch, tch, wh
Lesson 8: Words with Double Consonants
Lesson 9: Short e and Long e

Lesson 10: Short Vowels a, i, o, u
Lesson 11: Long Vowels a, i, o

REVIEW WORD LIST

1. anywhere	11. watch	21. beat	31. couple	41. bacon
2. catcher	12. whatever	22. contest	32. forgot	42. decide
3. chocolate	13. bottle	23. fence	33. into	43. drove
4. church	14. lettuce	24. season	34. river	44. invite
5. flashlight	15. odd	25. speak	35. tough	45. remote
6. kitchen	16. offer	26. them	36. trouble	46. smoke
7. pitcher	17. slippers	27. treat	37. window	47. station
8. shelter	18. supper	28. backpack	38. with	48. stole
9. somewhere	19. tomorrow	29. blanket	39. young	49. vacation
10. trash	20. alley	30. chop	40. April	50. whole

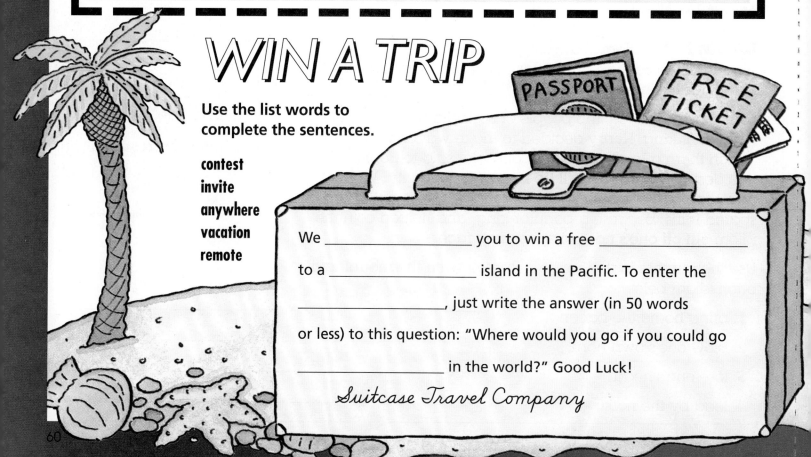

WIN A TRIP

Use the list words to complete the sentences.

contest
invite
anywhere
vacation
remote

We _____ you to win a free _____

to a _____ island in the Pacific. To enter the

_____, just write the answer (in 50 words

or less) to this question: "Where would you go if you could go

_____ in the world?" Good Luck!

Suitcase Travel Company

Nat's Story

couple   young   odd
them   decide   whatever
smoke

Nat is telling the story of *Aladdin* to his classmates, but he has forgotten a few of the details. Use the list words to complete his story.

ALADDIN AND THE MAGIC LAMP

Aladdin is a (1) man who finds a magic lamp. He rubs the lamp and an (2) fellow, called a genie, floats out in a puff of (3). The genie gives Aladdin (4) he asks for. Aladdin falls in love with the Emperor's daughter and must (5) how to win her. The genie helps (6), and the happy (7) are finally married.

1. _____
2. _____
3. _____
4. _____
5. _____
6. _____
7. _____

While in Los Angeles, Aponi sent her friend Ray this postcard. Use the list words to complete her message.

church   river   season
April   speak   station
window

1. _____
2. _____
3. _____
4. _____
5. _____
6. _____
7. _____

POSTCARD FROM L.A.

Dear Ray,

April 3, 19--

We arrived in Los Angeles on the first of (1). Our train pulled into the (2) at midnight. It's supposed to be the rainy (3), but each day is sunny. It's fun to (4) Spanish with my friend Carlota. Today we visited Watts Towers. They look like steeples on a (5). I can see them from my bedroom (6). Tomorrow we will find a (7) and do some fishing. Have fun.

Aponi

Household Chores

Complete the list of weekly chores using each list word once.

forgot with
offer trash
fence slippers
bottle alley

SUNDAY: Feed the fish. You (1) to do this last week.

MONDAY: Clean the hamster's water (2).

TUESDAY: Mend torn bedroom (3).

WEDNESDAY: Help Mom. Remember to (4) to wash dishes.

THURSDAY: Clean the tub (5) scouring powder.

FRIDAY: Take old newspapers and other (6) out to the (7).

SATURDAY: Paint the picket (8).

1. _____
2. _____
3. _____
4. _____
5. _____
6. _____
7. _____
8. _____

The Big Game

pitcher
stole
watch
catcher
beat
drove
into
tough
trouble

Kelly couldn't wait to write in her journal after the championship baseball game. Complete the sentences. Use each list word once.

We played the big game against Evanston yesterday and we _____ them by one run!!! Dad said it was an incredibly exciting game to _____ . It sure was a _____ game to play! We had a lot of _____ getting on base the first five innings, but then Chris got to first and _____ two bases. I _____ home the winning run! Our _____ struck out five of their batters, and our _____ tagged two runners sliding _____ home. The final score was 2-1.

A Family Meal

The local high school is offering a family cooking class. Complete the description using each of the list words once.

— Cooking Together 101 —

If you want to (1) your family to a great time, this course is for you. Come into the (2) and learn how to prepare an entire (3). You will learn how to make a delicious omelet, using eggs, (4) milk, and crisp (5). Children will enjoy making Caesar salad, using fresh garden (6). They will also learn how to (7) and arrange vegetables for a dip. Dessert will be a (8) cake you prepare without flour! Only five families per class.

| supper | chocolate | lettuce | bacon |
| kitchen | treat | chop | whole |

5. _____

2. _____   6. _____

3. _____   7. _____

1. _____   4. _____   8. _____

Camping Out

tomorrow   blanket
somewhere   flashlight
shelter   backpack

Use the list words to complete the conversation.

Place: Middle of the woods
Time: Twilight

1. _____

2. _____

3. _____

4. _____

5. _____

6. _____

Lewis: I'm glad we set up camp here. The trees will give us (1).

Clark: Can you help me get my arm out of this heavy (2)?

Lewis: Gosh, it's cold. I hope you packed an extra (3).

Clark: It may be in here, but I can't see anything, it's so dark. I need the (4).

Lewis: It's here (5), but I can't find it. It's too dark.

Clark: Let's just roll out our sleeping bags. We'll find everything (6), when it's light.

STRATEGY WORKSHOP

Meaning Helpers

DISCOVER THE STRATEGY   Even a short word like *every* can be hard to spell—until you discover where it comes from.

You don't hear the second **e** when you say **every,** but you do hear it when you say **ever. Ever** is a meaning helper for **every** because a sound clue in *ever* helps you spell *every*.

TRY IT OUT   Now try the Meaning Helper Strategy yourself. Follow the directions on the next page.

64

Work with a partner to figure out what sound clue in the top word helps you spell the bottom word. The first two pairs are done for you.

major
majority

The **long a** in **major** reminds me that **majority** is spelled with an **a** too. The sound of **a** is different in the two words, but the spelling of that sound is the same.

act
action

The sound of **t** in **act** reminds me that **action** is spelled with a **t** too.

1. press
   pressure

   _____

   _____

2. fast
   fasten

   _____

   _____

   _____

Write a meaning helper of your own for each word below. Mark the letter or letters that give the sound clue.

3. national

_____

4. election

_____

5. confession

_____

LOOK AHEAD   Look ahead at the next five lessons. Write two list words and the helpers that you could use with this strategy. Underline the letters that give the sound clues.

1. _____

2. _____

_____

_____

Related Words

Related words often have parts that are spelled the same but pronounced differently: **able, ability; sign, signal.**

■ **STUDY**   Say each word. Then read the sentence.

1. *able*   Is anyone **able** to do a flip?
2. *ability*   Gymnasts have that **ability.**
3. *sign*   The **sign** said "Railroad crossing."
4. *signal*   You must **signal** when you turn.
5. *mean*   Did you **mean** to make me laugh?
6. *meant*   I **meant** what I said about leaving.
7. *deal*   Will you **deal** the number cards?
8. *dealt*   She **dealt** six math fact cards.
9. *soft*   We play **soft,** relaxing music.
10. *soften*   Lotion will **soften** dry skin.

11. *relate*   Dogs **relate** well to people.
12. *relative* My cousin is my **relative.**
13. *heal*   A cut will **heal** in time.
14. *health*   Good **health** is important.
15. *meter*   A **meter** is about 39 inches.
16. *metric*   Do you have a **metric** ruler?
17. *compose* He can **compose** piano music.
18. *composition* He wrote a piano **composition.**
19. *crumb*   You ate every **crumb** of the cake!
20. *crumble* Sandcastles quickly **crumble.**

■ **PRACTICE**   Write the related word pairs. For each pair, first write the word that is easier for you to spell. The easier word should help you spell the related word.

■ **WRITE**   Choose two sentences to write an advertisement, slogan, or saying.

1. _____
2. _____
3. _____
4. _____
5. _____
6. _____
7. _____
8. _____
9. _____
10. _____
11. _____
12. _____
13. _____
14. _____
15. _____
16. _____
17. _____
18. _____
19. _____
20. _____

CHALLENGE!

direct	direction
personal	personality
invade	invasion

CONTRASTS   Write list words to complete the sentences.

1. A small bit of water is a drop.
   A small bit of bread is a ___.
2. Lack of rest and a virus may cause sickness.
   Rest and medicine may bring about ___.
3. If you fail at something, you are unable to do it.
   If you finally succeed, you are ___ to do it.
4. A person who helps you is kind.
   A person who harms you is ___.
5. You use your voice in spoken language.
   You use your hands in ___ language.
6. Apples should be sweet and hard.
   Raisins should be sweet and ___.

SYNONYMS   Write the list word that means the same as the underlined word or words. Use the Spelling Dictionary.

7. I wrote a <u>short essay</u> about my dog.
8. Please shuffle and <u>pass out</u> the division facts cards.
9. The <u>arrangement of beats</u> in a polka is very quick.
10. Mozart was able to <u>put together</u> twenty-two operas.
11. She was able to <u>tell</u> the exact details of the event.
12. Is that what you <u>intended</u> to say?
13. The cut will <u>become well</u> in a few days.
14. Dogs have the <u>power</u> to hear high-pitched sounds.
15. A red light is a <u>sign giving notice</u> to stop.
16. The old wall was beginning to <u>decay</u>.
17. Asia uses the <u>measurement-that-counts-by-tens</u> system.

STRATEGIC SPELLING
Using the Meaning Helper Strategy

Take a Hint
Watch out for the mean ant in meant.

18.–20. Meaning helpers can help you spell words. Write the list words related to *soft, relate,* and *deal.* Mark the letters that match the underlined letters in the helpers.

1. _____
2. _____
3. _____
4. _____
5. _____
6. _____
7. _____
8. _____
9. _____
10. _____
11. _____
12. _____
13. _____
14. _____
15. _____
16. _____
17. _____

18. _____
19. _____
20. _____

≡	Make a capital.
/	Make a small letter.
∧	Add something.
ℓ	Take out something.
⊙	Add a period.
⌗	New paragraph

PROOFREAD A PERSUASIVE PARAGRAPH

Min and her friends are trying to convince their principal to allow music during lunch. They are writing their reasons on index cards to be delivered on a cafeteria tray. Correct the five spelling errors Min has made.

PROOFREADING TIP

Min wrote *brother* when she meant to write something else. Always proofread your writing for words that are spelled correctly but have the wrong meaning.

> It is meen not to let us listen to music at lunch. Good music is good for our helth. It helps us relax and be abel to face the next class. We will only play sof music. It won't brother anyone.
>
> Min Yi

WRITE A PERSUASIVE PARAGRAPH

Think of something you would like to persuade someone to do or to allow you to do. Write about it. Try to use list words and a personal word.

Word List

crumb	meter
crumble	metric
sign	deal
signal	dealt
soft	able
soften	ability
mean	relate
meant	relative
heal	compose
health	composition

Personal Words

1. _____

2. _____

Review

CONTEXT CLUES   Mr. Chambers asked his students to list their talents and good qualities. One of his students made the list below. Write the boxed word that completes each sentence in the list.

able	ability
sign	signal
mean	meant
deal	dealt
soft	soften

My Talents and Good Qualities

I have the (1) to make friends easily.
I am never (2) or spiteful towards anyone.
I have (3), shiny hair.
When I am misunderstood, I always take the time to explain what I (4).
I am (5) to do a cartwheel and a handstand.
I have helped my mother the times she has (6) out food at the homeless shelter. I spend a good (7) of my free time doing volunteer work like that.
I obey every street (8) and traffic (9) when riding my bike.
I know how to (10) the hurt feelings of others with kind words.

1. _____
2. _____
3. _____
4. _____
5. _____
6. _____
7. _____
8. _____
9. _____
10. _____

Word *Study*

TRIPLETS   Here's a challenging vocabulary game called **Triplets.** It's a game in which you supply the one word that is often associated with three others. For example, what list word would you associate with the three words below?

post   language   up

The answer is **sign,** as in **signpost, sign language,** and **sign up.** Here are more for you to try. Remember, the missing word always goes in front. Use the boxed words for help.

soft	night	whole	music	dry

1. drink	boiled	soap
2. cleaner	run	ice
3. gown	crawler	mare
4. video	hall	box
5. milk	note	wheat

1. _____
2. _____
3. _____
4. _____
5. _____

Consonant Sounds /j/, /ks/, /kw/

SPELLING FOCUS

The sound /j/ can be spelled **ge** and **dge**: chan**ge**, e**dge**. The sounds /ks/ and /kw/ can be spelled **xc**, **x**, and **qu**: e**xc**ept, e**x**plain, **qu**ick.

■ **STUDY**   Say each word. Then read the sentence.

1. _change_   Leaves **change** colors in autumn.
2. _village_   The country **village** was quiet.
3. _edge_   He stood at the **edge** of the cliff.
4. _except_ ✳   Everyone **except** me went home.
5. _excited_   She is **excited** about the trip.
6. _explain_   Can a book **explain** how to draw?
7. _expect_   Scientists **expect** an earthquake.
8. _Texas_   Alaska is larger than **Texas.**
9. _quick_   We enjoy a **quick** morning jog.
10. _equal_   Give them **equal** shares.

11. _charge_   Plumbers **charge** by the hour.
12. _bridge_   The **bridge** crosses the river.
13. _fudge_   Smooth, rich **fudge** is a treat.
14. _excellent_   The concert was **excellent.**
15. _relax_   Try to **relax** and go to sleep.
16. _extra_   He did the work for **extra** credit.
17. _queen_   That country is ruled by a **queen.**
18. _quart_   This bottle holds one **quart.**
19. _liquid_   Cough syrup is in **liquid** form.
20. _quilt_   The **quilt** is made of cloth scraps.

■ **PRACTICE**   Sort the list words by writing
- eight words with the sound /ks/ spelled **x** or **xc**
- six words with the sound /j/ spelled **ge** or **dge**
- six words with the sound /kw/ spelled **qu**

■ **WRITE**   Use two sentences in a paragraph.

1. _____
2. _____
3. _____
4. _____
5. _____
6. _____
7. _____
8. _____
9. _____
10. _____
11. _____
12. _____
13. _____
14. _____
15. _____
16. _____
17. _____
18. _____
19. _____
20. _____

CHALLENGE!

advantage
pledge
excess
explosion
question

✳ **WATCH OUT FOR FREQUENTLY MISSPELLED WORDS!**

TONGUE TWISTERS   Write the list word that would best complete each tongue twister.

1. Fran fasts Fridays, frequently forgetting flavorful ____.
2. The ____ quickly quashed the quarrelsome quibbler.
3. Tula took trips to ____ a total of ten times.
4. Beside the bay ____, Binita built a bungalow.
5. Running relentlessly, Russ will rarely ____ or rest.
6. Chang's chum can ____ cheese into cheesecake.
7. This Vermont ____ is veiled in the vast verdant valley.
8. Lassie lapped at the ____ in the ladle.
9. Ed is edgy at the ____ of the edifice.

WORD SEARCH   Find the ten list words in the puzzle below. They may be printed down or across. Write them.

```
c e x c e l l e n t e e
h x e q u a r t e a x x
a p e x t r a q u i c k
r e x p l a i n q u e e
g c e x c i t e d e p p
e t q u i l q u i l t x
```

STRATEGIC SPELLING

20. Write a list word that is related in spelling and meaning to the words in the box.

_____

equator
equally
equation

Finish the sentences with words from the box.

21. Divide this _____ among you.

22. (2 x 2) + 3 = 7 is a math _____.

23. The _____ circles the earth.

1. _____
2. _____
3. _____
4. _____
5. _____
6. _____
7. _____
8. _____
9. _____
10. _____
11. _____
12. _____
13. _____
14. _____
15. _____
16. _____
17. _____
18. _____
19. _____

FREQUENTLY MISSPELLED WORDS
FREQUENTLY MISSPELLED WORDS

Because they sound alike, *except* and *accept* are often confused. Make an **ex**tra effort to remember the **ex** in **ex**cept.

Symbol	Meaning
≡	Make a capital.
/	Make a small letter.
∧	Add something.
ℓ	Take out something.
⊙	Add a period.
¶	New paragraph

PROOFREAD A RECIPE Read the following recipe. Correct four misspellings and one place where *good* is used incorrectly.

Here's a recipe for very good fuge.

In a pan over low heat mix together good:

2 tablespoons butter

2 cups marshmallows

2 cups exellent chocolate

2 cups sugar

Pour liqid into pan. Allow to cool. Cut into bars. For a good snack, freeze exdra pieces.

PROOFREADING TIP
Good food, good kids, good home are good ways to use the word good. Good describes a person, place, or thing. Use well to describe how you do something: cook well.

WRITE A RECIPE Think of something you enjoy eating. Find out how to make it and write the recipe. You might want to make the dish and share it with your classmates.

Word List

bridge	expect
queen	quick
except	explain
change	Texas
relax	charge
quart	equal
edge	excellent
extra	quilt
village	excited
liquid	fudge

Personal Words

1. _____

2. _____

Review

CONTEXT CLUES Isabella was in a hurry when she wrote this letter to her friend. Write the missing boxed words to complete her letter.

change	explain
village	expect
edge	Texas
except	quick
excited	equal

Dear Nina,

I'm having a great time on my trip in the Southwest. The weather here has been a nice (1) from the cold weather we left in Minnesota. Temperatures have been in the nineties every day (2) one day when it was over one hundred. Standing on the (3) of the Grand Canyon was awesome! Nothing is (4) to its beauty. I saw a Pueblo Indian (5) where the people live in houses called adobes. When I see you I'll (6) how they are made. Tomorrow we make a (7) stop in Santa Fe where we catch a flight to Dallas, (8). We (9) to see a rodeo there. I'm (10) about that! I'll write again soon.

Love,
Isabella

1. _____
2. _____
3. _____
4. _____
5. _____
6. _____
7. _____
8. _____
9. _____
10. _____

Using a *Dictionary*

FINDING THE RIGHT MEANING If someone said, "I can't eat without my bridge," would you understand the person? *Bridge* has many meanings. If you look it up in a dictionary, you might find these definitions. ⟶

The second definition is followed by a **sentence.** This sentence helps you to see how the word is used.

At the end of the entry, each definition is identified by its **part of speech** (whether noun, verb, adjective, etc.). These are called part-of-speech labels.

Look at the entry for *bridge* again. Write the number of the definition that answers each question below.

1. Which definition of *bridge* fits the meaning, "I can't eat without my bridge"? ___
2. Which definition of *bridge* is part of a stringed instrument? ___
3. Which definition is a verb? ___

bridge (brij), **1** something built over a river, road, or railroad, so that people can get across. **2** to build a bridge over: *The engineers bridged the river.* **3** the false tooth or teeth in a mounting fastened to natural teeth. **4** a thin, arched piece over which the strings of a violin and other stringed instruments are stretched. 1, 3–4 *n.,* 2 *v.,* **bridged, bridg•ing.**

1. _____
2. _____
3. _____

73

Adding -s and -es

SPELLING FOCUS

Add **-s** to words ending in a **vowel** and **y** and to most words: **monkeys, flowers.** Change **y** to **i** and add **-es** to words ending in a **consonant** and **y: supplies.** Add **-es** to words ending in **sh, ch, s, ss, x: beaches.**

■ **STUDY**   See whether **-s** or **-es** is added to each list word.

monkey	1.	monkeys
flower	2.	flowers
friend	3.	friends ✳
supply	4.	supplies
enemy	5.	enemies
eyelash	6.	eyelashes
beach	7.	beaches
circus	8.	circuses
class	9.	classes
tax	10.	taxes

tiger	11.	tigers
holiday	12.	holidays
delay	13.	delays
hobby	14.	hobbies
memory	15.	memories
mystery	16.	mysteries
ash	17.	ashes
bunch	18.	bunches
glass	19.	glasses
suffix	20.	suffixes

■ **PRACTICE**   Sort the words by writing
- five words in which **y** has been changed to **i**
- nine other words in which **-es** is added
- six words in which **-s** is added

■ **WRITE**   Choose ten words to write in sentences.

1. _____
2. _____
3. _____
4. _____
5. _____
6. _____
7. _____
8. _____
9. _____
10. _____
11. _____
12. _____
13. _____
14. _____
15. _____
16. _____
17. _____
18. _____
19. _____
20. _____

CHALLENGE!

accidents
skis
injuries
libraries
couches

✳ **WATCH OUT FOR FREQUENTLY MISSPELLED WORDS!**

MAKING COMPARISONS   Complete each comparison using a list word.

1. The children chattered like ____ in a tree.
2. Her sweet perfume smelled like fresh ____.
3. The long threads were as thin and dark as ____.
4. Their faces were as dry and gray as ____.
5. The play had more problems than one of my math ____.
6. The two round puddles shined like a pair of ____.
7. The floor was as sandy as ten ____.
8. Deep-sea photography is like having two ____ in one.
9. They ate the roast like ferocious, snarling ____.

WORD ASSOCIATIONS   Write the list word that you would associate with the words or phrases below. Use the Spelling Dictionary for help.

10. stops along the way
11. grapes in groups
12. July 4, Thanksgiving
13. groups at war
14. clowns and acrobats
15. money citizens pay
16. sleeping bags, canteens
17. good pals
18. puzzling secrets
19. -ment, -ly, -ous
20. things remembered

STRATEGIC SPELLING

Building New Words

Write the plural form of each word. Remember what you learned.

21. scratch   _____

22. guess   _____

23. play   _____

1. _____
2. _____
3. _____
4. _____
5. _____
6. _____
7. _____
8. _____
9. _____
10. _____
11. _____
12. _____
13. _____
14. _____
15. _____
16. _____
17. _____
18. _____
19. _____
20. _____

Take a Hint
Here's another way to remember when to add **-es:**
Say the plural form aloud. If the ending you hear adds a syllable, the ending you add is **-es:**
watch•es   tax•es

75

≡	Make a capital.
/	Make a small letter.
∧	Add something.
ℯ	Take out something.
⊙	Add a period.
¶	New paragraph

PROOFREAD A DESCRIPTION

Byron wrote this description of reggae, his favorite music. Read what he wrote, and then correct three misspellings and one pronoun error.

PROOFREADING TIP

My friends and I means the same thing as we. Byron should use one or the other, never both.

> In Jamaica, my homeland, my freinds and I we listen to reggae music. Reggae has a strong beat, like rock music. It is not as hard as rock, though, because it was born on island beachs. It is like the blues, but brighter. It has the sound of sunshine and floweres.

Word List

friends	circuses
tigers	glasses
flowers	classes
holidays	taxes
delays	suffixes
monkeys	hobbies
ashes	enemies
eyelashes	memories
beaches	mysteries
bunches	supplies

Personal Words

1. _____

2. _____

WRITE A DESCRIPTION
Write a description of your favorite music. Use list words and personal words.

_____

_____

_____

_____

_____

_____

_____

_____

Review

WORD ASSOCIATIONS Write the boxed word that belongs in each group.

1. leopards, zebras, ___
2. chin, nose, ___
3. students, learning, ___
4. foes, rivals, ___
5. allowances, wages, ___
6. carnivals, fairs, ___
7. buddies, pals, ___
8. sunbathers, lifeguards, ___

CATEGORIZING Write the boxed word that is a name you would give to each group.

9. pens, paper, ruler
10. roses, daisies, petunias

monkeys	eyelashes
flowers	beaches
friends	circuses
supplies	classes
enemies	taxes

1. _____
2. _____
3. _____
4. _____
5. _____
6. _____
7. _____
8. _____
9. _____
10. _____

Multicultural *Connection*

ENVIRONMENT People of all nations use flowers to express feelings and to symbolize love. The flowers pictured below are national flowers. Write the boxed word that matches each description. Use your Spelling Dictionary to look up the flowers you don't know.

1. a small flower that grows in Austria, made famous in a song

2. a bright, showy flower that grows in the tropics of Costa Rica

| lotus |
| almond blossom |
| cattleya orchid |
| edelweiss |

3. a kind of water lily found in India

4. the flower of the almond tree, often seen in Israel

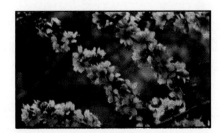

1. _____
2. _____
3. _____
4. _____

Using Just Enough Letters

SPELLING FOCUS

Pronouncing a word correctly and picturing how it looks can help you avoid writing too many letters.

■ **STUDY** Say each word. Then read the sentence.

1. coming — He is **coming** to my house.
2. always ✳ — Jokes **always** make me laugh.
3. almost — Our team **almost** lost the game.
4. didn't ✳ — You **didn't** wash your hands.
5. upon ✳ — Birds perch **upon** the fence.
6. wasn't — Dinner **wasn't** ready yet.
7. until ✳ — Can you wait **until** later?
8. during — Bears hibernate **during** the winter.
9. want ✳ — Do you **want** this sweater?
10. father — The **father** played with his son.

11. hamster — Her pet is a furry, little **hamster.**
12. a lot ✳ — Our family likes to ski **a lot.**
13. ugly — What an **ugly,** old car!
14. washed — The floor needs to be **washed.**
15. hotel — We stayed at a **hotel** in the city.
16. missed — I think we **missed** the bus.
17. eleven — The carton has only **eleven** eggs.
18. crazy — Stunt people do **crazy** things.
19. lazy — She felt **lazy** all day.
20. feelings — I may have hurt his **feelings.**

1. _____
2. _____
3. _____
4. _____
5. _____
6. _____
7. _____
8. _____
9. _____
10. _____
11. _____
12. _____
13. _____
14. _____
15. _____
16. _____
17. _____
18. _____
19. _____
20. _____

■ **PRACTICE** Sort the list words by writing
- the only two-word form
- one word that has three syllables
- three words that have one syllable
- fifteen words that have two syllables

■ **WRITE** Choose two sentences to write a riddle.

CHALLENGE!

delivery
magnet
replied
drowned
mustard

✳ **WATCH OUT FOR FREQUENTLY MISSPELLED WORDS!**

CLASSIFYING   Write the list word that fits in each group.

1. sister, mother, ____
2. ten, ____, twelve
3. inn, resort, ____
4. wish, desire, ____
5. in the course of, at the time, ____
6. foolish, nutty, ____
7. emotions, thoughts, ____
8. careless, not working, ____
9. guinea pig, gerbil, ____

WORDS IN CONTEXT   Write the missing list words to complete the paragraph below.

Once (10) a time, there was a little boy who thought of himself as an (11) duckling, although his grandmother always told him, "You're truly a handsome fellow." She (12) kidding, but the boy (13) believe her. He would frown at himself in a mirror (14) his face would begin to hurt. Other children would ask him to play quite (15), but he would (16) find an excuse to smile and say, "Not today, thanks." One day a little girl invited him to a party. He (17) didn't go, but his grandmother convinced him that the girl would feel hurt if he stayed home. When he finally arrived at the party, his friend rushed to him, saying, "I was worried you weren't (18)! We would have (19) your friendly face!"

STRATEGIC SPELLING
Using the Meaning Helper Strategy

wishy-washy
washable
washcloth

20. Write a list word that is related to the words in the box. _____

Now write words from the box that fit the clues.

21. Use it when you take a bath. _____

22. If asked an opinion, don't be this. _____

23. Your play clothes should definitely be this. _____

1. _____
2. _____
3. _____
4. _____
5. _____
6. _____
7. _____
8. _____
9. _____
10. _____
11. _____
12. _____
13. _____
14. _____
15. _____
16. _____
17. _____
18. _____
19. _____

≡	Make a capital.
/	Make a small letter.
∧	Add something.
ℓ	Take out something.
⊙	Add a period.
¶	New paragraph

PROOFREAD A WARNING One morning the sign below appeared beside the cage of Scratch the Hamster. Correct four misspellings and one place where the punctuation is wrong.

PROOFREADING TIP

Remember that *it's* has an apostrophe because it's short for *it is.* Say *it is* aloud when you write *it's* or *its.* If *it is* doesn't fit, take out the apostrophe.

> ## WARNING
>
> *This hamster is on strick untill it's cage is cleaned. Hamsters have feellings too.*
>
> *Please, allways be aware of its needs!*

WRITE A WARNING Think of a warning sign you would like to write. Try to use your list words and your personal words.

Word List

hamster	eleven
a lot	didn't
ugly	upon
washed	crazy
hotel	lazy
always	wasn't
father	almost
missed	want
until	feelings
coming	during

Personal Words

1. _____

2. _____

Review

ANTONYMS   Complete each phrase by writing the boxed word that means the opposite of the underlined word.

coming	wasn't
always	until
almost	during
didn't	want
upon	father

1. not a <u>mother</u>, but a ___   2. not <u>going</u>, but ___

DRAW YOUR OWN CONCLUSIONS   Write the boxed word that matches each clue.

3. before, ___, after
4. This word is used in the following phrase that starts many fairy tales: *Once ___ a time.*
5. This word means the same as *nearly.*
6. was + not = ___
7. ___, sometimes, never
8. This word means the same as *desire.*
9. did + not = ___
10. This word means "up to the time when."

1. _____
2. _____
3. _____
4. _____
5. _____
6. _____
7. _____
8. _____
9. _____
10. _____

Word *Study*

WORD PLAY   Janna thinks that the word *ugly* looks just like what it means. "It's an ugly word," she says. "Just look at that open, gaping **u** and the hanging **g** and **y**. It just says 'ugly' to me!" Janna drew the word *ugly* to illustrate her point.

Lee had other ideas. "That's a neat drawing, Janna," he said, "but I don't see it that way. I think there's some beauty to be found in the word *ugly.*" Lee drew the word his way.

Now it's your turn. Find a way to make a word look like what it means. You might want to take Lee's approach and do the opposite.

Contractions

SPELLING FOCUS

In contractions, an apostrophe replaces omitted letters. **We will** becomes **we'll**; **I am** becomes **I'm.**

■ **STUDY** A **contraction** is a shortened form of two words. Say each pair of words and then say its contraction.

we + will	=	1. *we'll*
I + am	=	2. *I'm* ✳
I + would	=	3. *I'd*
you + would	=	4. *you'd*
I + will	=	5. *I'll*
we + have	=	6. *we've*
it + is	=	7. *it's* ✳
that + is	=	8. *that's* ✳
what + is	=	9. *what's*
does + not	=	10. *doesn't*

he + will	=	11. *he'll*
she + will	=	12. *she'll*
they + will	=	13. *they'll*
they + would	=	14. *they'd*
he + would	=	15. *he'd*
would + have	=	16. *would've*
could + have	=	17. *could've*
would + not	=	18. *wouldn't*
should + not	=	19. *shouldn't*
let + us	=	20. *let's* ✳

■ **PRACTICE** Sort the list words by writing
- five words ending in **-'ll**
- four words ending in either **-'ve** or **-'m**
- four words ending in **-'d**
- seven words ending either in **-'t** or **-'s**

■ **WRITE** Choose ten words to write in sentences.

1. _____
2. _____
3. _____
4. _____
5. _____
6. _____
7. _____
8. _____
9. _____
10. _____
11. _____
12. _____
13. _____
14. _____
15. _____
16. _____
17. _____
18. _____
19. _____
20. _____

CHALLENGE!

it'll
who'll
might've
mustn't
we'd

✳ **WATCH OUT FOR FREQUENTLY MISSPELLED WORDS!**

HOMOPHONES Write the contraction that sounds just like each word below.

1. heed
2. weave
3. aisle
4. eyed
5. heel
6. lets

CREATING CONTRACTIONS Write the contractions for the words below.

7. they will
8. we will
9. what is
10. they would
11. that is
12. could have
13. would have
14. she will

DON'T QUOTE ME Write list words to help the famous people below complete sentences they might have said.

15. Nathan Hale: "____ sorry I have but one life to give."
16. Rosa Parks: "Would I give up my seat on the bus? I ____!"
17. Mohandas Gandhi: "One should resist oppression, but one ____ use violence to do so."
18. Pablo Picasso: "Painting isn't beautiful, ____ magical."
19. Confucius: "Do to others what ____ want done to you."
20. Amelia Earhart: "Peace comes with courage. It ____ come easily."

STRATEGIC SPELLING
Building New Words

1. _____
2. _____
3. _____
4. _____
5. _____
6. _____
7. _____
8. _____
9. _____
10. _____
11. _____
12. _____
13. _____
14. _____
15. _____
16. _____
17. _____
18. _____
19. _____
20. _____

Add the contraction for *will* to the base words. Remember what you learned.

Base word	Contraction with 'll
21. you	_____
22. who	_____

Did You Know?
I is a capital because in old handwritten manuscripts, a small *i* would often be lost or attached to a neighboring word. A capital *I* helped separate it.

≡	Make a capital.
/	Make a small letter.
∧	Add something.
ℯ	Take out something.
⊙	Add a period.
⁋	New paragraph

PROOFREAD A SIGN The photograph below contains a misspelled word. Since a question is being asked, the punctuation is also incorrect. Write the word correctly as well as the punctuation mark.

PROOFREADING TIP
When making a sign, it's easy to make a mistake in a word. Be sure you carefully proofread your sign before others see it.

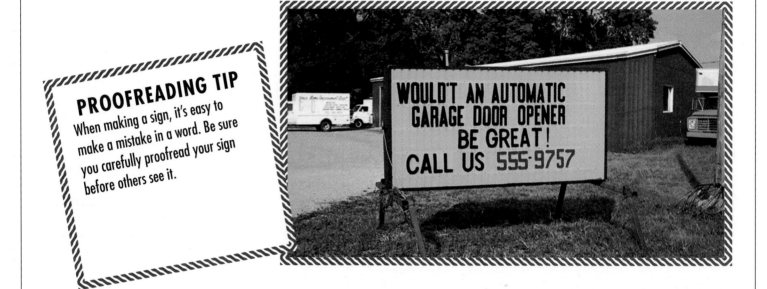

WRITE A SIGN Isn't there a question you'd like to ask in a big way? Use a few list words to create your message.

Word List

I'm	it's
I'd	that's
you'd	what's
they'd	let's
he'd	wouldn't
I'll	shouldn't
he'll	doesn't
she'll	we've
we'll	would've
they'll	could've

Personal Words

1. _____

2. _____

Review

CONTEXT CLUES   Write the missing boxed words to complete the paragraph below.

we'll	we've
I'm	it's
I'd	that's
you'd	what's
I'll	doesn't

(1) convinced that my dog Rusty is the world's naughtiest dog! That (2) mean I don't love him. After all, (3) been great pals ever since he was a pup, and (4) always be the best of friends. But (5) rather he didn't get into so much mischief! (6) never forget the time he saw the kid across the street with a big ice cream cone. There isn't any treat that Rusty loves more than ice cream, (7) for sure! Well, he ran lickety-split toward that kid, jumped all over him, and started licking his cone. Then there was the time that Rusty jumped into the bathtub when Dad was giving my younger brother Joel a bath. I bet (8) have laughed like I did though if you saw how Dad couldn't get ahold of Rusty. What a mess! You never know (9) going to happen next with Rusty around, but you can bet (10) going to be BIG TROUBLE!

1. _____
2. _____
3. _____
4. _____
5. _____
6. _____
7. _____
8. _____
9. _____
10. _____

Word *Study*

PYRAMID SENTENCES   **Pyramid sentences** start with one word, the subject, and get longer and longer. Each word that is added must begin with the same letter. Arranged one atop the other, the sentences look like a pyramid. Here's an example:

Subject word: *she'll*

She'll sing.

She'll sing songs.

She'll sing six songs.

Shelly says she'll sing six silly songs.

Now you try writing your own pyramid sentences. Begin with one of these words: *They'll, I'm, It's, He'd,* or *We'll.*

_____

_____

_____

_____

Review

Lesson 13: Related Words
Lesson 14: Consonant Sounds /j/, /ks/, /kw/

Lesson 15: Adding -s and -es
Lesson 16: Using Just Enough Letters
Lesson 17: Contractions

REVIEW WORD LIST

1. ability	11. soft	21. quart	31. friends	41. missed
2. able	12. change	22. quick	32. glasses	42. want
3. compose	13. charge	23. quilt	33. holidays	43. washed
4. composition	14. edge	24. relax	34. memories	44. didn't
5. crumb	15. excellent	25. Texas	35. a lot	45. doesn't
6. heal	16. excited	26. village	36. always	46. I'm
7. health	17. explain	27. beaches	37. eleven	47. it's
8. meter	18. extra	28. bunches	38. father	48. let's
9. relative	19. fudge	29. classes	39. feelings	49. shouldn't
10. signal	20. liquid	30. flowers	40. lazy	50. we'll

R℞ for Good Health

excellent   lazy   we'll   heal   charge   health

The students in health class put together the rules below. Supply the missing words and see how the rules apply to you.

1. _____
2. _____
3. _____
4. _____
5. _____
6. _____

Take (1) of your own life. Eat sensibly! Exercise!

To maintain good (2), always get plenty of rest.

Don't be (3)! Get out and do things!

Exercise is an (4) way to reduce stress.

If a sore doesn't (5), see your doctor.

If we follow these simple rules, (6) all stay healthy.

Daily Record
Mon, May 7

5:30	(1) _____ up and dressed.
5:40	Breakfast: two (2) _____ of orange juice. 7-grain cereal, and ½ (3) _____ of 2% milk
6:30	30 sit-ups
7:00	My (4) _____ comes in and says, "Son, (5) _____ talk."
7:05	I tell him I'm not (6) _____ to take the time.
7:30	I run 5 miles, worrying about hurting Dad's (7) _____.
8:30	Home to change clothes for school.
9:00	Take a shortcut that (8) _____ go anywhere.
10:00	I'm so late for school, I've missed two (9) _____! Tomorrow will be better.

N'Jabi decided to keep a record of his daily routine. Complete the entry for Monday, May 7.

quart   glasses   father
able   feelings   classes
I'm   doesn't   let's

1. _____
2. _____
3. _____
4. _____
5. _____
6. _____
7. _____
8. _____
9. _____

GOOD SPORTS

Use the words below to complete each person's statement.

1. _____
2. _____
3. _____
4. _____

signal
missed
beaches
always

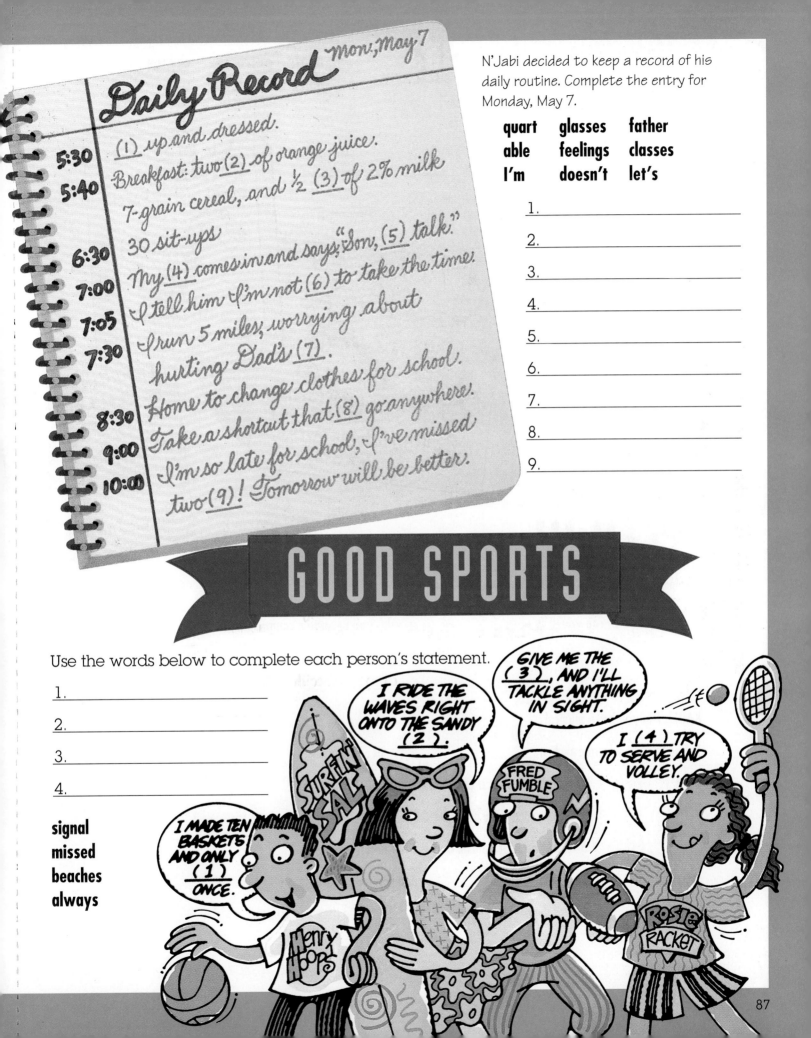

I MADE TEN BASKETS AND ONLY (1) _____ ONCE.

I RIDE THE WAVES RIGHT ONTO THE SANDY (2) _____.

GIVE ME THE (3) _____, AND I'LL TACKLE ANYTHING IN SIGHT.

I (4) _____ TRY TO SERVE AND VOLLEY.

SURFIN' SAL
FRED FUMBLE
Henry Hoops
ROSIE RACKET

Off the Shelf

a lot   extra   change

quick   shouldn't   want

The items below are missing words.
Complete each item with a list word.

1. _____
2. _____
3. _____
4. _____

5. _____
6. _____

WHEAT CRUNCHIES
Breakfast of Eaters

with (5) helpings of honey clusters

the ROACHES SING the BEETLES

"I liked it (3)."
— Paula McCartney

"You'll (4) to hear more!"
— Ringlet Starr

SLICK SHOES
"If you want to be (1), wear Slick. They'll (2) the way you run... for the better!"

MY FLIGHTY LIFE
by Carl Canary

"You (6) miss this one!"

Interview

Karli loves music and wondered what it would be like to discuss it with a famous composer. She wrote this imaginary interview with J. S. Bach.

KARLI: Mr. Bach, can you _____ **why you became a composer?**

J. S.: Yes. I _____ want to do anything in my life

but _____ music.

KARLI: Did you have musical _____ **at a young age?**

J. S.: I believe so. I wrote my first _____ as a young man.

didn't
meter
ability
compose
excited
it's
explain
soft
composition

KARLI: What was it about music that _____ **you?**

J. S.: Everything! The notes, the _____ , the harmonies!

KARLI: You write music that is loud and triumphant

or _____ **and romantic. Which do you prefer?**

J. S.: I think _____ all a challenge. Music is my life.

88

Visiting the Lone Star State

Rafael gave a talk to his class about a place that is very important to him. Use the list words to complete his sentences.

- EL PASO
- PECOS
- SOCORRO

holidays   friends   relative   Texas
eleven   memories   village

I love the state of _____ .

I have wonderful _____ of El Paso. I spend all my school _____ there.

My good _____ Juana and Paul live in Pecos.

I have _____ cousins who live in the small _____ of Socorro.

I am the only _____ who doesn't live in this state.

School Fund-Raiser

Martin Luther King, Jr. School is having its annual fund-raiser. Use the list words to finish the posters.

fudge   washed   liquid
quilt   bunches   edge
flowers   crumb   relax

1. _____
2. _____
3. _____
4. _____
5. _____
6. _____
7. _____
8. _____
9. _____

Raffle Tickets
TAKE A CHANCE ON THIS BEAUTIFUL HANDMADE (1). NOTICE THE SCALLOP ALONG EACH (2).

Fresh garden (5)
Daisies, Roses, Snapdragons, and more!! Buy two (6) in a big bouquet, get one free! Hurry while the supply lasts!!

QUENCH YOUR THIRST
25¢ each
Sodas, apple juice, and other (9) refreshments. Straw free.

Homemade Chocolate (3) for sale here. You'll gobble up every (4)! Fifty cents apiece

CAR WASH #2.50
We'll have it (7) in 5 minutes. You just sit back and (8).

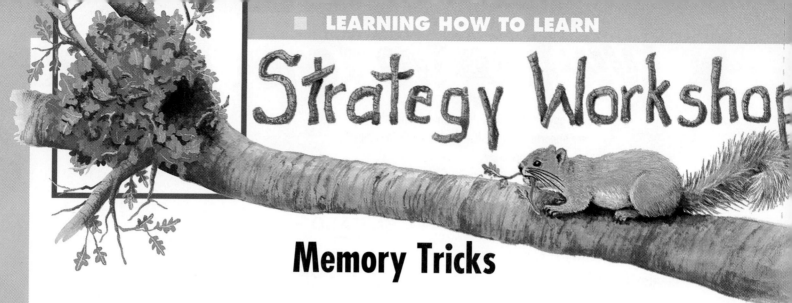

Strategy Workshop

Memory Tricks

DISCOVER THE STRATEGY Some words seem so tricky to spell that we need to outsmart them with tricks of our own. Follow these steps.

| 1. Mark the letters that give you a problem. | 2. Find words you know with those same letters. | 3. Use your problem word and the word you know in a phrase or sentence. |

Your memory trick might be more than one word. It might rhyme. Just be sure you can spell the helping word and that the problem letters match. Here are more memory tricks.

wheat—Heat the wheat.

liquid—quick liquid
young—You are young.
bubbles— big beautiful bubbles

TRY IT OUT Now practice the memory-tricks strategy yourself. Follow the directions on the next page.

Complete each memory
trick using a word from the box to the right.

1. Ride _____ the lion.

2. A couple is _____.

3. Flick the kitchen _____.

4. Give _____ lettuce.

switch

on

Bruce

plenty

With a partner, write your own memory tricks for each pair
of words below. It's all right if they sound silly. The point is
to find ways to remember how to spell tricky words.
Underline the matching letters.

5. hotel—Elvis _____

6. blanket—thank _____

7. window—down _____

Make a memory trick for one of the words in the box to the
right. Follow steps 2 and 3 on page 90. Mark the matching
letters.

8. _____

_____

cable

closet

season

tomorrow

LOOK AHEAD Look ahead at the next five lessons. Find
one list word that looks hard to spell and write a memory
trick for it. Share your trick with the class.

_____

_____

Getting Letters in Correct Order

SPELLING FOCUS

Watch for letter combinations that are hard to keep in order, and pay special attention to those parts: **fri̲end, sa̲id.**

■ **STUDY** Say each word. Then read the sentence.

1. *piece* — He took the last **piece** of pie.
2. *friend* ✳ — She always helps a **friend.**
3. *field* — Wheat grows in this **field.**
4. *said* ✳ — Who **said** it was going to snow?
5. *again* ✳ — I'd like to see that movie **again.**
6. *asked* — No one **asked** for my opinion.
7. *only* — She works **only** on Tuesdays.
8. *brought* ✳ — He **brought** chips to the party.
9. *heard* ✳ — Have you **heard** this song?
10. *build* — Birds **build** nests in trees.

11. *believe* ✳ — Do you **believe** her story?
12. *heart* — My uncle has a kind **heart.**
13. *weird* — Elves wear **weird** hats.
14. *height* — He's a boy of average **height.**
15. *weight* — Lift that ten-pound **weight.**
16. *neighbor* — I haven't met my new **neighbor.**
17. *rattle* — Shake the baby's **rattle.**
18. *pickle* — A good **pickle** tastes sour.
19. *toes* — The baby grabbed her **toes.**
20. *hospital* ✳ — Nurses work at the **hospital.**

■ **PRACTICE** Decide which of the list words you use most in your writing. Then write them in order, from the ones you use most to the ones you use least. Underline any letter combinations that are hard for you to keep in order.

■ **WRITE** Use two sentences in a paragraph.

1. _____
2. _____
3. _____
4. _____
5. _____
6. _____
7. _____
8. _____
9. _____
10. _____
11. _____
12. _____
13. _____
14. _____
15. _____
16. _____
17. _____
18. _____
19. _____
20. _____

CHALLENGE!

interview
poetry
sword
tongue
unusual

✳ **WATCH OUT FOR FREQUENTLY MISSPELLED WORDS!**

EQUATIONS   Write each list word using the math clues.

1. a + gain =
2. on + lye – e =
3. we + bird – b =
4. ask + led – l =
5. rat + tile – i =
6. fried – d + nd =

7. is – i + aid =
8. pick + led – d =
9. outfield – out =
10. built – t + d =
11. be + lie – e + eve =
12. neigh + born – n =

HOMOPHONES   Write the list word that sounds like each word below.

13. herd
14. peace
15. wait
16. tows
17. hart

Strategic Spelling

Using the Memory Tricks Strategy

Use memory tricks to help you spell. Write a list word to complete each trick. Underline the matching letters.

18. <u>eight</u> feet in _____

19. <u>p</u>at<u>i</u>ents <u>i</u>n tract<u>i</u>on in a _____

20. I _____ grapes, <u>h</u>oney, and <u>te</u>a to the

   party.

1. _____
2. _____
3. _____
4. _____
5. _____
6. _____
7. _____
8. _____
9. _____
10. _____
11. _____
12. _____
13. _____
14. _____
15. _____
16. _____
17. _____

Take a Hint
Is it **peace** or **piece?**
Just remember:
Slice a **pie**ce of **pie.**

PROOFREAD A DESCRIPTION

While blindfolded, Bria felt an object and then wrote a description of it. First correct three misspellings and two careless errors in her description below. Then write the name of the object. Hint: It's a list word.

PROOFREADING TIP
Bria tried so hard to get the description right that small words were left out. Such mistakes are easy to catch if you proofread.

It is a long peice of plastic with a round part on top.

Its weight is about two ounces.

Its hight about five inches.

It makes wierd sound when you shake it.

What is it? _____

WRITE A DESCRIPTION Play this guessing game with your classmates. While blindfolded, each player feels a different object and writes a description of that object. After everyone has written descriptions, read them aloud one by one and guess the names of the objects.

_____

_____

_____

_____

_____

_____

_____

Word List

believe	heard
friend	heart
piece	rattle
field	pickle
weird	brought
height	asked
weight	toes
neighbor	build
said	only
again	hospital

Personal Words

1. _____

2. _____

Review

WORDS IN CONTEXT Write the missing boxed words to complete the dialogue below.

piece	asked
friend	only
field	brought
said	heard
again	build

"Have you (1)?" (2) Louie. "There's a new pizza place called Pepe's Premium Pizza Palace across from the baseball (3) on Fifth Street. You can get a (4) of pizza there for (5) seventy-five cents."

"Oh, I bet that's the place that Ramon was telling me about," Ricky replied. "He (6) the pizza is great and he can hardly wait to get back there (7). I heard that the owners are planning to (8) a video arcade right next door too."

"Let's go over there for lunch," said Louie. "I (9) some money with me. It'll be my treat."

"Thanks! You're a great (10)!" Ricky said, just as his stomach let out an approving growl. "My stomach thanks you too."

1. _____
2. _____
3. _____
4. _____
5. _____
6. _____
7. _____
8. _____
9. _____
10. _____

Word *Study*

AFFIXES Affixes are added to words to change their meanings. An affix added to the beginning of a word is called a **prefix**. An affix added to the end of a word is called a **suffix**. Look at the table below.

PREFIXES			SUFFIXES		
	Meaning	Example		Meaning	Example
un-	not	(unhappy = not happy)	**-less**	without	(hopeless = without hope)
re-	again	(replay = play again)	**-ly**	in a ___ way	(slowly = in a slow way)
mis-	badly	(misbehave = behave badly)	**-ness**	being ___	(happiness = being happy)

Use the list words below and the affixes in the chart to make new words that will finish the sentences. One sentence will need a word with two affixes.

build   friend   heard   weight

1. The cat's noisy meowing was ___ by its sleeping owner.
2. The astronauts floated around in a ___ state.
3. The beavers were able to ___ their home after it was destroyed by a flood.
4. I backed away from the growling, ___ dog.

1. _____
2. _____
3. _____
4. _____

Vowels with r

The vowel sound in **fourth** and **storm** is the same, but it is spelled differently: **our, or**. The same is true of **serve** and **dirty**: **er, ir**.

■ **STUDY** Say each word. Then read the sentence.

1.	*fourth*	Our team took **fourth** place.
2.	*course*	Sign up for a Spanish **course**.
3.	*storm*	The **storm** blew down trees.
4.	*morning* ✳	I woke up early this **morning**.
5.	*forest*	Bears may live in this **forest**.
6.	*serve*	You **serve** yourself at a buffet.
7.	*herself*	She finished the job **herself**.
8.	*certain*	I am **certain** the car will run.
9.	*dirty*	We got **dirty** planting flowers.
10.	*first* ✳	He wanted to be the **first** in line.

11.	*pour*	Let me **pour** you some tea.
12.	*fourteen*	This tank has **fourteen** fish.
13.	*court*	We waited for a tennis **court**.
14.	*Florida*	Hurricanes often hit **Florida**.
15.	*form*	Fill out an application **form**.
16.	*nerve*	He had the **nerve** to sing a solo.
17.	*perfect*	It was **perfect** weather for running.
18.	*girlfriend*	She invited a **girlfriend** to stay.
19.	*thirsty*	Salty food makes me **thirsty**.
20.	*skirt*	She wore a red **skirt** and blouse.

■ **PRACTICE** Sort the list words by writing
- five words with **er**
- five words with **or**
- five words with **ir**
- five words with **our**

■ **WRITE** Choose four sentences to rewrite as questions.

CHALLENGE!

resources
unfortunately
commercial
determine
whirl

1.
2.
3.
4.
5.
6.
7.
8.
9.
10.
11.
12.
13.
14.
15.
16.
17.
18.
19.
20.

✳ **WATCH OUT FOR FREQUENTLY MISSPELLED WORDS!**

MAKING CONNECTIONS   Write the list word that
answers each question.

1. What follows second and third?
2. In what kind of place could you see many trees?
3. What type of clothing is often worn with a blouse?
4. What do you call that special female pal?
5. What does a waiter do with the meal you order?
6. When you play basketball, what do you play it on?
7. What comes next: myself, yourself, himself,____?
8. If something is absolutely wonderful, what is it?

POETRY   Write the list words that complete the poem.

Early one (9) in their Michigan dorm,
The students could hear the raging (10).
They hadn't the (11) to go out the door,
Because rain continued to pour and (12).
Then the temperature dropped to a cold (13).
Snow mounds began to (14) all over the green.
Said one, "I'm (15) now of nature's force.
Mother Nature always takes her own (16)."
Well, they did the same—on the (17) bus they could reach.
They arrived in sunny (18) and headed for the beach.

Strategic Spelling

Building New Words

Write *dirty* and *thirsty*. Write the forms of these words
that complete the chart. **Remember:** In words that end
in **y,** you change the **y** to **i** before adding **-er** or **-est.**

1.
2.
3.
4.
5.
6.
7.
8.
9.
10.
11.
12.
13.
14.
15.
16.
17.
18.

> **Take a Hint**
> If you think it may **rain,**
> But you're not quite cert**ain,**
> Spare yourself some p**ain.**
> Open up the curt**ain.**

Spelling Word	Add -er	Add -est
19.		
20.		

≡	Make a capital.
/	Make a small letter.
∧	Add something.
℮	Take out something.
⊙	Add a period.
⨍	New paragraph

PROOFREAD AN ADVERTISEMENT

The ad below was written for a small travel magazine. Correct four misspelled words and two incorrect verbs.

PROOFREADING TIP
The writer used the verbs swam and saw incorrectly. It's swim, swam, (have) swum. Check a dictionary for how to handle see.

Have you ever swam in the ocean?

Have you ever eaten fresh lobster?

Have you ever saw grate blue herons flying?

No? Then you must visit **Flordia!**

It is the perfict vacation for anyone thursty for sun and fun!

Call us today. **Travel Masters**

WRITE AN ADVERTISEMENT

Write an advertisement for a place you think others might like to visit. Use a few list words and personal words.

Word List

pour	nerve
morning	dirty
course	first
Florida	serve
storm	girlfriend
fourth	certain
forest	thirsty
fourteen	perfect
form	skirt
court	herself

Personal Words

1. _____

2. _____

Review

WORDS IN CONTEXT   Write the boxed word that completes each person's statement.

fourth	serve
course	herself
storm	certain
morning	dirty
forest	first

1. **TV Weatherman:** "A severe ___ warning is in effect for Greenfield County until 10:00 P.M."
2. **Teacher:** "The ___ and ___ grades will be performing together at this year's fall concert."
3. **Waitress:** "I'm happy to ___ you this evening. May I take your order?"
4. **Softball Coach:** "If Marilyn wants to be on the softball team, she must train ___ to be on time for practice."
5. **News Reporter:** "At the top of the news this ___ is the President's visit to Chicago."
6. **Park Ranger:** "I am ___ that you will enjoy the many hiking trails, plants, and wildlife in the ___."
7. **Student:** "I plan to take a ___ in history at college."
8. **Laundromat Worker:** "Our brand-new washing machines will do a good job cleaning those ___ clothes."

1. _____
2. _____
   _____
3. _____
4. _____
5. _____
6. _____
   _____
7. _____
8. _____

Word *Study*

ONOMATOPOEIA   This big word is pronounced **on′ ə mat′ ə pē′ ə.** It's what we call words like *buzz, hum,* and *splash.* When you use **onomatopoeia,** the words sound like the sounds they describe. Read the poem aloud. Emphasize the words that are examples of onomatopoeia.

> *Whack! The tennis ball is served.*
> *It whizzes 'cross the net.*
> *Bing! It bounces on the court.*
> *Wham! It's hard to get.*
> *Then...thud!*
> *Oh...*
> *No!*
> *It's collapsed into the net.*

Now use onomatopoeia to write words you might use to describe the sounds of

1. walking on leaves in wet tennis shoes
2. bees building a honeycomb
3. dropping pebbles in a puddle
4. eating soup and salad

1. _____
2. _____
3. _____
4. _____

Vowel Sounds in *put* and *out*

SPELLING FOCUS

The vowel sound in **put** is spelled **oo** in **took** and **u** in **bush.** The vowel sound in **out** is spelled **ow** in **power** and **ou** in **loud.**

■ **STUDY**   Say each word. Then read the sentence.

1. stood — A man **stood** at the door.
2. took ✳ — They **took** a nap after lunch.
3. wood — Oak and pine are types of **wood.**
4. bush — The **bush** has shiny leaves.
5. July — It is usually hot in **July.**
6. power — Leaders have a lot of **power.**
7. however — Paint it **however** you wish.
8. loud — Babies don't like **loud** noises.
9. house ✳ — We live in an old brick **house.**
10. outside ✳ — The children played **outside.**

11. cushion — The cat sat on a soft **cushion.**
12. butcher — A **butcher** sells meat.
13. pudding — Vanilla **pudding** tastes good.
14. football — Can you catch a **football?**
15. brook — We waded in the **brook.**
16. shower — Do you take a bath or a **shower?**
17. crowd — A **crowd** of people waited in line.
18. mountain — She climbed the **mountain.**
19. cloud — He drew a white, puffy **cloud.**
20. proud — They are **proud** of their children.

■ **PRACTICE**   Sort the list words by writing
- six words with **ou**   - five words with **u**
- four words with **ow**   - five words with **oo**

■ **WRITE**   Choose ten words to write in sentences.

Sidebar numbered list 1–20 (blank lines)

CHALLENGE!

barefoot
jury
coward
thousand
announced

✳ **WATCH OUT FOR FREQUENTLY MISSPELLED WORDS!**

SYLLABLE SCRAMBLE Each group of letters is one syllable of a two-syllable word. Match one from each column to make list words.

1. moun		ball
2. butch		ly
3. foot		er
4. cush		ding
5. Ju		tain
6. pud		ion

RHYME TIME Write the list words that rhyme with the underlined words and make sense in the sentences. Circle the list word that ends differently than its rhyming word.

The tiny <u>mouse</u> crept through the (7).
With one swift <u>push</u> I fell into the (8).
Lee <u>Loud</u> looked up at a fluffy white (9).
The actors <u>bowed</u> before the cheering (10).
"Milk a <u>cow</u>? <u>Never</u>!" "You may have to, (11)."
I (12) a <u>book</u> and read beside the (13).
Tired Ms. <u>Good</u> (14) beside the cut (15).
<u>Gower</u> lacked the (16) to turn off the dripping (17).
Mr. <u>Doud</u> shouted out (18) because he was so (19).

Strategic Spelling

Seeing Meaning Connections

Write the words from the box that fit the definitions.

20. a person who is driven away from home and friends _____

21. not inside; outdoors _____

22. a way of looking at things; point of

view _____

Words with *out*
outlook
outside
outcast

1. _____
2. _____
3. _____
4. _____
5. _____
6. _____
7. _____
8. _____
9. _____
10. _____
11. _____
12. _____
13. _____
14. _____
15. _____
16. _____
17. _____
18. _____
19. _____

Take a Hint
If you have trouble with **wood** and **would**, remember the two round knotholes in **wood**.

≡	Make a capital.
/	Make a small letter.
∧	Add something.
ℓ	Take out something.
⊙	Add a period.
¶	New paragraph

PROOFREAD A LIST Lamont has written a list of the things he must do Saturday morning. Correct four misspelled words and two words that should be capitalized.

PROOFREADING TIP
Lamont has developed a "lazy-lower-case" habit. He forgets to capitalize people's names and the days of the week. Don't let this happen to you.

saturday chores

1. Take a shouwer.

2. Help auntie clean the hous.

3. Make puding for the party.

4. Practice foot ball.

WRITE A LIST Write a list of the things you plan to do this weekend. Use some of your list words and a few personal words.

Word List

took	shower
cushion	mountain
football	power
July	proud
brook	house
butcher	however
stood	cloud
pudding	crowd
bush	loud
wood	outside

Personal Words

1. _____

2. _____

Review

CROSSWORD PUZZLE Complete the crossword puzzle by writing the boxed word that matches each definition.

stood	power
took	however
wood	loud
bush	house
July	outside

Across

1. past tense form of the verb *take*
5. a woody plant
7. past tense form of the verb *stand*
8. in whatever way
10. strength

Down

2. outdoors
3. the opposite of quiet
4. the seventh month of the year
6. a building in which people live
9. parts of trees used for building houses and making furniture

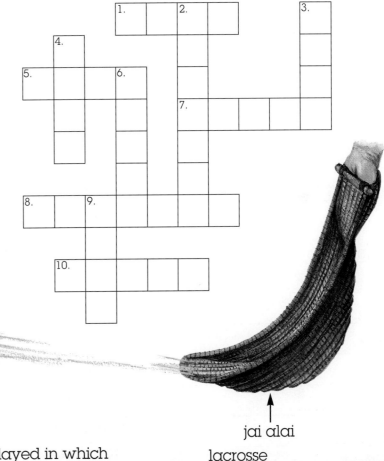

jai alai

lacrosse

Multicultural *Connection*

SPORTS All over the world, sports are played in which players try to move a ball from one place to another. Use the pictures and the labels at the right to help you name each sport described. Your Spelling Dictionary may also help.

soccer

1. North American Indians invented this game. It is played with a small rubber ball and sticks, or "crosses." It is called ___.

2. South Americans play a very fast game using a small, hard ball called a "pelota." Curved baskets are worn on the hands. The game is called ___.

3. This is the most popular game in the world. It is played without using the hands. Most Africans and Europeans call it "football," but you may know it as ___.

1. _____
2. _____
3. _____

Vowel Sounds in *few* and *moon*

SPELLING FOCUS

The vowel sound in **few** can be spelled **u-consonant-e**, **ew**, or **u**: ex<u>cu</u>se, f<u>ew</u>, p<u>u</u>pil. The vowel sound in **moon** can be spelled **oo** or **ui**: c<u>oo</u>l, j<u>ui</u>ce.

■ **STUDY** Say each word. Then read the sentence.

1.	*huge*	Blue whales are **huge** animals.
2.	*excuse*	She had no **excuse** for being late.
3.	*few*	There are a **few** apples left.
4.	*usual*	He took the **usual** route home.
5.	*pupil*	I am a fourth grade **pupil**.
6.	*cool*	Marble feels smooth and **cool**.
7.	*mood*	My dad is in a good **mood**.
8.	*fruit*	Cherries are a kind of **fruit**.
9.	*suit*	The man wore a business **suit**.
10.	*juice*	I drink orange **juice** for breakfast.

11.	*confuse*	I **confuse** pigeons with doves.
12.	*nephew*	My sister's son is my **nephew**.
13.	*curfew*	I must be in by my 9:00 **curfew**.
14.	*fuel*	We need to **fuel** the car with gas.
15.	*menu*	You order food from a **menu**.
16.	*shoot*	They **shoot** baskets at practice.
17.	*school* ✳	Our **school** is on the corner.
18.	*shampoo*	Should we **shampoo** the rug?
19.	*bruise*	The **bruise** on her leg was purple.
20.	*cruise*	We went on a Caribbean **cruise**.

■ **PRACTICE** Sort the list words by writing
- five words with **oo**
- six words with **u-consonant-e** or **ew**
- five words with **ui**
- four words with **u**

■ **WRITE** Choose two sentences to write an advertisement, slogan, or saying.

CHALLENGE!

commute
universe
reunion
fireproof
pursuit

1. _____
2. _____
3. _____
4. _____
5. _____
6. _____
7. _____
8. _____
9. _____
10. _____
11. _____
12. _____
13. _____
14. _____
15. _____
16. _____
17. _____
18. _____
19. _____
20. _____

✳ **WATCH OUT FOR FREQUENTLY MISSPELLED WORDS!**

ANALOGIES Write the list word that completes each phrase.

1. hot and warm, cold and ____
2. most and many, least and ____
3. aunt and uncle, niece and ____
4. small and tiny, large and ____
5. carrot and banana, vegetable and ____
6. apple and sauce, orange and ____
7. teeth and toothpaste, hair and ____
8. train and schedule, restaurant and ____
9. doctor and patient, teacher and ____

TONGUE TWISTERS Write the list word that would best complete each tongue twister.

10. Being bucked by a bronco brought about Brian's ____.
11. The sensational singer sported a silky silver ____.
12. Should Shelly snap the shutter and ____ the shy sheep?
13. Curt's camp counselor calls "Come in!" at ____.
14. Maybe Maya managed to maintain a merry ____.
15. Chemistry quiz questions ____ and confound Cornelius.
16. Chris chartered a craft to ____ the Caribbean.
17. The extravagant explorers had an ____ for the expensive expedition.

Strategic Spelling

Seeing Meaning Connections

Write the list word that completes each sentence. The underlined word is a clue. Circle the letters in each list word that are the same as in the underlined word.

18. The schoolwork at our ____ is very challenging.
19. I am usually on time if I take the ____ route.
20. We had to stop and refuel when we ran out of ____.

1. ____
2. ____
3. ____
4. ____
5. ____
6. ____
7. ____
8. ____
9. ____
10. ____
11. ____
12. ____
13. ____
14. ____
15. ____
16. ____
17. ____
18. ____
19. ____
20. ____

Did You Know?
The word *curfew* comes from the French words *covrir*, to "cover," and *feu*, "fire." When the curfew bell rang, people covered, or put out, their fires each night.

≡	Make a capital.
/	Make a small letter.
∧	Add something.
ℯ	Take out something.
⊙	Add a period.
⌯	New paragraph

PROOFREAD DIRECTIONS The owner of Cozy's Café left these directions for her after-school assistant. Correct four misspelled words and add three missing end marks.

PROOFREADING TIP

Cozy forgot to use an exclamation mark in her final sentence. What other mark did she forget (twice) ?

> P. J.,
>
> How was shcool Please squeeze oranges and cut up apples. Type up a new menu to include frut salad and fresh orange joos. Are you in the mude to make one of your special soups They are terrific
>
> Cozy

WRITE DIRECTIONS Isn't there something you'd like to ask someone to do in writing? Use spelling words and personal words to write your directions.

Word List

bruise	pupil
cool	few
juice	fuel
school	excuse
fruit	nephew
mood	huge
suit	curfew
shoot	confuse
cruise	usual
shampoo	menu

Personal Words

1. _____
2. _____

Review

WORDS IN CONTEXT   Maybe you have seen advertisements for vacation spots much like the one below. Write the boxed words to complete the advertisement.

huge	cool
excuse	mood
few	fruit
usual	suit
pupil	juice

Is the hot weather putting you in a bad (1)? Do you need to get away for a (2) days? Imagine this:

- Taking a dip in the ocean to (3) off
- Having fresh (4), including slices of watermelon, honeydew, and bananas, with your breakfast every morning
- Sipping a cool fruit (5) as you relax under a palm tree
- Being a (6) in one of Peter Orca's famous scuba diving classes

The Sand and Surf Hotel in southern Florida has a special limited offer. Instead of the (7) tiny rooms you find at other vacation spots, you can stay in a (8) room at a very low cost. So don't make the (9) that you can't afford a vacation. Call a travel agent NOW and make your reservation. See you at the Sand and Surf soon, and don't forget your bathing (10)!

1. _____
2. _____
3. _____
4. _____
5. _____
6. _____
7. _____
8. _____
9. _____
10. _____

Word *Study*

COLLECTIVE NOUNS   You know the phrase, "a herd of elephants," but did you know a group of geese is called a "gaggle"? Words like *herd* and *gaggle* are called **collective nouns.** Sometimes they reflect a quality possessed by the subject. This is why we speak of a *pride* of lions—because they seem proud to us.

Find the collective noun at the right that names each group below. Your Spelling Dictionary will help you.

1. Just one is called a goldfish.
   Two are goldfish or goldfishes.
   As a group, they are called a ___ .
2. One alone is a bee.
   More than one are bees.
   As a group, they are called a ___ .
3. One is called a fox.
   Two or more are called foxes.
   As a group, they are called a ___ .

swarm
school
skulk

1. _____
2. _____
3. _____

Homophones

A homophone is a word that sounds exactly like another word but has a different spelling and meaning: **wood, would.**

■ **STUDY** Say each word. Then read the sentence.

1. wood   Put some **wood** on the fire.
2. would ✳   He asked if I **would** help.
3. too ✳   She was **too** tired to stay awake.
4. to   Come **to** the meeting at noon.
5. two   He has **two** dogs and a cat.
6. there ✳   I've never been **there** before.
7. their ✳   The girls brought **their** guitars.
8. they're ✳   Ask them if **they're** twins.
9. your   Did you leave **your** bike here?
10. you're ✳   She asked when **you're** going.

11. beat   The drummer **beat** his drum.
12. beet   You can eat a **beet** cooked or raw.
13. break   Eggs **break** easily.
14. brake   Always **brake** at a stop sign.
15. clothes   He bought some new **clothes.**
16. close   Remember to **close** the window.
17. piece   I cut a **piece** of cheese.
18. peace   People dream of world **peace.**
19. thrown   She was **thrown** from a horse.
20. throne   The queen sat on her **throne.**

■ **PRACTICE** First write the homophone groups that may be difficult for you to keep straight. Then write the rest of the homophones.

■ **WRITE** Choose two sentences to write a dialogue, or conversation, between two or more people.

1. _____
2. _____
3. _____
4. _____
5. _____
6. _____
7. _____
8. _____
9. _____
10. _____
11. _____
12. _____
13. _____
14. _____
15. _____
16. _____
17. _____
18. _____
19. _____
20. _____

CHALLENGE!

guessed	guest
aisle	isle
waist	waste

✳ **WATCH OUT FOR FREQUENTLY MISSPELLED WORDS!**

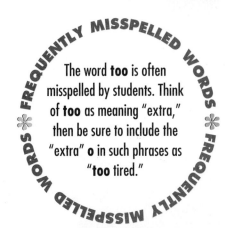

HOMOPHONE PHOTOS
Write the list word that labels each photograph. Below that word, write another list word that sounds just like it.

1. _____

2. _____

3. _____

4. _____

5. _____

6. _____

HOMOPHONE QUOTES
Complete the statements of the people below by writing list words that sound alike.

King: "I was so unpopular, I was (7) from my (8)."
Teacher: "If they stay (9), I know (10) going to miss (11) bus."
Twins: "The (12) of us would like (13) ride the bus (14)."
Driver: "If I (15) suddenly, the dishes in the back will (16)."
Dentist: "Tino, (17) going to have to brush (18) teeth more."

Strategic Spelling

Using the Memory Tricks Strategy

Use memory tricks to help you spell. Write a list word to complete each trick. Underline the matching letters.

19. a _____ of p̲i̲e

20. _____ for p̲e̲ople a̲l̲l over

7. _____

8. _____

9. _____

10. _____

11. _____

12. _____

13. _____

14. _____

15. _____

16. _____

17. _____

18. _____

☰	Make a capital.
/	Make a small letter.
∧	Add something.
ℓ	Take out something.
⊙	Add a period.
¶	New paragraph

PROOFREAD AN OUTLINE Sara is giving a speech tomorrow. Read her outline. Correct four misspelled words and two errors in capitalization.

PROOFREADING TIP
Sara knows that the first word in each main topic and subtopic of her outline must be capitalized. Proofreading would have helped her do just that.

How to Build a Birdhouse
I. Gather your materials
    A. Seven squares of wod (sides, bottom, roof)
    B. Hammer and nails
II. assemble you're materials
    A. Cut hole in one peace
    B. Nail four sides together (opening in front)
    C. nail bottom to sides
    D. Nail the last to pieces on top for roof
III. Paint your birdhouse

WRITE AN OUTLINE Write an outline of a speech you would like to give. Use list words.

Word List

beat	your
beet	you're
break	thrown
brake	throne
wood	to
would	too
clothes	two
close	there
piece	their
peace	they're

Personal Words

1. _____

2. _____

Review

POETRY Write the boxed words that complete the poem.

wood	there
would	their
too	they're
to	your
two	you're

Hair, oh hair,
It's just not fair!
Give me (1) hair, (2) hair,
Any hair but MY hair!

I'd say (3) lucky, (4) lucky (5),
To have such a fine-looking, stylish hairdo.
Mine is neither here nor (6),
Usually it's ho-hum hair.

Wait! Look in that window. STOP!
See that head made of (7) with a wig on top?
It's curly! I do declare,
I simply MUST have that hair!

Could you, (8) you spare a dollar or (9),
And help me (10) get a brand-new exciting hairdo?

1. _____
2. _____
3. _____
4. _____
5. _____
6. _____
7. _____
8. _____
9. _____
10. _____

Using a *Dictionary*

HOMOGRAPHS If you looked up *brake* in a dictionary, here is what you would find: ⟶

There is more than one entry for *brake*. *Brake* is a **homograph.** Homographs are spelled exactly alike, but they have different word histories and different meanings. The raised number alerts you to this.

Study the entries for *brake*. Write *brake¹* or *brake²* to answer each question below.

1. Which entry can be more than one part of speech?
2. Which entry has an example sentence?
3. Which entry would you find in a forest?

brake¹ (brāk), **1** anything used to slow or stop the motion of a wheel or vehicle by pressing or scraping or by rubbing against. **2** show or stop by moving a brake: *The driver braked the speeding car and it slid to a stop.* 1 *n.,* 2 *v.,* **braked, brak•ing.**

brake² (brāk), **1** a thick growth of bushes; thicket. *n.*

1. _____
2. _____
3. _____

111

Review

Lesson 19: Getting Letters in Correct Order   **Lesson 22:** Vowel Sounds in few and
Lesson 20: Vowels with r   moon
Lesson 21: Vowel Sounds in put and out   **Lesson 23:** Homophones

REVIEW WORD LIST

1. again	11. rattle	21. perfect	31. pudding	41. shampoo
2. believe	12. toes	22. skirt	32. shower	42. suit
3. friend	13. weight	23. storm	33. few	43. usual
4. heard	14. dirty	24. butcher	34. fruit	44. clothes
5. heart	15. Florida	25. cloud	35. fuel	45. there
6. height	16. forest	26. crowd	36. huge	46. they're
7. hospital	17. fourteen	27. cushion	37. juice	47. too
8. neighbor	18. fourth	28. football	38. menu	48. two
9. pickle	19. morning	29. July	39. nephew	49. wood
10. piece	20. nerve	30. mountain	40. school	50. your

CLARINETISTS' COMPLAINT

Band members are filing an official complaint with their leader.
Write the words they left out.

usual
suit
clothes
believe
crowd

Dear Mr. Seifworth,

We, the Woodwind Section, (1) it is unfair that we
must wear (2) pants to play in school concerts. The (3)
comes to hear us play, not to admire our (4). Please
consider letting us wear our (5) school clothes at
future concerts.

Thank you,
The Woodwinds

1. _____

2. _____

3. _____

4. _____

5. _____

Labels

Tess received a small label maker and went around her house labeling items. Match the name of each item to the number next to it.

football
heart
forest
skirt
cushion
shower
fourteen

1. _____
2. _____
3. _____   5. _____
4. _____   6. _____   7. _____

Descriptions

Guess what each person is describing below. Write your answers.

cloud
hospital
wood
storm
nephew

1. _____
2. _____
3. _____
4. _____
5. _____

She's my dad's sister, and I'm her (1).

It may look fluffy and white, but a (2) is simply water vapor. I predict there will be a major (3) moving in from the east.

There's nothing like the smell of freshly cut pine (4).

I spend long hours operating in the (5).

113

Wally

– a cartoon by Sam
Help Sam finish his comic strip about
a big baby named Wally.

dirty   rattle   shampoo   friend   nerve   huge   toes

1. _____
2. _____
3. _____
4. _____
5. _____
6. _____
7. _____

Wally is bigger than most babies. Actually, he is (1).

He can wiggle his gigantic (2). He makes music by shaking his (3).

Wally loves mud puddles!

I'm all (4)!

But he hates (5)!

You have some (6) messing with my hair!!!

He is a (7) to all animals.

Pen Pals

Read Marissa's card to her pen pal in Moscow, Russia.
Supply the missing words.

fourth   school   height   your   too   they're   July   weight   again

Chicago

May 2, 20__

Dear Svetlana,

I enjoyed reading _____ letter. Here are some facts about me: My birthday is _____ 22. My _____ is 4 feet 2 inches. My _____ is 62 pounds. I am in the _____ grade. I go to _____ on a bus. I like to wear sweatshirts because _____ so comfortable. Please write once _____. I want to hear more about you _____!

Sincerely,
Marissa

PETITE POEMS

1. _____
2. _____
3. _____
4. _____
5. _____
6. _____
7. _____
8. _____

Read each short poem below and supply the missing word.

$hopping List

Denzel left this list for Jacqui. Write the missing items.

few	butcher	fruit	Florida	juice
two	pickle	perfect	pudding	

• fresh orange juice from _____

• a large dill_____

• oranges, apples, bananas, and other _____

• one gallon of sweet apple _____ —not cider

• six red roses—must be _____ !

• one stick of butter and_____ loaves of bread

• just a _____ sprigs of parsley

• ready-made thick chocolate_____

• Have the _____ cut up a three-pound chicken.

Moscow

Here's a handy driving rule:
Don't go on the highway
  when you're low on (1).

  When you've lost something,
  you look everywhere.
  The last place you look, it's sure
  to be (2).

  Did I hear the squawks of the
  early bird? For an hour and a half
  it was all I (3)!

  Do yourself a great big favor.
  Get to know your next-door (4).

It's easy to order a fine meal when you,
Take a good look at the restaurant's (5).

If this arguing doesn't cease,
The cake will vanish; no one gets a (6).

The storm came up without a warning,
And rocked the city early one (7).

Here's one thing you can always count on:
A hill is never as large as a (8)!

115

STRATEGY WORKSHOP

Pronouncing for Spelling

DISCOVER THE STRATEGY 1 To avoid making the mistake Josh made in the cartoon below, use this strategy:

1. Pronounce the word carefully and correctly. Listen to the sound of each letter.
2. Pronounce the word again as you write it.

TRY IT OUT Now practice this strategy yourself.

Pronounce each word in dark type slowly and correctly. Pay special attention to the sounds of the underlined letters. Pronounce each word again as you write it.

1. Say **s<u>u</u>rprise** (NOT su-prise) _____

2. Say **pic<u>t</u>ure** (NOT pi-ture) _____

3. Say **stren<u>gth</u>** (NOT strenth) _____

4. Say **differ<u>e</u>nt** (NOT diff-rent) _____

5. Say **chas<u>ing</u>** (NOT chas-in) _____

DISCOVER THE STRATEGY 2 Pronouncing the
word correctly won't work for a word like *thumb*.
How can you remember to include the silent **b**? Use
the "secret pronunciation" strategy below.

1. Pronounce any silent letters to yourself. Don't worry if the
word sounds funny. Say the **b** in *thumb* and the **k** in *knit*.
Say "thum-**b**" and "**k**-nit."

2. Exaggerate or change a sound in the word. You might
pronounce *million* by exaggerating the smaller word *lion*
inside it. Say "mil-**li-on**" to yourself.

TRY IT OUT Now practice this strategy.

With a partner, make up secret pronunciations for the words
below. Pay special attention to the underlined letters. Write
each word correctly. Say its secret pronunciation to yourself.

1. lamb
2. knit
3. wrist
4. guess
5. everyone

6. talk
7. once
8. hour
9. clothes
10. movie

1. _____
2. _____
3. _____
4. _____
5. _____
6. _____
7. _____
8. _____
9. _____
10. _____

LOOK AHEAD Look ahead at the next five lessons. Write
four list words you could use these strategies with. Mark the
part of each word that you'll pay special attention to when
you pronounce it.

1._____   3._____

2._____   4._____

117

Including All the Letters

Some words have more letters than you might expect. To spell these words, pronounce each syllable carefully.

■ **STUDY** Say each word. Then read the sentence.

1. often — Cats **often** sleep most of the day.
2. might ❋ — We **might** go fishing next week.
3. they ❋ — The girls can go if **they** want to.
4. remember — Did he **remember** my name?
5. finally ❋ — The package **finally** arrived.
6. really ❋ — She sees things as they **really** are.
7. several — He invited **several** close friends.
8. everyone ❋ — Not **everyone** agreed with me.
9. interesting — That's an **interesting** clock.
10. everybody ❋ — I saw **everybody** at the party.

11. known — Dogs are **known** to be loyal.
12. caught ❋ — The player **caught** the ball.
13. surprised — He was **surprised** to see her.
14. island — Puerto Rico is an **island.**
15. swimming ❋ — I went **swimming** in the pool.
16. camera — She got film for her **camera.**
17. December — Snow may fall in **December.**
18. evening — The air cools in the **evening.**
19. beginning — The baby is **beginning** to crawl.
20. February — **February** 14 is Valentine's Day.

1.
2.
3.
4.
5.
6.
7.
8.
9.
10.
11.
12.
13.
14.
15.
16.
17.
18.
19.
20.

CHALLENGE!

broccoli
kindergarten
cabinet
serious
temperature

■ **PRACTICE** Sort the list words by writing
- four words with one syllable
- five words with two syllables
- eight words with three syllables
- three words with four syllables

■ **WRITE** Choose ten words to write in sentences.

❋ **WATCH OUT FOR FREQUENTLY MISSPELLED WORDS!**

PUZZLE IT OUT What do you shoot people with that makes them smile? When you write the list words that match the clues, the answer to this riddle will appear in the box.

1. the twelfth month
2. truly; actually
3. call back to mind
4. early part of night
5. astonished; shocked
6. grabbed; took and held
7. The answer to the riddle is a ____.

1. _ _ _ _ _ _ _ _
2. _ _ _ _ _ _ _
3. _ _ _ _ _ _ _ _
4. _ _ _ _ _ _ _
5. _ _ _ _ _ _ _
6. _ _ _ _

7. _____
8. _____
9. _____
10. _____
11. _____
12. _____
13. _____
14. _____
15. _____
16. _____

SYLLABLE ALERT Write the list word that starts and ends with the same letter and has the same number of syllables as each word below.

8. ballooning
9. keen
10. eventfully
11. tray
12. sweeping
13. exercise
14. inward
15. open
16. moat

Pronouncing for Spelling

We sometimes misspell words because we say them wrong. Write *February*, *finally*, *interesting*, and *several*. Now say each word carefully. Be sure to pronounce the underlined syllable.

17. _____
18. _____
19. _____
20. _____

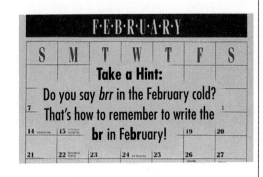

F·E·B·R·U·A·R·Y

S	M	T	W	T	F	S

Take a Hint:
Do you say *brr* in the February cold? That's how to remember to write the **br** in February!

≡	Make a capital.
/	Make a small letter.
∧	Add something.
ℓ	Take out something.
⊙	Add a period.
¶	New paragraph

PROOFREAD A MATH PROBLEM

Ms. Yasutaki's class is keeping a math journal. Read the journal entry below and correct four misspelled words and add the missing quotation marks.

I multiplied 22 X 15 in 3 seconds! Everyone was suprised by my speed. They asked, How do you do it? I finely told them this secret: "You know 22 X 10 is 220. Half of 220 is 110. So just add them up to get 330.

Math is intresting if you now the shortcuts!

PROOFREADING TIP

A speaker's exact words are called a **quotation.** Quotations begin with a capital letter and have quotation marks at the beginning (") and end (") of the speaker's words.

WRITE A MATH PROBLEM

You probably have a math shortcut or interesting problem you'd like to share. Use list words as well as personal words.

_____
_____
_____
_____
_____
_____

Word List

camera	surprised
finally	might
really	often
known	island
everybody	caught
everyone	evening
they	swimming
remember	several
February	beginning
December	interesting

Personal Words

1. _____

2. _____

Review

often	really
might	several
they	everyone
remember	interesting
finally	everybody

SYNONYMS Write the two boxed words that have similar meanings.

1. _____   2. _____

DEFINING WORDS Write the boxed word that means the same as the underlined word or words in each sentence.

3. Our team <u>at last</u> has won a game against the mighty Falcons.
4. Eddie was absent from school for <u>more than two or three</u> days when he had the flu.
5. The program about the grizzly bears in Yellowstone National Park was <u>holding my attention</u>.
6. I <u>frequently</u> stop to talk with Mrs. Griffin when I see her out in her yard.
7. Do you <u>truly</u> think that I bake good cookies?
8. I <u>will possibly</u> want to go bike riding with my friends on Saturday.
9. Do you <u>call back to mind</u> what time the train is due to arrive this evening?
10. The kittens are hungry and <u>the animals spoken about</u> need a good home.

3. _____
4. _____
5. _____
6. _____
7. _____
8. _____
9. _____
10. _____

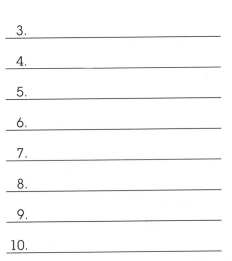

Using a *Dictionary*

WORDS THAT AREN'T ENTRIES You won't find **inflected forms**, words like *surprised* and *dirtiest,* as entry words in most dictionaries. If a dictionary included words like these as entries, it would be too large and heavy to use! To find inflected forms, look for the base words. You will find *dirtiest* at the end of *dirty* and *surprised* at the end of *surprise.*

Write the entry word you would look for in order to find the definition of each word below.

1. smuggled
2. funnier
3. speeches
4. largest

dirt•y (dėr/tē), **1** soiled by dirt; not clean: *I got dirty emptying the garbage.* **2** not fair or decent: *Fooling me was a dirty trick. adj.,* **dirt•i•er, dirt•i•est.**

sur•prise (sər prīz/), **1** a feeling caused by something that happens suddenly. **2** to cause to feel surprise; astonish: *The news surprised us.* **3** something unexpected: *I have a surprise for you. 1 n., 2,3 v.,* **sur•prised, sur•pris•ing.**

1. _____
2. _____
3. _____
4. _____

Compound Words

SPELLING FOCUS

A compound word is made of two or more words. Keep all the letters when spelling compounds: **base + ball = baseball.**

■ **STUDY** Say each word. Then read the sentence.

1. *baseball* We play **baseball** in the summer.
2. *basketball* ✳ The **basketball** player is very tall.
3. *upstairs* She's using the **upstairs** phone.
4. *myself* ✳ I saw **myself** on television.
5. *highway* Traffic on the **highway** is heavy.
6. *classroom* Students filled the **classroom.**
7. *anyway* I was late but went **anyway.**
8. *newspaper* He wrote a **newspaper** article.
9. *something* ✳ You have to eat **something.**
10. *sometimes* ✳ Doctors **sometimes** get sick.

11. *chalkboard* She wrote on the **chalkboard.**
12. *earrings* These are real gold **earrings.**
13. *nighttime* Bats fly during the **nighttime.**
14. *motorcycle* He rode on a **motorcycle.**
15. *downstairs* Dad is vacuuming **downstairs.**
16. *softball* All her friends play **softball.**
17. *weekend* Do you work this **weekend?**
18. *classmate* Ask a **classmate** for help.
19. *doorbell* The **doorbell** rang twice.
20. *driveway* Park the car in the **driveway.**

■ **PRACTICE** Write the words in alphabetical order.

■ **WRITE** Choose two sentences to include in a paragraph.

CHALLENGE!

courtroom
ourselves
heartbroken
teammate
skateboard

1.
2.
3.
4.
5.
6.
7.
8.
9.
10.
11.
12.
13.
14.
15.
16.
17.
18.
19.
20.

✳ **WATCH OUT FOR FREQUENTLY MISSPELLED WORDS!**

CLASSIFICATIONS   Add the list words that belong in each group. The words already listed are clues.

Sports	School	Time
football	*homeroom*	*weeknight*
1. _____	4. _____	6. _____
2. _____	5. _____	7. _____
3. _____	*schoolmate*	*sometime*

JOINING WORDS   Find two words in each sentence that can be joined to make a list word. Write the word.

8. Because I was so worried, I was not my old self.
9. Were there any sights along the way?
10. The dog ran to the door when the bell rang.
11. The good news is that I got an A on my paper.
12. Here are some crackers for that thing in the cage.
13. I got up and walked to the stairs near the porch.
14. When the sirens blast, my ear always rings.
15. There are some of us who enjoy good times.
16. The chalk was ordered by a member of the board.
17. He fell and went rolling down the stairs.
18. The washer's motor failed, so the cycle didn't finish.

8. _____
9. _____
10. _____
11. _____
12. _____
13. _____
14. _____
15. _____
16. _____
17. _____
18. _____

STRATEGIC SPELLING

Seeing Meaning Connections

Write the word from the box that answers each question.

Words with *way*
driveway
runway
highway

19. Where does an airplane take off? _____
20. Where do cars go whizzing along? _____
21. Where might a car be parked? _____

Did You Know?
Today, basketball players throw a ball through a net to score points. When the game was invented in 1891, they used a real basket. This is how the game got its name.

123

☰	Make a capital.
/	Make a small letter.
∧	Add something.
ℯ	Take out something.
⊙	Add a period.
¶	New paragraph

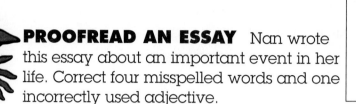

PROOFREAD AN ESSAY Nan wrote this essay about an important event in her life. Correct four misspelled words and one incorrectly used adjective.

PROOFREADING TIP

Nan forgot this rule about using the adjectives more and most: Don't use more or most with words that end in -er or -est.

> My Proud Moment
>
> I play basket ball in the Adapted Athletics Program. At first it was hard dribbling from my wheelchair, but I soon got more better at it. Once, I faked out my classmat, Pete. I drove my self around him and swished the ball trough the net. I felt like Supergirl!

WRITE AN ESSAY Write about one of your proud moments. Use your spelling words and a personal word.

_____
_____
_____
_____
_____
_____
_____
_____

Word List

basketball	upstairs
something	downstairs
sometimes	newspaper
baseball	softball
anyway	weekend
chalkboard	classroom
earrings	classmate
nighttime	doorbell
myself	driveway
motorcycle	highway

Personal Words

1. _____

2. _____

WORDS IN CONTEXT Write the missing boxed words to complete the following letter.

baseball	classroom
basketball	anyway
upstairs	newspaper
myself	something
highway	sometimes

Dear Jessica,

It's supposed to rain on Saturday, but I'm glad you're coming for a visit (1). Here are directions to my house.

Go to the intersection of Davis Street and Grant Avenue. Get on the (2) that takes you north to Cedar City. You will be on this road for about thirty miles.
Get off at the Dillard Street exit and turn left at the first stoplight. You will see a park with a (3) court on the corner. That's where I (4) shoot baskets either with a few other kids on my block or all by (5).
My house is the white one across from the (6) field. The Little League will probably be in the middle of a game.

I'll be looking for you from my (7) window. When you get here, we'll check the movie section in the (8) to see what's playing. If you'd rather do (9) else, that's all right. Oh, I almost forgot. My school will be open on Saturday, so I'll show you all the neat stuff in my new (10).

Your friend,
Marguerita

1. _____
2. _____
3. _____
4. _____
5. _____
6. _____
7. _____
8. _____
9. _____
10. _____

Multicultural *Connection*

ARTS Throughout history, people have worn jewelry. Read about the handcrafted jewelry pictured at the right. Then complete each description below by writing the name of one of the items pictured.

1. The ancient Egyptians used colored gemstones in jewelry, such as this beautiful pin, or ___.
2. The Greeks valued fine metalwork and often used lacelike *filigree,* or ornamental gold or silver wire, as seen in the center of this ___.
3. Carved jade and metal ornaments like this white jade hanging ornament, or ___, were popular in China .
4. The Inca of South America worked with gold and silver. This ___ shows their craftsmanship in making strings of ornaments for wearing around the neck.

earring

pendant

brooch

necklace

1. _____
2. _____
3. _____
4. _____

Suffixes -ful, -ly, -ion

When adding **-ful**, **-ly**, or **-ion** to most base words, the base stays the same: **slowly**. To words ending in **y**, change **y** to **i**: **beautiful**. To words ending in **e**, drop the **e** when the suffix begins with a vowel: **location**.

■ **STUDY** What happens when each suffix is added?

power + ful	=	1. *powerful*
peace + ful	=	2. *peaceful*
beauty + ful	=	3. *beautiful* ✳
slow + ly	=	4. *slowly*
safe + ly	=	5. *safely*
day + ly	=	6. *daily*
sudden + ly	=	7. *suddenly*
careful + ly	=	8. *carefully*
act + ion	=	9. *action*
locate + ion	=	10. *location*

cheer + ful	=	11. *cheerful*
pain + ful	=	12. *painful*
thought + ful	=	13. *thoughtful*
week + ly	=	14. *weekly*
late + ly	=	15. *lately*
truthful + ly	=	16. *truthfully*
hopeful + ly	=	17. *hopefully*
invent + ion	=	18. *invention*
correct + ion	=	19. *correction*
pollute + ion	=	20. *pollution*

■ **PRACTICE** Sort the list words by writing
- nine words with the suffix **-ly**
- six words with the suffix **-ful**
- five words with the suffix **-ion**

■ **WRITE** Use three words to write about a friend.

Lines:
1.
2.
3.
4.
5.
6.
7.
8.
9.
10.
11.
12.
13.
14.
15.
16.
17.
18.
19.
20.

CHALLENGE!

grateful
suspenseful
completely
exactly
separation

126

✳ **WATCH OUT FOR FREQUENTLY MISSPELLED WORDS!**

SUFFIX ADDITION   Write the list word that has each meaning and ending shown below.

1. gladness and joy + ful
2. seven days + ly
3. feeling hope + ly
4. not early + ly
5. quiet and still + ful
6. without warning + ly
7. good looks + ful
8. not fast + ly
9. feeling hurt + ful
10. free from harm + ly
11. strength and might + ful
12. twenty-four hours + ly

1. _____
2. _____
3. _____
4. _____
5. _____
6. _____
7. _____
8. _____
9. _____
10. _____
11. _____
12. _____

WORD FORMS   Add -**ion**, -**ly**, or -**ful** to the base words below to make list words. Write the list words. Circle the word in which the spelling changed when the suffix was added.

13. act _____

14. thought _____

15. pollute _____

16. invent _____

17. truthful _____

18. careful _____

STRATEGIC SPELLING

Using the Meaning Helper Strategy

Use meaning helpers to help spell hard words. Write the list word that goes with each meaning helper. Mark the letter that matches the underlined sound clue.

19. correct

20. locate

_____   _____

Did You Know?
The word *pollution* comes from a Latin word meaning "soiled," "dirty."

127

≡	Make a capital.
/	Make a small letter.
∧	Add something.
ℯ	Take out something.
⊙	Add a period.
¶	New paragraph

PROOFREAD CAPTIONS Hassan and his friend Bill have written captions for the photos they took on their camping trip. Correct four misspellings and one sentence that contains more than one negative word.

PROOFREADING TIP

No and *not* are **negative words.** Contractions formed with the adverb *not* are also negative words. Use ONLY ONE negative word per sentence.

> *Here we are in beatiful Mesa Verde.*

> *We carfully climb the ladder to the house.*

> *Our campsite is in a peacefull locashun.*

> *This deer didn't have no fear of humans.*

WRITE A CAPTION Think about a photo that shows you and a friend doing something. Draw a picture of it. Then write a caption for the picture. Use a spelling word and a personal word.

Word List

peaceful	lately
thoughtful	daily
powerful	truthfully
cheerful	carefully
painful	hopefully
beautiful	invention
safely	correction
slowly	action
weekly	pollution
suddenly	location

Personal Words

1. _____

2. _____

Review

ANALOGIES Write the boxed word that completes each analogy.

powerful	daily
peaceful	suddenly
beautiful	carefully
slowly	action
safely	location

1. Eagerly is to anxiously as thoroughly is to __.
2. Narrow is to wide as ugly is to __.
3. Edge is to rim as place is to __.
4. Politely is to courteously as unexpectedly is to __.
5. Week is to weekly as day is to __.
6. Lazy is to hardworking as hostile is to __.
7. Gently is to roughly as swiftly is to __.
8. Stillness is to calmness as movement is to __.
9. Generously is to selfishly as dangerously is to __.
10. Tricky is to clever as mighty is to __.

1. _____
2. _____
3. _____
4. _____
5. _____
6. _____
7. _____
8. _____
9. _____
10. _____

Word *Study*

CODES Many different kinds of codes can be used to disguise what we write. Can you read the message below?

When you understand how the **tick-tack-toe code** works, the message is easy to read.

A	B	C
D	E	F
G	H	I

J•	K•	L•
M•	N•	O•
P•	Q•	R•

S••	T••	U••
V••	W••	X••
Y••	Z••	

All the letters of the alphabet are on three tick-tack-toe grids. To spell a word in code, look at where the letter is on the grid. Then draw the lines that appear around it. If there are dots, draw those too. So, B = ⊔ M = ⊡ F = ⊏
Now read the words above and write them.

_____   _____   _____

129

Suffixes -less, -ment, -ness

SPELLING FOCUS

When **-less, -ment,** or **-ness** is added to most base words, the base stays the same: **goodness.** If the base word ends in a **consonant** and a **y,** the **y** is changed to **i** before adding the suffix: **business.**

■ **STUDY** What happens when each suffix is added?

help + less	=	1. *helpless*
care + less	=	2. *careless*
hope + less	=	3. *hopeless*
pay + ment	=	4. *payment*
state + ment	=	5. *statement*
move + ment	=	6. *movement*
good + ness	=	7. *goodness*
soft + ness	=	8. *softness*
bright + ness	=	9. *brightness*
busy + ness	=	10. *business*

spot + less	=	11. *spotless*
breath + less	=	12. *breathless*
worth + less	=	13. *worthless*
use + less	=	14. *useless*
pave + ment	=	15. *pavement*
treat + ment	=	16. *treatment*
punish + ment	=	17. *punishment*
great + ness	=	18. *greatness*
fair + ness	=	19. *fairness*
dark + ness	=	20. *darkness*

1.
2.
3.
4.
5.
6.
7.
8.
9.
10.
11.
12.
13.
14.
15.
16.
17.
18.
19.
20.

CHALLENGE!

assignment
appointment
announcement
homelessness
consciousness

■ **PRACTICE** Sort the list words by writing
- seven words ending in **-ness**
- six words ending in **-ment**
- seven words ending in **-less**

■ **WRITE** Choose ten words to write in sentences.

ADDING ENDINGS Complete each sentence by adding **-less**, **-ment**, or **-ness** to the word in parentheses.

1. (busy)   She was out of town on ___.
2. (pay)   He just made his last car ___.
3. (help)   The trapped fox was ___.
4. (use)   This old map is ___.
5. (move)   I watched the dancer's graceful ___.
6. (great)   The child was destined for ___.
7. (state)   The lawyer began her closing ___.
8. (hope)   Our unfortunate situation looked ___.
9. (good)   He helped us out of the ___ of his heart.
10. (worth)   Throw away that ___ old inner tube.
11. (breath)   I ran so fast I was soon ___.
12. (pave)   We rode our bikes on the concrete ___.
13. (fair)   In all ___, I don't want to take sides.
14. (soft)   The child loved the ___ of the blanket.

MATCH UP Match each word with one of the suffixes below to form a list word. Write each word.

ness	less	ment

15. care   18. spot
16. treat   19. dark
17. bright   20. punish

STRATEGIC SPELLING

Building New Words

Add the suffix to each base word to make a new word.

Base word	Suffix	New word
21. home	-less	_____
22. enjoy	-ment	_____
23. cold	-ness	_____

1. _____
2. _____
3. _____
4. _____
5. _____
6. _____
7. _____
8. _____
9. _____
10. _____
11. _____
12. _____
13. _____
14. _____
15. _____
16. _____
17. _____
18. _____
19. _____
20. _____

Take a Hint
It's easy to leave out the **i** in **business** because you don't say it. Just remember this phrase: Take the **bus in** when you have **busin**ess in town.

131

≡	Make a capital.
/	Make a small letter.
∧	Add something.
ℓ	Take out something.
⊙	Add a period.
¶	New paragraph

PROOFREAD A COMIC STRIP

LaDonna and Jake created a superhero named WizKid, who fights crime by using brain power. Read WizKid's words and correct four misspellings and two careless errors.

> What is this I see on the pavment? It's a hepless bird with clipped wings!

> This is the work of my flightless foe, the Ostrich! Little bird, can you lead me that worthes evildoer?

> Release those nestlings, Ostrich! You've clipped your last wing! Get ready your punisment!

PROOFREADING TIP

LaDonna and Jake made a great superhero, but they also made two super errors. Words such as *to* and *for* may be small, but they should never be left out.

WRITE A COMIC STRIP

Practice writing your own comic strip dialogue. Use list words.

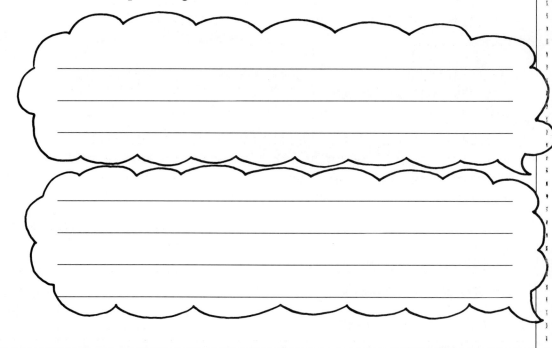

Word List

pavement	darkness
statement	brightness
movement	business
payment	breathless
treatment	careless
punishment	spotless
greatness	helpless
fairness	useless
goodness	hopeless
softness	worthless

Personal Words

1. _____

2. _____

PUZZLE IT OUT What is a name for action figures that are brave, strong, and good? Write the boxed words that match the clues. Then use the numbered letters to solve the riddle.

helpless	movement
careless	goodness
hopeless	softness
payment	brightness
statement	business

1. shininess
2. amount of money paid
3. motion
4. the opposite of badness
5. fluffiness
6. unable to take care of oneself
7. the opposite of confident
8. work; occupation
9. done without enough thought or effort
10. remark; declaration

1. _ _8_ _ _ _ _ _ _1_
2. _ _ _ _7_ _ _ _
3. _ _ _ _10_ _ _ _ _
4. _ _ _ _ _4_ _ _
5. _ _9_ _ _ _ _
6. _ _ _3_ _ _ _ _
7. _6_ _ _ _ _ _
8. _ _2_ _ _ _ _
9. _ _ _5_ _ _ _
10. _11_ _ _ _ _ _ _ _

_1_ _2_ _3_ _4_ _5_ _6_ _7_ _8_ _9_ _10_ _11_

Word *Study*

HAIKU Long ago in Japan, a contest was held in which competitors added lines to existing poems. Those who created the best lines won. The name **haiku** (hī′ kü) comes from this contest. Read the two haiku below.

The falling flower
I saw drift back to the branch
was a butterfly.

Poor crying cricket,
perhaps your little husband
was caught by our cat.

A haiku is usually three lines long and often describes a scene in nature. The first line has five syllables, the second line has seven syllables, and the third line has five syllables.

Write your own haiku.
Start with the line at the right.
Use a dictionary if you need
help counting syllables.

Raindrops on a leaf

_____

_____

Prefixes dis-, in-, mis-, re-

When prefixes **dis-**, **in-**, **mis-**, and **re-** are added to words, make no change in the spelling of the base word: **dis + like = dislike.**

■ **STUDY**   Notice that each base word below does not change when a prefix is added.

dis + like	=	1. *dislike*
dis + appear	=	2. *disappear*
in + complete	=	3. *incomplete*
in + dependent	=	4. *independent*
in + correct	=	5. *incorrect*
mis + place	=	6. *misplace*
mis + spell	=	7. *misspell*
mis + led	=	8. *misled*
re + build	=	9. *rebuild*
re + use	=	10. *reuse*

dis + trust	=	11. *distrust*
dis + honest	=	12. *dishonest*
dis + agree	=	13. *disagree*
in + visible	=	14. *invisible*
in + active	=	15. *inactive*
mis + treat	=	16. *mistreat*
mis + behave	=	17. *misbehave*
re + act	=	18. *react*
re + place	=	19. *replace*
re + call	=	20. *recall*

1. _____
2. _____
3. _____
4. _____
5. _____
6. _____
7. _____
8. _____
9. _____
10. _____
11. _____
12. _____
13. _____
14. _____
15. _____
16. _____
17. _____
18. _____
19. _____
20. _____

CHALLENGE!

disobedience
incredible
inconvenient
misfortune
recycling

■ **PRACTICE**   Sort the list words by writing
- five words with **dis-**
- five words with **re-**
- five words with **in-**
- five words with **mis-**

■ **WRITE**   Choose ten words to write in sentences.

SUPER ANTONYMS   Complete each statement with a list word that means the opposite of the underlined word.

1. Superguy said, "I <u>like</u> good guys, but I ___ criminals."
2. Spygirl stated, "I <u>trust</u> that you won't ___ me."
3. X-ray Man boasted,"What is <u>visible</u> to me is ___ to you."
4. Wiseguy said, "<u>Treat</u> others <u>well</u> and they won't ___ you."
5. Plastic Woman asked, "Do you <u>agree</u> or ___with me?"
6. Supergirl warned, "The <u>honest</u> are rewarded, but the ___ are never happy."

PREFIX ADDITION   Write the list word that has each beginning and meaning indicated below.

7. re + do something
8. dis + come into sight
9. in + without mistakes
10. mis + put down
11. re + put into service
12. in + finished
13. mis + went in front of
14. in + ready to do things
15. re + put down
16. mis + act politely
17. in + needing help
18. re + speak or shout
19. mis + write words
20. re + put pieces together

STRATEGIC SPELLING

Building New Words

Add the prefix **dis-** or **re-** to each word to make a new word. Remember what you learned.

21. able   _____

22. design   _____

23. charge   _____

24. band   _____

Take a Hint
Miss Pell will never misspell the word misspell!

1. _____
2. _____
3. _____
4. _____
5. _____
6. _____
7. _____
8. _____
9. _____
10. _____
11. _____
12. _____
13. _____
14. _____
15. _____
16. _____
17. _____
18. _____
19. _____
20. _____

☰	Make a capital.
/	Make a small letter.
∧	Add something.
℮	Take out something.
⊙	Add a period.
¶	New paragraph.

PROOFREAD A LETTER Editors at a textbook publisher received the letter below. Correct four misspellings and four handwriting errors.

PROOFREADING TIP

People appreciate hearing your opinion, but they have to be able to read what you write. Make it easy for them—always cross your t's and loop your l's.

April 8, 20__

Dear Editors,

Your spelling book is fun and some times challenging, but we all have sertain lessons we dislik. We enjoy finding words other wrilers mispell.

Sincerely,

Lill School Fourth Graders

WRITE A LETTER Let the editors of one of your textbooks know what you think of their product. Use list words.

Word List

disappear	misplace
distrust	misspell
dishonest	mistreat
disagree	misled
dislike	misbehave
invisible	react
incorrect	replace
incomplete	recall
inactive	rebuild
independent	reuse

Personal Words

1. _____

2. _____

Review

dislike	misplace
disappear	misspell
incomplete	misled
independent	rebuild
incorrect	reuse

WORD ASSOCIATIONS   Write the boxed word that you would associate with each situation described below.

1. a town repairing buildings that were damaged by a tornado
2. a child choosing activities he likes instead of just doing what everyone else wants to do
3. a student accidentally adding an extra letter as she is writing a word
4. a man saving a piece of paper to write on again
5. a student handing in a written assignment with missing answers
6. a customer discovering that a salesperson directed him to the wrong department
7. a student giving the wrong answer on a math test
8. a child not eating broccoli
9. a child forgetting where she left her library book
10. a boat sinking into a lake

1. _____
2. _____
3. _____
4. _____
5. _____
6. _____
7. _____
8. _____
9. _____
10. _____

Word *Study*

SYNONYMS   Words that have the same meanings are called **synonyms**. The words in dark type in the sentences below are synonyms.

When I rub my powerful ring, my assistant will **disappear.**

When I rub my powerful ring, my assistant will **vanish.**

Write the list word that is a synonym for each underlined word below.

1. I'm sorry that the number I gave you was <u>wrong</u>.
2. Doctors often <u>differ</u> about the way to treat patients.
3. You've made a good start, but your work is <u>unfinished</u>.
4. I cannot <u>remember</u> the words to that song.

1. _____
2. _____
3. _____
4. _____

Review

Lesson 25: Including All the Letters
Lesson 26: Compound Words
Lesson 27: Suffixes -ful, -ly, -ion
Lesson 28: Suffixes -less, -ment, -ness
Lesson 29: Prefixes dis-, in-, mis-, re-

REVIEW WORD LIST

1. camera	11. remember	21. nighttime	31. thoughtful	41. worthless
2. caught	12. several	22. something	32. brightness	42. disagree
3. December	13. surprised	23. beautiful	33. business	43. disappear
4. evening	14. swimming	24. carefully	34. fairness	44. dislike
5. everybody	15. baseball	25. daily	35. greatness	45. incomplete
6. everyone	16. classmate	26. invention	36. hopeless	46. independent
7. finally	17. classroom	27. painful	37. pavement	47. invisible
8. interesting	18. downstairs	28. peaceful	38. spotless	48. rebuild
9. island	19. myself	29. powerful	39. statement	49. recall
10. often	20. newspaper	30. suddenly	40. treatment	50. reuse

Adopt-a-Pet

brightness
newspaper
independent
daily
dislike
rebuild

These animals are looking for good homes. Read their stories and supply the words that are missing.

1. _____
2. _____
3. _____
4. _____
5. _____
6. _____

Rico

Rico is a quiet cat. He's a bit of a loner and very (1). The (2) of his wide, green eyes will delight you. Rico likes kids but would (3) living with another cat.

Mim

When Mim first arrived, she distrusted everyone. Help her (4) her trust by giving her a loving home. Mim must have (5) exercise. She loves to fetch the (6)!

Tricks of the Trade

Read the chapter subtitles from the book *Magic to Annoy Those Around You*. Write the words that have been left out.

reuse	**downstairs**	**everybody**	
invisible	**December**	**caught**	**disappear**

1. _____

2. _____

3. _____

4. _____

5. _____

6. _____

7. _____

1. Writing on your Grandpa's best shirt with ____ ink

2. New ways to ____ old paper towels

3. Ten foolproof ways to grab cookies without getting ____

4. Making your little sister ____ without a trace

5. Throwing your voice all the way ____ when you are upstairs

6. Convincing ____ at home that you're asleep when you're not

7. Creating ____ snowstorms in July with the spurting whipped-cream trick

classmate
powerful
baseball
island
several
camera
swimming

Necessities of Life

Use list words to complete the list below.

I would want these things along if I were stranded on a desert _____ :

- my _____ cap—for cool dips in the sea
- my _____ Alex—for good company
- a _____ — to capture the sights
- a _____ to toss around with Alex
- _____ books—about wilderness camping
- a _____ speedboat—for escape— HA HA!

Jack and the Beanstalk and the Three Little Pigs had their sides of the story told, but what do the giant and the wolf have to say? You supply the missing words.

Story Book Secrets

Daily Report ★★★★★★★ Read all about it!

Giant Tells All

Bigtown, Austria—The giant of the beanstalk legend has (1) agreed to share his story. He feels that the (2) the press has given him lacks (3). "I strongly (4) with what's been written about me," he said. "Jack stole my (5) harp and golden eggs! He brought disorder to my once quiet, (6) household. He gets to be the hero, and I'm the (7) one! Well, I'm here to defend (8)!"

From the Trial of B. B. Wolf

Bailiff: Do you swear that the (1) you are about to give is the whole truth, and nothing but the truth?

Wolf: I do.

Bailiff: Be seated.

Defense Lawyer: Tell us, Mr. Wolf, do you (2) the night of August 6?

Wolf: Yes, I think about it (3). It is the night I huffed and puffed and blew. . . .

Defense Lawyer: To be sure, but how were you feeling that particular (4)?

Wolf: I had a terrible cold. My sinuses were blocked and very (5). Whenever I sneezed, a house fell to the (6)!

Defense Lawyer: So it wasn't your intention to destroy the homes of these squealing piglets?

Wolf: Certainly not! I am a peaceful wolf who minds his own business.

disagree beautiful fairness
peaceful treatment finally
myself worthless

1. _____
2. _____
3. _____
4. _____
5. _____
6. _____
7. _____
8. _____

painful pavement statement
recall evening often

1. _____
2. _____
3. _____
4. _____
5. _____
6. _____

The Leszczynsky family is celebrating the birthday of their dog, Spot. Supply the words that are missing from the card they wrote.

1. _____
2. _____
3. _____
4. _____
5. _____

surprised spotless
everyone nighttime
remember

BIRTHDAY GREETINGS
to One Fine Canine

You know (1) said that we were thoughtless,
For naming you Spot, although you are (2)!

Will you be (3) to find steak in your bowl,
And to have us take you for a (4) stroll?

Just (5), dear old Spot,
We all love you quite a lot!

Hugs and kisses,
Your Family

140

Benjamin Banneker— American Genius

page 1

By Yael Rubin

Learning about Benjamin Banneker was very (1). He became famous for the (2) of his mathematical abilities.

He was (3) taught to read and write by his grandmother. He was further educated in the (4) of a Quaker school. George Ellicott, who owned a large flour mill (5), also encouraged Benjamin's (6) pursuit of knowledge.

Write the words that are missing from Yael's report on a famous American.

business
carefully
interesting
thoughtful
classroom
greatness

1. _____
2. _____
3. _____
4. _____
5. _____
6. _____

page 2

At the age of 24, Benjamin built a clock that struck the hour. This clock is thought to be the first such (7) made in the United States.

Later, Benjamin was appointed by George Washington to help plan Washington, D.C. The chief architect had (8) left the project, so the work was (9). The architect had taken the plans with him, and re-creating them seemed (10). Benjamin came to the rescue, drawing all the plans from memory. The building of the capital city is (11) people can thank Benjamin Banneker for.

invention   hopeless   suddenly
incomplete   something

7. _____
8. _____
9. _____
10. _____
11. _____

141

Choosing the Best Strategy

DISCOVER THE STRATEGY You've learned that it is important to use the Steps for Spelling when studying spelling words. Don't forget to also use the strategies you've learned when a spelling word gives you a problem. Read about the strategies in the chart below.

Steps for Spelling	**Divide and Conquer**	**Memory Tricks**
Use the step-by-step strategy for studying most spelling words. 1. Look. 2. Spell. 3. Think. 4. Picture. 5. Look. 6. Cover and write.	Divide long words into shorter pieces. choc/o/late un/known	Link the tricky word with a helper you can spell. <u>You</u> are <u>you</u>ng. <u>qu</u>ick l<u>i</u>q<u>ui</u>d
Problem Parts	**Pronouncing for Spelling**	**Meaning Helpers**

Identify the problem part and study it extra hard.
    <u>w</u>rong   laug<u>h</u>ed
	Pronounce the word correctly, say a silent letter, or exaggerate a sound.
	    Say "thum<u>**b**</u>." Say "mil-<u>**li-on**</u>."
		Find a related word that gives you a sound clue.
		      ev<u>e</u>r—every a<u>ct</u>—a<u>ct</u>ion

TRY IT OUT Now it's time to practice choosing the best strategies. Read the exercises below and on the next page. Write the name of each strategy. Use the chart.

1. Which tricky strategy helps you remember the two **r**'s in *arrives*?

   _____

2. Which strategy helps you conquer a long word like *caterpillar?*

_____

3. Which strategy helps you remember to pronounce the **o** in *favorite?*

_____

4. Name the meaningful strategy that is helpful when trying to remember that *operation* is spelled with a **t.**

_____

5. Which strategy would you use if a certain part of the word were giving you a spelling problem?

_____

Compare your results with others in your class. It's fine to have different choices as long as you can explain them.

LOOK AHEAD Look ahead at the next five lessons. Find three words that look hard to spell. Write the word and the strategy you would use to help spell each word.

1. _____   _____

2. _____   _____

3. _____   _____

Vowels with No Sound Clues

SPELLING FOCUS

In many words, the vowel sound gives no clue to its spelling: m**a**chine, mom**e**nt, an**i**mals, ir**o**n, s**u**pport.

■ **STUDY** Say each word. Then read the sentence.

1. machine — We need an answering **machine**.
2. especially ✳ — I love fruit, **especially** bananas.
3. usually — Pandas **usually** eat bamboo.
4. probably ✳ — Prices will **probably** rise.
5. giant — This **giant** pillow is too big.
6. moment — Talk to me for just a **moment**.
7. animals — A zoo has many **animals**.
8. iron — You must **iron** those pants.
9. support — He offered her his **support**.
10. suppose — I **suppose** we'll be invited.

11. buffalo — We saw **buffalo** on the plains.
12. Canada — **Canada** is our northern neighbor.
13. canoe — We often **canoe** down this stream.
14. relatives — My **relatives** live in the South.
15. stomach — I hear my **stomach** growling!
16. cement — The sidewalk is made of **cement**.
17. yesterday — We did that lesson **yesterday**.
18. favorite ✳ — Blue is my **favorite** color.
19. welcome — Cities always **welcome** visitors.
20. August — School may begin in **August**.

■ **PRACTICE** Sort the words by writing those you know how to spell. Then write the ones you think are difficult. You can use a memory trick like this for learning hard words: The **stomach** is an eating **machine**. Tell which strategy you will use for learning the hard words.

■ **WRITE** Choose ten words to write in sentences.

1. _____
2. _____
3. _____
4. _____
5. _____
6. _____
7. _____
8. _____
9. _____
10. _____
11. _____
12. _____
13. _____
14. _____
15. _____
16. _____
17. _____
18. _____
19. _____
20. _____

CHALLENGE!

dictionary
separate
multiplication
salmon
recognize

✳ **WATCH OUT FOR FREQUENTLY MISSPELLED WORDS!**

DRAWING CONCLUSIONS   Write a list word that fits each clue below.

1. A bricklayer uses this material to keep things in place.
2. If you want to paddle down a river, do it in this.
3. These people may be your aunts, uncles, and cousins.
4. When friends come to visit, greet them with a big one.
5. This is what you call the one you like more than others.
6. Use this to straighten out a wrinkled shirt.
7. A fairy tale might include one of these large fellows.
8. This is the month before September.
9. To sew a dress quickly, learn to operate one of these.
10. Sit-ups firm up the muscles in this part of your body.
11. This country is the United States' neighbor to the north.

SYNONYMS   Write the list word that means the same as the words below. Use the Spelling Dictionary for help.

12. particularly; chiefly
13. assume; believe
14. help; comfort
15. instant; short time
16. normally; customarily

1. _____
2. _____
3. _____
4. _____
5. _____
6. _____
7. _____
8. _____
9. _____
10. _____
11. _____
12. _____
13. _____
14. _____
15. _____
16. _____

STRATEGIC SPELLING
Choosing the Best Strategy

Write *yesterday, probably, buffalo,* and *animals.* Which strategy could help you spell all four words? Name the strategy and tell why you chose it. Compare choices with a partner. For a list of strategies, see page 142.

17. _____   19. _____

18. _____   20. _____

Name of strategy: _____

Why I chose it: _____

_____

FREQUENTLY MISSPELLED WORDS

To be an **especial**ly good speller, include the word *special* inside *especially* whenever you write it.

☰	Make a capital.
/	Make a small letter.
∧	Add something.
ℯ	Take out something.
⊙	Add a period.
¶	New paragraph.

PROOFREAD A LETTER Anya wrote this letter home after her first day at camp. Correct five misspelled words, one of which is an incorrectly formed plural.

PROOFREADING TIP

Remember, to make words that end in a consonant and **y** plural, you must change the **y** to **i** and add **-es.**

July 8, 20__

Dear Mom and Aunt Carol,

I arrived yesterdey. Flies are everywhere. My canoe tipped over. The food is relly bad. I supose one day I'll have fond memorys of camp, but so far it's not my favrite place.

Love,

Tenderfoot

Word List

animals	canoe
buffalo	machine
especially	moment
favorite	relatives
giant	stomach
August	cement
suppose	yesterday
usually	probably
iron	support
Canada	welcome

Personal Words

1. _____

2. _____

WRITE A LETTER Pretend you are at camp. Write a letter home telling all about your first day. Use list words.

_____
_____
_____
_____
_____
_____
_____

Review

machine	moment
especially	animals
usually	iron
probably	support
giant	suppose

CROSSWORD PUZZLE Complete the crossword puzzle by writing the word that matches each definition.

Across

3. help
5. living things that are not plants
8. likely
9. huge
10. a very short space of time

Down

1. more than others
2. press
4. commonly; ordinarily
6. consider as possible
7. an object for doing work

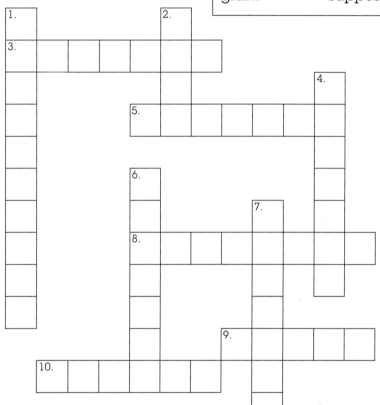

Using a *Dictionary*

FINDING A WORD WHEN YOU CAN'T SPELL IT

Many sounds in the English language can be spelled lots of different ways. Take the sound /s/, for example. It can be spelled **s**upport, **c**ement, **sc**ent, li**st**en, wal**tz,** and about six other ways. So if you wanted to look up *sword* and only knew it began with the sound /s/, what would you do?

You'd check the Spellings of English Sounds chart in your dictionary (and in this book on page 245). It shows you all the ways any given sound in English can be spelled.

Look at each pronunciation below. Write the word you would look up in the dictionary to find its spelling. If you are unsure, check the Spellings of English Sounds chart. Then check your Spelling Dictionary for the correct spelling.

1. (hwēt)   2. (brij)   3. (fō′tō)

1. _____   2. _____   3. _____

Vowels in Final Syllables

SPELLING FOCUS

The vowels in final syllables often sound alike but are spelled differently: **peopl_e_, mod_el_; broke_n_, commo_n_.**

■ **STUDY**   Say each word. Then read the sentence.

1. *other*   Where's my **other** shoe?
2. *number*   The runner wore the **number** ten.
3. *color*   I painted the room a different **color.**
4. *doctor*   The **doctor** looked at the X ray.
5. *people* ✳   She loves meeting new **people.**
6. *simple*   Spelling **simple** words is fun.
7. *model*   He is a **model** for all soldiers.
8. *broken*   I threw away the **broken** glass.
9. *sudden*   The siren gave a **sudden** warning.
10. *common*   Cake is a **common** dessert.

11. *October*   **October** evenings are often cool.
12. *another* ✳   Pass me **another** rye roll, please.
13. *motor*   The **motor** in a car makes it run.
14. *angle*   Set the boards at a right **angle.**
15. *title*   What is the story's **title?**
16. *barrel*   The pickles are stored in a **barrel.**
17. *angel*   She drew wings on the **angel.**
18. *oven*   Cookies are baking in the **oven.**
19. *gallon*   We bought a **gallon** of cider.
20. *button*   Would you **button** my cuffs?

■ **PRACTICE**   Sort the list words by writing
■ seven words that end with **or** and **er**
■ seven words that end with **el** and **le**
■ six words that end with **en** and **on**

■ **WRITE**   Choose two sentences to include in
a paragraph.

1. _____
2. _____
3. _____
4. _____
5. _____
6. _____
7. _____
8. _____
9. _____
10. _____
11. _____
12. _____
13. _____
14. _____
15. _____
16. _____
17. _____
18. _____
19. _____
20. _____

CHALLENGE!

receiver
counselor
article
citizen
cinnamon

✳ **WATCH OUT FOR FREQUENTLY MISSPELLED WORDS!**

THINK AND PRACTICE ■

CONTEXT CLUES   Write the list word that ends like the underlined word and completes the sentence.

1. An ___ with wings was carved into each door <u>panel</u>.
2. Tex was my ___ when I learned how to <u>yodel</u>.
3. The little <u>squirrel</u> jumped into the wooden ___.
4. To cure a <u>pimple</u>, try this ___ solution.
5. No one ___ than <u>Mother</u> will be waiting.
6. The <u>inventor</u> built a new automobile ___.
7. My <u>cotton</u> shirt is missing a ___.
8. I would not <u>bother</u> to look for ___ pen.
9. Drinking tea with <u>lemon</u> is ___ in many countries.
10. A ___ rainstorm will <u>sadden</u> picnickers.
11. The poor little <u>chicken</u> had a ___ wing.

ABBREVIATIONS   Write the list word that corresponds to each abbreviation below. Use the Spelling Dictionary if you need help.

12. Dr.
13. Oct.
14. gal.
15. no.

CATEGORIZING   Write the list word that names the category to which you would assign each group below.

16. men, women, children
17. turquoise, mauve, orange
18. your highness, her majesty
19. gas, electric

STRATEGIC SPELLING
Seeing Meaning Connections

20. Write a list word that is related to the words in the box.

rectangle
triangle

Write the words from the box that fit the definitions.

21. a three-sided shape _____

22. a four-sided shape _____

| 1. |
| 2. |
| 3. |
| 4. |
| 5. |
| 6. |
| 7. |
| 8. |
| 9. |
| 10. |
| 11. |
| 12. |
| 13. |
| 14. |
| 15. |
| 16. |
| 17. |
| 18. |
| 19. |
| 20. |

Did You Know?
The word *angel* comes from a Greek word meaning "messenger."

149

Make a capital.

 Make a small letter.

∧ Add something.

Take out something.

⊙ Add a period.

¶ New paragraph

PROOFREAD A CARD Indira received this card from a friend at school. Correct five misspelled words and two careless errors.

PROOFREADING TIP

You may leave out words when you're writing a card you're in a hurry to mail. Take a minute to proofread. Your reader will thank you.

GET WELL SOON!

I sorry about your brokin leg. Does it hurt? Is your docter nice? All the peopel at shcool miss you a lot. Hurry back. I want sighn your cast.

Michael

WRITE A CARD Pretend you are Indira. Write a response to your friend's card. Use a few list words and some personal words.

Word List

people	sudden
gallon	another
color	button
broken	other
October	simple
angle	doctor
number	oven
barrel	title
motor	angel
model	common

Personal Words

1. _____

2. _____

Review

other	simple
number	model
color	broken
doctor	sudden
people	common

WORDS IN CONTEXT   Write the missing boxed words to complete the following news story.

Jimmy Thundercloud got quite a surprise during his demonstration of a (1) of the new XK-2000 vacuum cleaner at Mulberry's Department Store. "Most vacuum cleaners have a hard time picking up pet hair, but that task is (2) for the XK-2000," Mr. Thundercloud announced to the large (3) of (4) who were admiring the bright red (5) of the machine. Just as Mr. Thundercloud turned on the machine, the loud roar of the motor could be heard in all the (6) departments. All of a (7), the powerful suction turned the hose into a wild monster. It thrashed about wildly and hit Mr. Thundercloud in the arm with a loud *smack*.

"The arm is (8) and will be in a cast for about six weeks," says Mr. Thundercloud's (9).

A (10) reaction might be anger, but in an interview, Mr. Thundercloud chuckled and said, "I guess that machine just doesn't like me!"

1. _____
2. _____
3. _____
4. _____
5. _____
6. _____
7. _____
8. _____
9. _____
10. _____

Word *Study*

WORD WEBS   Suppose you wanted to write a report about spiders. The first thing you'd want to do is ask yourself what you know about them. "What do they look like? What do they do? What makes them special?" Your next step would be to create a **word web** like the one below.

eight-legged   *small*

spider

builds webs   *eats insects*

Now suppose you were a spider, spinning a word web about people. Write the words you would use in your web.

(1) _____   (2) _____

people

(3) _____   (4) _____

1. _____
2. _____
3. _____
4. _____

Capitalization and Abbreviation

Holidays, days and months of the year, titles, and words that are part of an address are always capitalized: **Christmas, May.** Abbreviations should be capitalized and followed by a period: **Dr., Rd., Sun.**

■ **STUDY** Notice that these words are capitalized. Some have periods.

1. Memorial Day
2. Christmas ✳
3. Sun.
4. May
5. June
6. September
7. Dec.
8. Dr.
9. Mrs.
10. Rd.
11. Hanukkah
12. Kwanzaa
13. Chinese New Year
14. Valentine's Day
15. November
16. Feb.
17. Wed.
18. Ms.
19. Mr.
20. Ave.

■ **PRACTICE** Sort the list words by writing
- six words that name holidays
- two words that name days
- six words that name months
- four words that name people
- two words that name types of streets

■ **WRITE** Choose three words to write an invitation to a holiday party.

CHALLENGE!

Fourth of July
St. Patrick's Day
English
Blvd.
etc.

1.
2.
3.
4.
5.
6.
7.
8.
9.
10.
11.
12.
13.
14.
15.
16.
17.
18.
19.
20.

✳ **WATCH OUT FOR FREQUENTLY MISSPELLED WORDS!**

ABBREVIATIONS   Write the abbreviation on your spelling list that stands for each word below.

1. doctor
2. avenue
3. December
4. Wednesday
5. February
6. mister
7. Sunday
8. road

IDENTIFICATION   Write the list word that matches each clue below.

9. This is the ninth month of the year.
10. On this day we remember those who have died.
11. This is the fifth month of the year.
12. This is the eleventh month of the year.
13. This is a title put in front of a married woman's name.
14. This is the sixth month of the year.
15. On this day we may send a card to a sweetheart.
16. This is a title put in front of a woman's name, married or unmarried.

1. _____
2. _____
3. _____
4. _____
5. _____
6. _____
7. _____
8. _____
9. _____
10. _____
11. _____
12. _____
13. _____
14. _____
15. _____
16. _____

STRATEGIC SPELLING

The Divide and Conquer Strategy

Sometimes it helps to study long words piece by piece. Write *Kwanzaa, Hanukkah, Christmas,* and *Chinese New Year*. Draw lines between the syllables. Then study each word syllable by syllable. Use a dictionary if you need help.

17. _____
18. _____
19. _____
20. _____

Did You Know?
Both **Hanukkah** and **Kwanzaa** can be spelled in different ways. You may also see **Hanukkah** spelled **Chanukah**. **Kwanzaa** may also be spelled **Kwanza**.

≡	Make a capital.
/	Make a small letter.
∧	Add something.
ℰ	Take out something.
⊙	Add a period.
⌐⌐	New paragraph

PROOFREAD AN ANNOUNCEMENT

The announcement below was posted on a school bulletin board. Find five misspelled words and four handwriting errors. Write them correctly.

PROOFREADING TIP

Did you stop and try to figure out what an aulhor and an audilorium were? Uncrossed t's can cause confusion. You can catch these errors if you proofread.

Ms Jan Dure to Speak on Novenber 5

Here the aulhor of <u>Hannah's Hannuka</u>, <u>Cal's Cristmas</u>, and <u>Kestra's Kwanzaa</u> speak aboul her wriling.

Time: Wed. 6:00 P.M.

Place: School Audilorium

WRITE AN ANNOUNCEMENT

Now it's your turn to write an announcement about a visiting author. Use list words and personal words.

_____

_____

_____

_____

_____

_____

_____

_____

Word List

Ms.	Hanukkah
Mr.	Christmas
Mrs.	Kwanzaa
Dr.	Chinese New Year
Ave.	Valentine's Day
Rd.	Memorial Day
Sun.	May
Wed.	June
Feb.	September
Dec.	November

Personal Words

1. _____

2. _____

Review

MAKING INFERENCES Complete each group by writing the missing boxed word.

Memorial Day	September
Christmas	Dec.
Sun.	Dr.
May	Mrs.
June	Rd.

1. April, ___, June
2. Oct., Nov., ___
3. August, ___, October
4. Sat., ___, Mon.
5. May, ___, July

MAKING ASSOCIATIONS Write the boxed word that you would associate with each group of words below.

6. December, tree, celebration
7. woman, married, title
8. person, professional, medicine
9. street, address, abbreviation
10. holiday, May, remembering

1. _____
2. _____
3. _____
4. _____
5. _____
6. _____
7. _____
8. _____
9. _____
10. _____

Multicultural *Connection*

HOLIDAYS People everywhere celebrate important occasions. Read the descriptions of the holidays below. Then answer the questions.

Hanukkah celebrates the recapturing of the great temple at Jerusalem over 2,000 years ago. Jewish writings describe how the Jews had barely enough lamp oil for one night in the temple, yet the lamp burned for eight days. Today, the menorah is lit in memory of this. Also called the "Festival of Lights," Hanukkah is celebrated in November or December.

Christmas celebrates the birth of Jesus, also called Christ. According to the Bible, Jesus was born in a stable and welcomed with gifts from wise men and shepherds. Christians believe Jesus is their savior. Small stable scenes are often seen at Christmas. It comes on December 25.

Kwanzaa is a yearly African American holiday created in 1966. It celebrates black people and their history. There are seven principles of Kwanzaa. The kinara, or candle holder, holds seven candles, one for each principle. Kwanzaa lasts from December 26 through January 1.

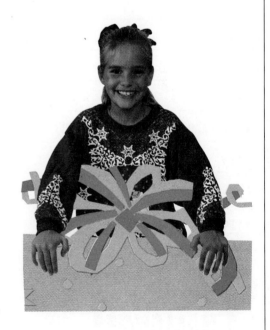

1. Which holiday celebrates African traditions?
2. Which holiday celebrates the birth of Jesus?
3. Which holiday is also called the "Festival of Lights"?

1. _____
2. _____
3. _____

Possessives

1. _____
2. _____
3. _____
4. _____
5. _____
6. _____
7. _____
8. _____
9. _____
10. _____
11. _____
12. _____
13. _____
14. _____
15. _____
16. _____
17. _____
18. _____
19. _____
20. _____

SPELLING FOCUS

To form possessives of
- singular nouns, add an **apostrophe** and **s: baby's**
- plural nouns that end in **s**, add only an **apostrophe: babies'**

■ **STUDY** Say each word. Then read the sentence.

1. *Dad's*   April 25 is **Dad's** birthday.
2. *friend's* ✳   That's my **friend's** book.
3. *girl's*   That **girl's** drawing was good.
4. *girls'*   I can't find the **girls'** bathroom.
5. *teacher's*   I met my **teacher's** mother.
6. *teachers'*   This room is the **teachers'** lounge.
7. *baby's*   Wash the **baby's** bottle.
8. *babies'*   She saw all the **babies'** fathers.
9. *family's*   Look at my **family's** picture.
10. *families'*   We shared our **families'** stories.

11. *grandma's*   I have my **grandma's** ring.
12. *grandpa's*   Show me my **grandpa's** store.
13. *brother's*   He is my older **brother's** friend.
14. *brothers'*   This is my two **brothers'** room.
15. *boy's*   We found that **boy's** bicycle.
16. *boys'*   They are on the **boys'** soccer team.
17. *aunt's*   We're keeping my **aunt's** dog.
18. *aunts'*   These are my **aunts'** cars.
19. *lady's*   He returned the **lady's** purse.
20. *ladies'*   That store sells **ladies'** hats.

■ **PRACTICE** Sort the list words by writing
- twelve singular possessive nouns
- eight plural possessive nouns

■ **WRITE** Choose four sentences to rewrite as questions.

CHALLENGE!

someone's
boss's
James's
grandparent's
grandparents'

156

✳ **WATCH OUT FOR FREQUENTLY MISSPELLED WORDS!**

SINGULAR POSSESSIVES Complete each sentence by writing the singular possessive of the underlined word.

1. We found the boy cap under the chair.
2. I enjoyed the girl piano playing very much.
3. I visited my aunt office last Tuesday.
4. I accidentally scratched my brother car.
5. I listened to Dad advice.
6. The children loved their grandma lullabies.
7. She always followed her grandpa directions.
8. I stayed the night at my best friend house.

USING CONTEXT CLUES Write the list word that is a form of the word in parentheses to complete each sentence.

9. I found a (lady) ring at the bottom of the pool.
10. That makes five (lady) rings I've found this week!
11. My (family) way of spending free time is to go hiking.
12. Other (family) free time activities may differ from ours.
13. My math (teacher) classroom is full of large posters.
14. The other (teacher) classrooms have smaller posters.
15. I put the (baby) little jacket on a hook in the closet.

PLURAL POSSESSIVES Write the possessive of each word.

16. brothers _____

17. boys _____

18. aunts _____

19. babies _____

20. girls _____

1. _____
2. _____
3. _____
4. _____
5. _____
6. _____
7. _____
8. _____
9. _____
10. _____
11. _____
12. _____
13. _____
14. _____
15. _____

Take a Hint
Dad's is capitalized only when it is used as a name. *You read Dad's letter, but you borrow your dad's pen.*

STRATEGIC SPELLING
Building New Words

Write the words that complete the chart.

Singular	Singular Possessive	Plural Possessive
21. father	_____	_____
22. monkey	_____	_____

157

≡	Make a capital.
/	Make a small letter.
∧	Add something.
ℓ	Take out something.
⊙	Add a period.
¶	New paragraph

PROOFREAD AN OPINION Find four misspelled words in this opinion. Write them correctly. Fix two places where the subject and verb don't agree.

PROOFREADING TIP

I take, you take, but it takes. Be sure your subject (It) always agrees with your verb (takes).

Opinion Poll: Should Your TV Watching Be Restricted?

☑ *Yes*   ☐ *No*

Comments:

Watching to much TV is bad for you. It take away from the time you'd be doing important stuff. At my frends house, his family watch TV all day! I read, play basball, and help build my grandpas boat instead.

WRITE AN OPINION Do you think that you should restrict the amount of TV you watch? Write the reasons for your opinion. Use list words and personal words.

Word List

brother's	lady's
brothers'	ladies'
boy's	family's
boys'	families'
girl's	baby's
girls'	babies'
aunt's	grandma's
aunts'	grandpa's
teacher's	Dad's
teachers'	friend's

Personal Words

1. _____

2. _____

_____
_____
_____
_____
_____
_____
_____
_____

Review

CONTEXT CLUES Write the list word that completes each *if...then* sentence.

Dad's	teachers'
friend's	baby's
girl's	babies'
girls'	family's
teacher's	families'

1. If a teacher owns a house, then it is the ___ house.
2. If your friend is having a party, then it is your ___ party.
3. If some cars are owned by more than one family, then they are the ___ cars.
4. If a baby has a stuffed animal, then it is the ___ stuffed animal.
5. If some computers are owned by more than one teacher, then they are the ___ computers.
6. If two or more girls have lunches, then they are the ___ lunches.
7. If Dad has his own special chair, then it is ___ chair.
8. If a girl has her own telephone, then it is the ___ telephone.
9. If a family has a vegetable garden, then it is the ___ garden.
10. If several babies have blankets, then they are the ___ blankets.

1. _____
2. _____
3. _____
4. _____
5. _____
6. _____
7. _____
8. _____
9. _____
10. _____

Word *Study*

PALINDROMES Anna, Otto, and Ada have something in common. Their first names are **palindromes.** A palindrome is a word that reads the same backward and forward. To complete the puzzle below, you must write palindromes. You will find the names of the Palindrome Kids hiding in the puzzle.

Across
3. the sound made by a horn or whistle
6. 12 o'clock in the daytime
7. something done; a good ___ should be rewarded
8. a girl's name
9. a young dog

Down
1. a boy's name
2. a short word for *mother*
4. a girl's name
5. the sound made by a young bird

159

Easily Confused Words

SPELLING FOCUS

Some words are easily confused because they have similar pronunciations and spellings: **our, are.**

■ **STUDY** Say each word. Then read the sentence.

1. *set*   He **set** the alarm for 6:00.
2. *sit*   May I **sit** on this cushion?
3. *off* ✳   Please turn **off** the radio.
4. *of*   Half is part **of** a whole.
5. *when* ✳   Call me **when** you finish.
6. *win*   Not everyone can **win.**
7. *our* ✳   We love **our** new home.
8. *are* ✳   They **are** watching television.
9. *than*   Geese are bigger **than** ducks.
10. *then* ✳   Wash your hair, **then** comb it.

11. *lose*   They didn't **lose** the game.
12. *loose*   My shoelace is coming **loose.**
13. *were* ✳   I'd stay if I **were** you.
14. *we're* ✳   She says **we're** not going.
15. *where* ✳   He doesn't know **where** I live.
16. *quiet*   The woods were dark and **quiet.**
17. *quite*   The cat is not **quite** a year old.
18. *quit*   She **quit** a job that she hated.
19. *whose*   Tell me **whose** voice that was.
20. *who's*   He asked **who's** bringing the food.

■ **PRACTICE** First write the groups of words that are confusing for you. Then write the rest of the words.

■ **WRITE** Choose two sentences to write a rhyme.

1.
2.
3.
4.
5.
6.
7.
8.
9.
10.
11.
12.
13.
14.
15.
16.
17.
18.
19.
20.

CHALLENGE!

recent	resent
pedal	petal
diary	dairy

✳ **WATCH OUT FOR FREQUENTLY MISSPELLED WORDS!**

☰	Make a capital.
/	Make a small letter.
∧	Add something.
ℯ	Take out something.
⊙	Add a period.
⨍	New paragraph

PROOFREAD A SIGN   The sign in the photograph below contains a misspelled word. Can you find it? Write the word correctly.

PROOFREADING TIP

Be sure that words you've written with apostrophes really should have them. Read the words without the apostrophe—*who's* as *who is*, for example—to see if it's needed.

CREATE A SIGN   Do you have a favorite snack you'd like to tell everyone about? Draw a picture and use a word or two from the word list. Be sure to proofread your writing.

Word List

were	then
we're	than
where	lose
quiet	loose
quite	set
quit	sit
off	when
of	win
our	whose
are	who's

Personal Words

1. _____

2. _____

Review

WORDS IN CONTEXT   Write the boxed words that complete the following note.

set	win
sit	our
off	are
of	than
when	then

Dear Robert and Carrie,

I will be a little late getting home this evening. In case you (1) hungry, I (2) a bowl of fruit on the kitchen table. I plan to be home about 6:30, and (3) we will have (4) dinner. Remember, do not (5) in front of the television while you are doing your homework. The TV must be turned (6) until you have finished your work.

Carrie, did your team (7) the relay race today? You said your team had faster runners (8) the other team. Robert, did you do all right on that math test? I am anxious to see both (9) you (10) I get home.

Love,
Mom

P.S. Don't forget to feed Scuffy.

1. _____
2. _____
3. _____
4. _____
5. _____
6. _____
7. _____
8. _____
9. _____
10. _____

Word *Study*

USING EXACT WORDS   *Win* is a perfectly good word to use when describing a victory. But think how boring sportscasts would be if scores from baseball games were read using only *win* or *lose*.

> Cozy's Cafe had a 10-9 win against Dee's Diner.

> Harold's Hardware lost 3-5 to Main St. Lumber.

When sportscasters use words that are more exact and descriptive, we get a better (and more interesting) picture.

> Cozy Cafe slapped Dee's Diner with a 10-9 check that was the upset of the season.

> Main St. Lumber hammered away at Harold's Hardware to gain a 5-3 victory.

Use your own words to complete the sportscast below.

1. The Hawks' superior pitching _____ the Pigeons in the first five innings.
2. The Pigeons _____ but couldn't get a hit.
3. The Pigeons were _____ by the Hawks 6-0.

163

Review

Lesson 31: Vowels with No Sound Clues

Lesson 32: Vowels in Final Syllables

Lesson 33: Capitalization and Abbreviation

Lesson 34: Possessives

Lesson 35: Easily Confused Words

REVIEW WORD LIST

1. animals
2. August
3. buffalo
4. Canada
5. especially
6. favorite
7. giant
8. iron
9. machine
10. moment
11. probably
12. relatives
13. stomach
14. support
15. welcome
16. yesterday
17. angel
18. another
19. broken
20. button
21. common
22. model
23. number
24. oven
25. people
26. Ave.
27. Chinese New Year
28. Dr.
29. Hanukkah
30. Ms.
31. November
32. Rd.
33. Sun.
34. Valentine's Day
35. Wed.
36. baby's
37. boys'
38. Dad's
39. are
40. loose
41. lose
42. of
43. our
44. quit
45. quite
46. set
47. than
48. were
49. we're
50. win

WEEKLY CALENDAR

Wed.
Dad's
Rd.
Sun.
Dr.

Use the list words to complete the calendar.

_____	*Visit Arnetta.*
Mon.	*Board Meeting—21 Oak _____*
Tue.	*Pick up _____ shirts.*
_____	*Book Club—7 P.M.*
Thurs.	*Eye Exam—_____ Fowler 10 a.m.*

164

Offbeat Greetings

These days, greeting cards say more than just "Happy Birthday" and "Get Well." Supply the missing words in each card below.

baby's   August   probably
iron   Ave.   yesterday
loose   of

Congratulations!
It's your (1) first tooth! Let's hope it stays in there and doesn't get (2)!

HAPPY BIRTHDAY
(in advance)
I know it's July and you were born in (3), but I like to keep ahead (4) things!

Welcome to the Neighborhood!
You have (5) heard the rumors about Maple (6). Well, most of them are true!

DEAR FRIEND,
I'm sorry I didn't call you (7). I had to (8) my best shirt and that takes time. Maybe tomorrow... after I wash my hair.

1. _____
2. _____
3. _____
4. _____
5. _____
6. _____
7. _____
8. _____

BEING CATERED TO

Jake and Clare make healthy desserts for people giving parties. Supply the list words missing from their advertising brochure.

- Ja'Clare offers your (1) the healthiest and tastiest dessert it's ever had.
- Our treats come direct from our (2) to you!
- Choose from tarts, pies, custards, mousses, and any (3) of your (4) cakes.
- We work seven days a week and (5) always available for consultations.
- You'll find that (6) desserts are (7) the thing for parties, (8) the masterpiece we call Strawberry Rapture.

favorite
number
we're
especially
stomach
oven
our
quite

1. _____
2. _____
3. _____
4. _____
5. _____
6. _____
7. _____
8. _____

Happy Holidays

Use the list words to complete the holiday memories.

Hanukkah   **Chinese New Year**   **Valentine's Day**
angel   **relatives**   **moment**
giant

1. What I love best about Christmas is putting the _____ on the tree.

2. I love the glow of the candles in the menorah on _____.

3. My favorite memory of Kwanzaa is seeing all my friends and _____.

4. Memorial Day is a time I like to take a _____ to remember those who have died.

5. I enjoy welcoming in the new year with fireworks and a dragon parade during _____.

6. We always buy a _____ pumpkin to carve at Halloween. It's great!

7. I like getting those fancy, heart-shaped greetings on _____.

Canada   **button**
boys'   **animals**
machine   **model**
set

1. _____
2. _____
3. _____
4. _____
5. _____
6. _____
7. _____

Moving Out

The Russos are packed and ready to move, but they need help labeling all their belongings. Use each list word once.

Grandma's (1) collection

Mom's five-speed rowing (2)

Leonardo's (3) airplane kits

Dion's miniature tea (4)

(5) skates-sizes 5 and 6

Jenelle's stuffed (6)

Angela's map of (7)

Where the Buffalo Roam

Read the information below and supply the missing list words.

lose buffalo are than

quit were common

The American bison, also called the (1), once roamed over most of North America. In the 1700s there (2) thirty to sixty million buffalo in North America. A single herd might be twenty miles wide and more (3) fifty miles long. By the 1800s the slaughter of buffalo by the thousands was a (4) occurrence. It looked as though we might (5) the buffalo forever. By 1900 there were only 20 wild bison left in the United States. Laws were passed to ensure that people would (6) hunting them, and there (7) now parks and preserves that protect the buffalo.

1. _____
2. _____
3. _____

4. _____
5. _____
6. _____
7. _____

Election Time

Lynn Page is running for student council treasurer. Help her finish her campaign slogans.

1. _____
2. _____
3. _____
4. _____
5. _____
6. _____
7. _____
8. _____

people
Ms.
support
win
welcome
November
broken
another

If YOU vote for Lynn, we're all sure to (1)! Lend your (2) to one who understands money.

Attention: all (3) of voting age. When you vote in (4), be sure it's for (5) Page.

No more (6) promises!! You are all (7) to join LYNN to discuss the issues.

It's time for (8) point of view! Turn to Page!

Vocabulary, Writing, and Reference Resources

Cross-Curricular Lessons

Writer's Handbook

Spelling Dictionary

Writer's Thesaurus

English/Spanish Word List

Cross-Curricular Lessons

☟ SOCIAL STUDIES

☟ HEALTH

☟ SCIENCE

☟ READING

☟ MATHEMATICS

☟ WORK AND PLAY

location
latitude
parallels
equator
degrees
hemispheres
longitude
meridians
prime meridian
coordinates

_____

_____

Global Grid

Can you find Ecuador on a map? What about Egypt or Finland? Understanding the words in the list can help you find places in the world. Add your own words to the list. Use your Spelling Dictionary if you need help.

■ GETTING AT MEANING

Locating Places Look at globes A and B on the next page. Use them to help you complete the sentences.

1. _____

2. _____

3. _____

4. _____

5. _____

6. _____

7. _____

8. _____

9. _____

10. _____

hemispheres   latitude   equator   parallels

Globe A

The imaginary east-west lines on a map or globe are used to show (1). They are called (2). The (3) is at 0° latitude. It divides the Earth into two halves, or (4)—the Northern and Southern Hemispheres.

degrees   longitude   meridians   location
prime meridian   coordinates

Globe B

The imaginary north-south lines that go from pole to pole on a map or globe are used to show (5). They are called (6). The (7) is at 0° longitude. Both latitude and longitude are measured in (8). On a globe showing both parallels and meridians, the intersecting lines 20°S, 20°E that go through Africa are called (9). You can find any (10) on a map or globe when you know its coordinates.

A Parallels
Lines of Latitude

B Meridians
Lines of Longitude

■ SPELL WELL

Double Letters   Sometimes double letters can cause spelling problems. Write the words in the list that have double letters. Underline the double letters.

11. _____

12. _____

13. _____

Did You Know?
Suppose you wanted to circle the Earth at the equator. You would have to travel about 24,902 miles to complete your trip.

oak
dune
evergreens
cactus
needleleaf
moisture
forest
broadleaf
desert
sagebrush

_____

_____

Deserts and Forests

What makes a desert? What makes a forest? How are the two alike or different? Use the pictures below to find out. Add your own words to the list. Use the Spelling Dictionary.

■ GETTING AT MEANING

Using Picture Clues   Look at all of the illustrations. Use words from the list to complete each caption.

1. _____

2. _____

3. _____

4. _____

5. _____

cactus   desert   sagebrush   dune   moisture

One-seventh of all the Earth's land is dry, sandy <u>(1)</u>. The United States has deserts in the Southwest. Strong, dry winds can blow sand into a mounded <u>(2)</u>.

The dry, bushy <u>(3)</u> is found on western plains.

Although all living things require <u>(4)</u> to live, a <u>(5)</u> doesn't need much water. It grows in hot, dry regions.

evergreens   needleleaf   oak   forest   broadleaf

6. _____

7. _____

8. _____

9. _____

10. _____

A (6) is more than just trees. It includes shrubs, mosses, and flowers. The largest ones in the United States are in the North and East.

Trees with broad, flat leaves are called (7) trees. Their leaves change color and fall off. The (8) is this kind of tree.

Trees with leaves like thin, sharp needles are called (9) trees. These trees are also called (10) because they stay green all year.

■ SPELL WELL

Divide and Conquer Study long words piece by piece. Draw a line between the two base words in each compound below. Write each word.

11. needleleaf _____

12. evergreens _____

CREATE A DIORAMA
Make a three-dimensional desert or forest. First, research your chosen area. What kinds of plants and animals are found there? Next, get a shoe box and pictures, sand, clay, branches, and so on. Create the environment inside the box. Label your diorama.

173

The Great Lakes

The Great Lakes and the St. Lawrence Seaway are North America's major water highways. Read the list below to learn about them. Add your own words and sentences.

Lake Huron   **Lake Huron** borders Michigan and Canada.

Lake Ontario   **Lake Ontario** borders New York and Canada.

Lake Michigan   **Lake Michigan** borders Wisconsin, Illinois, Indiana, and Michigan.

Lake Erie   **Lake Erie** borders Michigan, Ohio, New York, Pennsylvania, and Canada.

Lake Superior   **Lake Superior** borders Michigan, Wisconsin, Minnesota, and Canada.

St. Lawrence Seaway **The St. Lawrence Seaway** is a waterway that connects the Great Lakes and the Atlantic Ocean.

Atlantic Ocean   **The Atlantic Ocean** is east of North and South America and west of Europe and Africa.

waterway   A **waterway** is a channel through which boats can navigate.

canal   An artificial waterway for navigation is a **canal.**

lock   An enclosed section of a canal in which the level of water can be changed is called a **lock.**

_____   _____

_____   _____

■ GETTING AT MEANING

Using Written Clues Complete each sentence using either **lock, canal,** or **waterway.**

1. The St. Lawrence Seaway is a major _____.

2. The ship at right is sailing through a _____.

3. The ship at left enters a _____ and the gates are then closed.

Labeling a Map   Label the Great Lakes, the St. Lawrence Seaway, and the Atlantic Ocean using the map below.

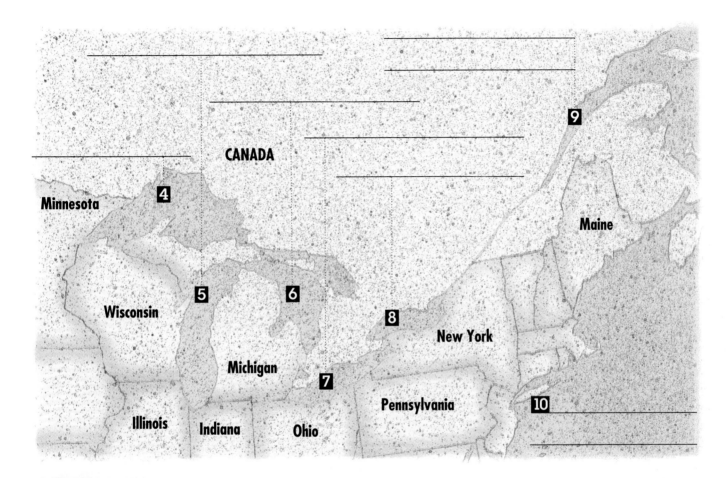

■ SPELL WELL

Divide and Conquer   Study the name of each lake syllable by syllable. Then write the names.

11. Lake Su • per • i • or _____

12. Lake On • tar • i • o _____

Lōōk into This

List the names of streams, rivers, lakes, and other bodies of water that influence your environment. Are they natural or made by people? Where do they begin and end? Present your findings in the form of a chart, map, or diagram.

Did You Know?

The first letters of the names of the Great Lakes spell a word that means "places where we live." What is that word? (Once you figure it out, you can use it to help you remember the names of all the Great Lakes!)

Using Natural Resources

Our natural resources are very important to our way of living. Read the sentences below to find out why. Add your own related words and phrases to the list.

energy	We use natural resources to create **energy** to do work.
electricity	**Electricity** is energy that powers lights and machines.
hydroelectric	**Hydroelectric** plants use water power to make electricity.
fuels	**Fuels** are resources that are burned to create energy or heat.
oil	**Oil** is our main fuel for running kinds of transportation.
gasoline	By cleaning and breaking down oil, we get **gasoline.**
natural gas	Another fuel, **natural gas,** is used for heating and cooking.
coal	We burn **coal** to create heat.
steel	**Steel** is a product of iron ore and carbon that is formed into sheets, beams, and other shapes.
products	Steel and gasoline are **products** that are made from natural resources.

_____ _____

_____ _____

■ GETTING AT MEANING

1. _____

2. _____

3. _____

4. _____

5. _____

Using Context Clues   Use the clues in the sentences above to help you choose the right list word for each blank below.

1. In manufacturing and industry, natural resources are made into finished ___.
2. Melting down the natural resource of iron ore and mixing it with carbon produces ___.
3. Factories may burn coal, oil, or other ___ to produce energy.
4. Burning coal turns water into steam that generates electrical ___.
5. The Earth's mineral fuels, including coal, oil, and ___, may be used up in the next few centuries.

Using Visual Clues Write the list word that best corresponds to each picture below.

6. _____

7. _____

8. _____

9. _____

10. _____

■ SPELL WELL

Seeing Meaning Connections The word *electric* is related to two list words. Finish each sentence by writing the correct list word.

11. Without _____ I couldn't

watch TV.

12. Hoover Dam is a _____

dam.

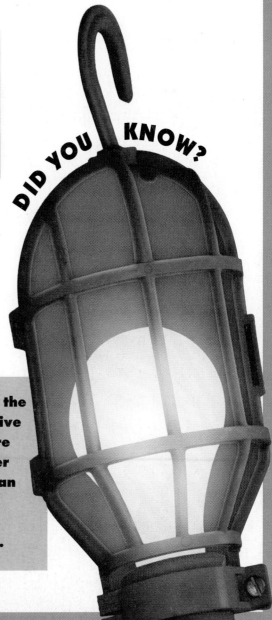

DID YOU KNOW?

People in the U.S. use five times more energy per person than any other people in the world.

Constitution
republic
democratic
participate
leaders
elected
represent
local
state
federal

_____

_____

Our Government

What's so special about the United States' government? Plenty! The words in the list will help you find this out. Add more government words to the list. Then do the exercises.

■ GETTING AT MEANING

Context Clues   Use the list words to complete what the people below are saying.

democratic   participate   represent   elected
leaders   republic

1. _____

2. _____

3. _____

4. _____

5. _____

6. _____

America's highest **(1)** are the President and Vice-President.

Government officials are **(2)** by citizens when they vote.

All citizens should take part in, or **(3)** in, elections.

Because the people run our government, we're a **(4)** country.

We also elect senators and representatives to **(5)** us in Congress.

We pledge allegiance to the flag and to the **(6)** for which it stands.

State the Facts
Use the list words to answer the questions.

state   federal   local   Constitution

7

What written plan gives Americans their power?

8

Do governors and lieutenant governors work on the state or local level?

9

Do the President and Vice-President work on the federal, state, or local level?

10

Do mayors and city council members work on the federal, state, or local level?

7. _____

8. _____

9. _____

10. _____

■ SPELL WELL

Divide and Conquer   Some long words are easier to study if you sound them out in syllables. Study each word below, saying it syllable by syllable. Then write the words.

11. Con • sti • tu • tion _____

12. par • tic • i • pate _____

CLASSMATE CONSTITUTION

What kind of government would work best in your classroom? Work in small groups to author a "Classroom Constitution" that establishes the kind of government you want. Think about the number of leaders, their powers, limitations, and responsibilities, as well as the role of the rights and responsibilities of classroom citizens. Use the Constitution of the United States as your guide.

Did You Know?

The Constitution of the United States is one of the oldest written constitutions. Many other countries have patterned their constitutions after it.

pueblo
adobe
corn
ceremony
pottery
Navajo
hogans
silver
weaving
reservation

_____

_____

Southwest American Indians

Many Southwest American Indians keep the traditions their ancestors kept hundreds of years ago. The list words reflect their past as well as their present life. Add your own words. Use the Spelling Dictionary as you do the exercises.

■ GETTING AT MEANING

Using Picture Clues Look at the illustrations. Complete the sentences using words from the list.

1. _____

2. _____

3. _____

4. _____

5. _____

| adobe | ceremony | pottery | pueblo | reservation |

These American Indians of New Mexico and Arizona get their name from the apartmentlike villages in which they live. Each village is called a (1). The pueblos are made of stone or sun-dried (2) bricks. In one religious (3), the Pueblo pray for harmony and order in the universe. The Pueblo make beautiful clay (4), which they sell to tourists who visit the (5).

6. _____

7. _____

8. _____

9. _____

10. _____

11. _____

12. _____

silver   hogans   weaving   Navajo   corn

The (6) are also American Indians of the Southwest. Many of them are farmers, growing (7) and raising sheep. Others are gifted at (8) wool into beautiful blankets, while others are engineers, teachers, and technicians. The Navajo are also famous for the artistic turquoise and (9) jewelry they make. A single ring can cost over $20,000. Many Navajo live in (10), shelters made of log frames covered with earth.

■ SPELL WELL

Seeing Meaning Connections Write the list word that completes each sentence. The underlined word is a clue.

11. That beautiful clay <u>pot</u> is just one of a large (11) collection.
12. A parcel of land <u>reserved</u> exclusively for American Indians is a (12).

Design Your Own Pottery
Each Pueblo village creates pottery using its own special design. Draw a pot and decorate it with your own one-of-a-kind design.

Inuit
seal
whale
walrus
polar bear
caribou
blubber
fur
tundra
kayak

_____

_____

Arctic Life

The Arctic is quite a place! How do people and animals live and travel there? The list words will help you answer these questions. Add your own Arctic words to the list.

■ GETTING AT MEANING

Using Photographs   Use list words to complete the caption for each photograph.

blubber   Inuit   kayak   polar bear   whale

Many of the people who live in the Arctic, such as the (1), zip around in snappy little snowmobiles!

1. _____

2. _____

3. _____

4. _____

5. _____

When the ice melts, an easy way to get around is to paddle a (2), a special boat.

The huge, snow-colored (3) looks at us as if to say, "Isn't the Arctic wonderful?"

This leaping (4) has a thick layer of fat called (5) that keeps it warm in cold water.

fur   tundra   walrus   caribou   seal

6. _____
7. _____
8. _____
9. _____
10. _____

The (6) has two huge teeth called tusks.

A sleek (7) tends to its pup.

The reindeer feeding on the grass is also called a (9)!

This girl will stay warm in a hood trimmed in animal (8).

The caribou stands on the treeless plain, called (10).

■ **SPELL WELL**

Rhyming Helpers   The rhyming helpers *meal* and *Mary Lou* can help you spell two list words. Write the list word that rhymes with each rhyming helper.

11. The polar bear
    Sniffs the air,
    Hoping for a meal.
    While diving for a codfish,

    It sees a lively _____.

12. "What are you doing,
    Mary Lou?"
    "Reading a book

    About _____."

TRY IT OUT

The Inuit are famous for their sculptures. They use soapstone, whalebone, and other material to carve animals or scenes from their environment. Try it yourself. Use clay or a bar of soap to carve something you see each day.

183

strengths
appreciate
weaknesses
decision
disagree
tears
result
psychologist
special
appearance

_____

_____

Know Yourself

You are one of a kind. The list words celebrate that. Add your own words to the list. Use the Spelling Dictionary for help.

■ GETTING AT MEANING

Talking About You   The friends in the comic strip are eager to share their wisdom with you, but the cartoonist left out words. Use the list words to complete their sentences.

1. _____   3. _____

2. _____   4. _____

184

5. _____   8. _____

6. _____   9. _____

7. _____   10. _____

■ SPELL WELL

Problem Parts   Some words cause problems because they are not spelled the way they sound. Write *psychologist* and *appreciate.* Underline any letters in these words that you think might cause spelling problems.

11. _____   12. _____

decision   psychologist   disagree   result   weaknesses

And what makes you mad? An argument? It's okay to (<u>6</u>) with people. You can't agree all the time.

And, like all of us, you have faults. Be aware of your (<u>7</u>). What needs improvement? Once you've made a (<u>8</u>) to improve a fault, ask family and friends to help.

If a problem is bigger than you can handle, a professional (<u>9</u>) may help you.

The (<u>10</u>) may be a happier, healthier you!

185

crosswalks
first aid
pedestrians
rescue
reflector
bicycle
hand signal
jaywalking
emergency
helmet

_____

_____

Being Safe

You've heard the phrase "safety first." Understanding the words in the list can help you put safety first in your life. Add your own words to the list. Use the Spelling Dictionary if you need help.

■ GETTING AT MEANING

Labeling Write a list word from the sign that identifies each numbered part of the picture.

reflector
bicycle
helmet
hand signal

1. _____
2. _____
3. _____
4. _____

186

Using Context Clues   As Sara rides to school, she is reviewing some of the safety rules she knows. Use the list words on the sign to complete Sara's thoughts.

- People who are walking, or (5), must follow safety rules.
- Pedestrians should cross streets only at (6), or specially marked places.
- Not crossing a street at a crosswalk is called (7).
- If someone is hurt in an accident, call the police and request an ambulance. A paramedic team will come to the (8).
- When driving a car or riding a bike, always pull over to the right side of the road and stop to allow an (9) vehicle to pass.
- Stand back and allow the paramedics to provide (10).

jaywalking
pedestrians
first aid
emergency
rescue
crosswalks

DETOUR

Did You Know?

Preventing accidents is the goal of safety engineers. These experts design structures and equipment to keep us safe at home, in school, on the job, and on the road.

5. _____   8. _____

6. _____   9. _____

7. _____   10. _____

■ SPELL WELL

Divide and Conquer   Sometimes it helps to study long words piece by piece. Study the following words syllable by syllable. Then write each one.

11. e • mer • gen • cy _____

12. pe • des • tri • an _____

bicuspid
cuspid
incisor
molar
enamel
epidermis
dermis
pore
sweat gland
oil gland

_____

_____

Your Body

■ GETTING AT MEANING

There's more to teeth than a dazzling smile, and more to skin than bone covering. Read about them below. Add more words to the list. Use your Spelling Dictionary for help.

Labeling Diagrams   Read about the teeth and skin. Then use list words to write the parts of each diagram.

The Teeth

The word **cuspid** means "tooth with a sharp point." A **bicuspid,** therefore, is a tooth with two sharp points. An **incisor** is a front tooth, and a **molar** is a back tooth. All of our teeth are protected by hard, white **enamel.**

1. _____

2. _____

3. _____

4. _____

5. _____
   (the hard covering)

188

The Skin

The **epidermis** is the outer layer of the skin. The **dermis** is the inner layer. Each tiny opening in the skin is called a **pore.** Sweat is released through the **sweat gland,** and oil is released through the **oil gland.**

6. _____

7. _____

8. _____

9. _____
(produces oil)

10. _____
(produces salty liquid)

■ SPELL WELL

Root Awareness   Some of your list words come from Greek and Latin words. Often, a word is easier to understand and remember if you look at its root, the word it came from. Complete the chart to create two list words.

Prefix	Root Word	List Word
	derm (skin)	11. _____
epi (on, upon)	derm (skin)	12. _____

Try to Talk Without Teeth!

Not only do we need our teeth to eat, we need them to talk. Slowly read this sentence out loud: *The tiny worm sat upon a log.* Write down the words in which your tongue touches your teeth. Next to each word, also jot down where your tongue touches your teeth.

reproduce
seed
conifers
ferns
spores
pollen
stamen
pistil
fertilize
fruit

_____

_____

Plant Reproduction

How do plants reproduce—that is, make other plants?
Use the list words and the diagrams to find the answer.
Add your own words to the list. Use the Spelling Dictionary.

■ GETTING AT MEANING

Plants from Seeds Many plants, like the cherry tree
below, reproduce by means of seeds. The diagram will
help you complete the sentences.

1. This flower will _____ by means of seeds.

2. The tiny grains made by the stamen are called _____ .

3. The flower's _____ makes these tiny grains.

4. Bees and butterflies carry pollen from the stamen to the _____ .

5. The pollen will _____ an egg at the bottom of the flower's pistil.

6. The fertilized _____ will grow inside the plant.

7. The _____ grows around the seed.
   It is the part we eat.

fertilize
*bee carries pollen
from flower to flower*

*pollen
combines
with egg
to make
seed*

fruit

*stamen
makes tiny
grains of
pollen*

seed

*pistil
makes eggs
that combine
with pollen*

Plants from Spores and Cones **Ferns** and mosses reproduce by means of **spores. Conifers** such as pine trees reproduce by means of cones. The male cone is smaller and softer. The female cone is larger and harder. Use the diagram to complete the sentences.

8. Unlike flowers, mosses and _____ have clusters of tiny cells under their leaves.

9. These cells are called _____ .

10. Spruce and pine are both _____ . They produce cones.

fern

spores
on the underside of a fern

■ SPELL WELL

Divide and Conquer
Long words are easy to spell if you divide them into smaller parts. Study each word below, syllable by syllable. Then write each word.

11. fer • ti • lize _____

12. re • pro • duce _____

13. con • i • fers _____

Plants Aplenty

What's your favorite plant? a garden flower? a wildflower? an exotic tree of the rain forest? Draw and paint or color your favorite plant on a big sheet of paper. Cut it out, and with your classmates' plants, create a classroom "botanical garden" on the wall. For fun, label your plant with its name, where it grows, and some interesting facts about it.

producers
consumers
herbivore
carnivore
omnivore
food chain
food web
predator
prey
decomposer

_____

_____

Living Together

Every living thing—plant and animal—depends in some way on other living things. The list words can help you find out how. Can you add others? Use your Spelling Dictionary.

■ GETTING AT MEANING

Looking at Pictures **Producers** make their own food. **Consumers** eat other living things.
Look at the picture below. Then answer the questions.

1. The dog, boy, and squirrel all eat food.

    What are they called? _____

2. Are plants such as lettuce and carrots producers

    or consumers? _____

3. What do you call an animal who eats

    only beef and chicken? _____

4. What is an animal who eats only leaves, fruit,

    and nuts called? _____

5. What is an animal who eats both fish

    and rice called? _____

6. What do you call the tiny organism that causes
    dead plants and animals to crumble and rot?

    _____

Seeing Connections Animals that are hunted and eaten are called **prey.** Animals that do the hunting and eating are called **predators.** A **food chain** shows a direct link between an animal and the thing it eats and is eaten by. A **food web** is a complex arrangement of food chains. Label each picture either **food chain** or **food web.** Answer the questions that follow.

7. _____

8. _____

9. Is the mouse in the food chain predator or prey? _____

10. Is the hawk in the food chain predator or prey? _____

■ **SPELL WELL**

Pronouncing Words Carefully We sometimes spell words wrong because we say them wrong. Say each word below. Be sure to pronounce the sounds of the underlined letters. Write the words.

11. her<u>b</u>ivore _____

12. carn<u>i</u>vore _____

13. omn<u>i</u>vore _____

Draw the Food Chain in Your Yard

Take a good look around your schoolyard or yard at home. Sketch some of the plant and animal life you see. Turn your sketches into an illustration of your yard's food chains. Does your yard also have a food web? Illustrate that too!

193

conduct
insulation
current
series circuit
parallel circuit
magnet
magnetism
poles
magnetic field
compass

_____

_____

Electricity and Magnetism

Electricity and magnetism are forces we use every day. The list words tell about each force. Look up unknown words in the Spelling Dictionary. Add other words to the list.

■ GETTING AT MEANING

Using Diagrams   Write the words **current, conduct, insulation, series circuit,** and **parallel circuit** to complete the explanation below the diagrams.

Plastic or rubber insulation prevents the flow of the electrical current.

Copper is a good conductor of electricity.

Parallel circuit

Series circuit

1. _____

2. _____

3. _____

4. _____

5. _____

Like a river, electricity flows in a (1). Copper wire is used to (2) the electricity. The wires are wrapped in plastic (3) so that they are safe to touch. When the electricity moves along one path, the circuit is a (4). When the electricity moves along two or more paths, the circuit is a (5).

Using Diagrams Use the words below to complete the sentences.

poles   magnetic field   magnetism   compass   magnet

A (6) is any piece of iron or steel that can pull iron or steel things to it. The magnet's power to attract is called (7). The parts of a magnet where the magnetism is the strongest are called the (8). The magnetic force curves out between a magnet's poles creating what is called a (9). A magnetic (10) helps travelers to find directions. The arrow on the compass will point to the north because the north-seeking pole of the needle is attracted to the magnetic north pole of the earth.

6. _____

7. _____

8. _____

9. _____

10. _____

Compass

Magnet

magnetic field

S

poles

N

■ **SPELL WELL**

Related Words Write the two list words that are related in spelling and meaning to *magnet.*

11. _____

12. _____

Did You Know?

About 500 species of fish send out electric charges. Electric eels are the best known. They stun their prey with a 350- to 650-volt charge!

meteorologist
forecast
barometer
wind vane
rain gauge
humidity
air mass
front
Fahrenheit
Celsius

_____

_____

Weather

The weather's "behavior" tells us how to behave. What we wear and do often depends on the weather. The list words name ways we find out about weather. Look up unfamiliar words in the Spelling Dictionary. Add more weather words to the list.

■ **GETTING AT MEANING**

Weather Report Finish writing the newscaster's and weather forecaster's cue cards by writing these list words. Use the thermometer on the next page to help you.

And now it's time for the weather (1). Here's Channel 2 (2), Connie Yu.

Thanks, Dave. Did you notice how damp the air was today? The (3) was so high! Watch out for the rain tonight—and it could freeze! That's because the temperature might drop to 32 degrees (4). That's the same as 0 degrees (5). Brrr!

humidity

meteorologist

forecast

Celsius

Fahrenheit

1. _____

2. _____

3. _____

4. _____

5. _____

Related Words Complete each sentence by writing the list word that is related to the underlined word or term.

rain gauge

wind vane

barometer

6. A _____ measures the <u>barometric</u>, or air, pressure.

7. A _____ measures the amount of <u>rainfall</u>.

8. Both a _____ and a <u>wind sock</u> can show wind direction.

Reading a Weather Map An **air mass** is a large body of air pushing into an area. A **front** is where two different air masses meet. Look at the map key. Then label the symbols on the map for **air mass** and **front**.

9. _____   10. _____

Weather Records

What's the coldest recorded temperature in your hometown? What's the warmest recorded temperature? Find out and share your information with your classmates.

■ **SPELL WELL**

Divide and Conquer Study these long words syllable by syllable. Then cover the words and write them.

11. me • te • o • rol • o • gist _____

12. Fahr • en • heit _____

landforms
mountains
plains
plateau
plates
volcano
faults
earthquake
seismograph
Richter scale

_____

_____

Landforms

Can you describe your natural surroundings? Are there any mountains or plains nearby? The list words will help you talk about landforms and the forces that cause them. Look up unfamiliar words in the Spelling Dictionary. Add two words of your own.

■ GETTING AT MEANING

Labeling   Read the explanations of these list words and look at the numbered pictures. Write the list word that identifies each picture.

Landforms are different shapes of land. **Plains** are flat areas of land, and a **plateau** is flat land that is higher than the land around it. **Mountains** are hills that rise at least 600 meters above the land around them. A **volcano** looks like a mountain with an opening on the top. Lava, ashes, and steam sometimes flow through this opening in the earth's crust.

1. _____

2. _____

3. _____

4. _____

5. These four shapes of land are called

_____ .

Scientific Vocabulary When writers use technical words, they often put clues in the sentences to help you understand what the terms mean. Using the underlined clues, write list words to complete this paragraph about earthquakes.

6. _____

7. _____

8. _____

9. _____

10. _____

Earth Notes

When the <u>earth shakes</u>, it is called an (6)__. An earthquake is caused by the shifting of <u>large sections of rock that make up the earth's surface</u> called (7)__. The earth's surface has <u>cracks</u> called (8)__. Earthquakes usually begin along these fault lines. An instrument called a (9)__ records how strong the earthquake is by drawing lines on <u>graph paper</u>. Scientists report their results using the (10)__, a <u>scale of measurement</u> that goes from zero for the weakest quake, up to 9 for the very strongest.

■ **SPELL WELL**

Divide and Conquer Study these long words syllable by syllable. Then cover the words and write them.

11. earth • quake _____

12. seis • mo • graph _____

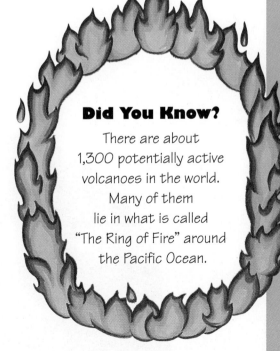

Did You Know?

There are about 1,300 potentially active volcanoes in the world. Many of them lie in what is called "The Ring of Fire" around the Pacific Ocean.

pupil
iris
retina
optic nerve
lens
eardrum
ear canal
outer ear
middle ear
inner ear

_____

_____

The Eyes and Ears

Our eyes and ears provide us with two important senses—seeing and hearing. The list words tell about the parts that make up our eyes and ears. Add other related words. Use your Spelling Dictionary for help.

■ GETTING AT MEANING

Labeling Diagrams   Read the paragraphs describing the parts of the eye and the parts of the ear. Write the list word that identifies each numbered part in the diagram.

The Eyes   We can see only certain parts of the eye: the white of the eye and the colored part called the **iris.** The iris has an opening in the middle called the **pupil,** which controls the amount of light that enters the eye. Right behind the iris is the **lens.** The lens works to make sure that the eye gets a sharp picture. The **retina** is the eye's "back wall." The retina changes the light coming in into electric signals. Then the **optic nerve** carries the electric signals to the brain.

1._____

2._____

3._____

4._____

5._____

The Ears

Ears are the sense organs that let us hear. The part of the ear on the outside of the head is part of the **outer ear.** The other part of the outer ear is the **ear canal.** This little "tunnel" leads from the outer ear to the **eardrum,** which separates the outer ear from the **middle ear.** Sound waves make the eardrum vibrate. These vibrations move through the middle ear to the inner ear. The middle ear has three tiny bones that link the eardrum to the **inner ear** deep inside the head. The inner ear is the part of the ear that sends messages to the brain. The brain then "hears" the sounds.

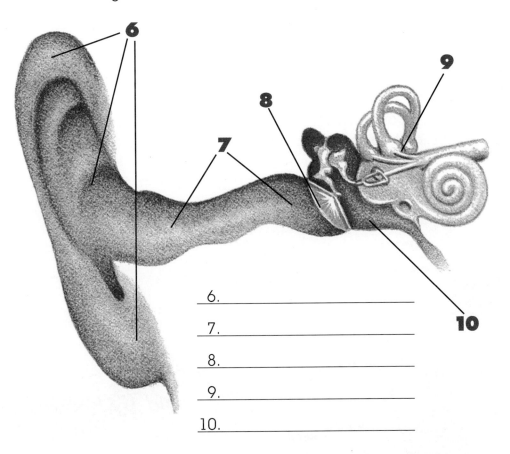

6. _____

7. _____

8. _____

9. _____

10. _____

■ SPELL WELL

Pronouncing Words Carefully

Some words are not spelled the way they're pronounced. Exaggerate the sounds of the underlined letters to help you remember them. Write the words.

11. retina _____

12. pupil _____

All Eyes and Ears

The animal kingdom is full of amazing eyes and ears. Check out eagles, owls, cats, insects, or lobsters to learn about their eyes. To learn about animals that "get an earful," check out foxes, bats, dogs, or elephants. Share what you find.

accomplishments
artist
celebrated
humor
confidence
determination
disappointment
expert
strategy
successful

_____

_____

Hopes, Dreams, and Wishes

What goals and achievements do you dream about and wish for? The words in the list will help you understand attitudes and actions that help make dreams come true. Look up unfamiliar words in the Spelling Dictionary. Add your own words to the list.

■ GETTING AT MEANING

Using Context Clues   Write the list words below to complete a recipe for success.

determination   1._____

disappointment   2._____

accomplishments   3._____

humor   4._____

expert   5._____

HoPES, DREAMS, and WiSHES

Start with your (1) —your talents and skills.
Add plenty of drive and (2) to help you focus on your goal.
Sprinkle in a few chuckles— (3) adds flavor to this dish.
Leave out (4) —so you won't give up.
Mix them all together to become an (5) at what you do—the very best.

Using Synonyms Write the list word that is similar in meaning to each group of words below.

successful   celebrated   strategy   artist   confidence

6. _____
painter, musician, sculptor

7. _____
famous, well-known

8. _____
method, plan

9. _____
self-trust, self-belief

10. _____
triumphant, fortunate,
well-off

■ SPELL WELL

Double Trouble Double letters can cause spelling problems. Write the words below. Underline the double letters in each word to help you remember them.

11. successful _____

12. accomplishments _____

13. disappointment _____

Did You Know?

Not all dreams come true overnight. Inventors Wilbur and Orville Wright experimented for about seven years before their first successful airplane flight!

assignments
collections
counselor
demonstrations
interview
experiment
exhibit
research
librarian
brainstorm

_____

_____

Many Ways of Learning

How do we learn new things? We learn in many different ways. The list words name just a few. Use the Spelling Dictionary to look up unknown words. Add your own words.

■ GETTING AT MEANING

Labeling Illustrations   Write the list word that identifies each picture.

interview   brainstorm

exhibit   assignments

experiment

1. _____

2. _____

3. _____

4. _____

5. _____

204

Completing Word Webs   Use the following list words
to finish the word webs.

librarian
demonstrations
counselor
research
collections

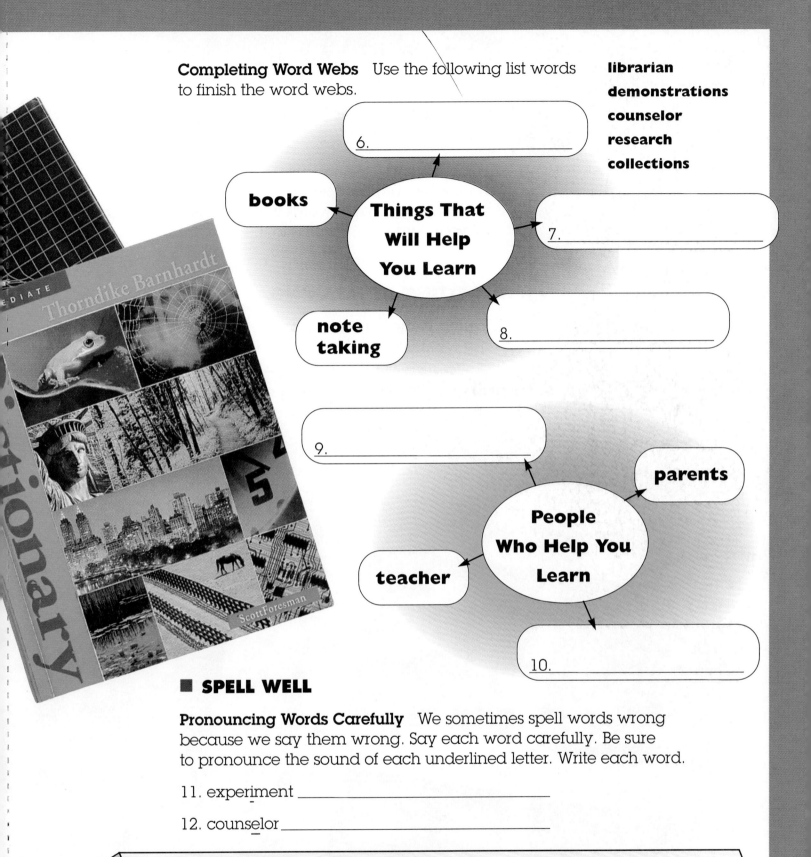

6. _____

books

**Things That
Will Help
You Learn**

7. _____

note
taking

8. _____

9. _____

**People
Who Help You
Learn**

parents

teacher

10. _____

■ SPELL WELL

Pronouncing Words Carefully   We sometimes spell words wrong
because we say them wrong. Say each word carefully. Be sure
to pronounce the sound of each underlined letter. Write each word.

11. experiment _____

12. counselor _____

Create the Perfect Learning Environment

Suppose you could create the perfect place where you could learn everything you wanted
to know. Where would it be? What would it look like? What would you have there? Who would
you have there? Draw or write a description of your "perfect learning place."

family
parents
children
home
shared
chores
love
childhood
memories
scrapbook

_____

_____

How Families Matter

What makes families special? Read the list of words,
and look up unknown words in the Spelling Dictionary.
Add your own family words to the list.

■ GETTING AT MEANING

Labeling Photographs Everyone's family is different.
Using what you know about families, write the list word
that describes each photograph in John's scrapbook.

home   **family**   **chores**   **parents**   **children**

1. _____

2. _____   4. _____

3. _____   5. _____

Using Context Clues Use these list words to complete the note that John's parents wrote to him in the front of his scrapbook.

love   **shared**   **childhood**
memories   **scrapbook**

6. _____

7. _____

8. _____

9. _____

10. _____

Dear John,

We can't believe that you are nine years old already! Your (6) is going so quickly! For your birthday we would like you to have this (7). It is full of photos, and it holds (8) of many happy times we have (9) together. Happy 9th birthday! We (10) you!

Mom and Dad

Conduct Interviews

Interview the older members of your family. Ask them to tell you about their early memories of childhood. Take notes as they speak. Share these memories with the class.

■ **SPELL WELL**

Related Words
Write the two list words that are related in spelling and meaning to *child*.

11. _____

12. _____

cafeteria
concert
curtains
furniture
office
library
orchestra
skateboarding
spider web
water fountain

_____

_____

Your Own Universe

The words in the list name just ten of the thousands of things that are part of your universe. Add your own words. Use the Spelling Dictionary if you need help.

■ GETTING AT MEANING

Context Clues School is a big part of your universe. Look at the bulletin board notices from Maple School. Complete them with list words.

THANK YOU, P.T.A. PARENTS!
Thanks to a generous gift from the P.T.A., students will not go thirsty during recess. Take a sip from the new (1) on the playground.

You're Invited!

Enjoy an evening of music. The band and the (2) will have a combined (3) on Saturday, May 22, at 7:30 P.M.

REMINDER!
No (4) on school grounds.
Thank you!

1. _____
2. _____
3. _____
4. _____

HELP WANTED!

We still need help with the fourth-grade play, *Charlotte's Web*. These jobs are still open.

Stage Crew: Responsible for opening and closing the (5) between acts.

Set Design: Responsible for building a (6) for Charlotte the spider.

5. _____

6. _____

7. _____

8. _____

9. _____

10. _____

FOR SALE

Used art table $10.00
File Cabinets $15.00
Money from the sale of the (7) will be used to buy new books for the (8).

$10.00

$15.00

HOT DOG HEAVEN

The Student Council will be selling hot dog lunches every Wednesday. Tickets are $1.75 each and may be purchased in the principal's (9) before school or in the (10) during the lunch hour.

home

music

Take a Look at Your Universe

School is only one part of your universe. Create word webs to show other parts of it—home, sports, hobbies, fashion, and so on. Share your webs with friends or display them on a bulletin board.

nature

sports

fashion

■ SPELL WELL

Pronouncing for Spelling Some words are not spelled the way they're pronounced. Exaggerate the sounds of the underlined letters in each word below. Then write the words.

11. orchestra _____

12. furniture _____

cathedral
Chartres
church
temple
Parthenon
marble
jewels
tomb
Taj Mahal
honor

_____

_____

Looking at the World in New Ways

Imagine that you are at the Parthenon, the Cathedral of Notre Dame, or the Taj Mahal. What would you notice about it? The list words tell about these three monuments. Add words about other world-famous buildings. Use your Spelling Dictionary for help.

■ GETTING AT MEANING

Using Photographs Complete the caption under each postcard. Use the words in the brick.

The (1) is in Athens, Greece. The ancient Greeks built this beautiful (2) to honor Athena, the goddess of wisdom. The Greeks built the entire structure of white (3). Inside stood a huge gold-and-ivory statue of Athena.

temple   marble

Parthenon

1. _____

2. _____

3. _____

cathedral   Chartres
church   jewels

4. _____

5. _____

6. _____

7. _____

The city of (4) in France is world famous for its (5), called the Cathedral of Notre Dame. The great (6) has more than 100 stained-glass windows so richly colored that they shine like (7).

The (8) is in Agra, India. The Indian ruler Shah Jahan had this beautiful (9) built in the mid-1600s. It was constructed in (10) of his wife, Mumtaz Mahal. It has a domed roof and four prayer towers.

tomb   honor
Taj Mahal

8. _____

9. _____

10. _____

■ SPELL WELL

Capital Letters Three of your list words are proper nouns. Write them. Remember to capitalize the words.

11. _____

12. _____

13. _____

Design a Monument

The Parthenon was erected to honor Athena. Farmers in Enterprise, Alabama, erected a monument to the boll weevil in 1919. By destroying their crops, the insect forced them to grow new and different crops. As a result, the farmers became richer. Think of someone you'd like to design a monument to honor. Draw the monument and write an inscription.

211

compassionate
debris
devastate
emergency
extraordinary
panic
pressure
recover
siren
tremendous

_____

_____

Tales of Courage

Many situations call for courage. The words in the list bring to mind some sounds, sights, and feelings of such situations. Add some of your own words of courage.

■ GETTING AT MEANING

Using Context Clues Use the list words at the right to complete the phone call.

siren
pressure
emergency
panic
recover

Hi, Aunt Betty! Guess what?
I'm a heroine, but I hardly remember what happened!
When I saw Gram fall on the stairs and hit her head,
I knew it was an (1). I managed not to (2). I ran to the phone and dialed 911. Giving my name and address helped me (3) my control. But until I heard the (4) and saw the paramedics pull up in the fire truck, I really felt the (5). I couldn't do anything for Gram—just wait and hold her hand. Anyhow, the doctor said I saved her life. And our newspaper gave me a commendation. Say hello to Uncle Jack.
Bye for now!

1. _____

2. _____

3. _____

4. _____

5. _____

More Context Clues Complete the paragraph with these list words. The underlined words may help you.

debris   compassionate   extraordinary   tremendous   devastate

A powerful earthquake can <u>destroy</u>, or <u>(6)</u>, a city. The <u>awesome</u>, <u>(7)</u> force of the earth moving can topple buildings. <u>Building materials</u>, <u>crushed automobiles</u>, <u>broken pipes</u>, and other <u>(8)</u> can block the streets. At times like this, <u>ordinary</u> citizens show <u>(9)</u> courage to help their neighbors. And <u>concerned</u> people from all over the country show their <u>(10)</u> nature by sending food, clothing, and money to aid the victims of an earthquake.

6. _____

7. _____

8. _____

9. _____

10. _____

■ SPELL WELL

Divide and Conquer Study the words below syllable by syllable. Then cover them and write them.

11. com • pas • sion • ate _____

12. ex • traor • di • nar • y _____

Did You Know?

Courage comes from a Latin word that means "heart."

operation key
number keys
display
memory recall
memory plus
memory minus
key sequence
error
clear key
equals key

_____

_____

1. _____

2. _____

3. _____

4. _____

5. _____

6. _____

7. _____

The Calculator

Do you, your parents, or your friends use calculators? The words in the list tell all about these small, remarkable machines. Add your own words. Use the Spelling Dictionary for help.

■ GETTING AT MEANING

Understanding a Calculator Read the paragraphs below. Then write list words to complete the sentences.

The **number keys** and each **operation key** are used to give information to the calculator. The order in which you press the keys is the **key sequence.** The answer to the problem appears in the **display** after you press the **equals key.**

Press the **clear key** once if you make a mistake entering numbers. An "E" will appear in the display if you make an **error** like trying to divide by zero.

Marta wanted to add the number of muffins she sold on Monday and Tuesday. She pressed the (1) 3 and 5, and the number 35 appeared in the (2). She pressed the "+" (3) before she entered 27. When 24 appeared in the display, she realized that she had pressed the 4 by mistake. She pressed the (4) once and then entered the correct numbers. The answer appeared after she pressed the (5). 35 ⊞ 27 ⊟ is the (6) Marta entered to solve her problem. If the answer to her problem had been greater than eight digits long, or she had tried to divide by zero, an "E" in the display would have told her that she had made an (7).

muffins 25¢

214

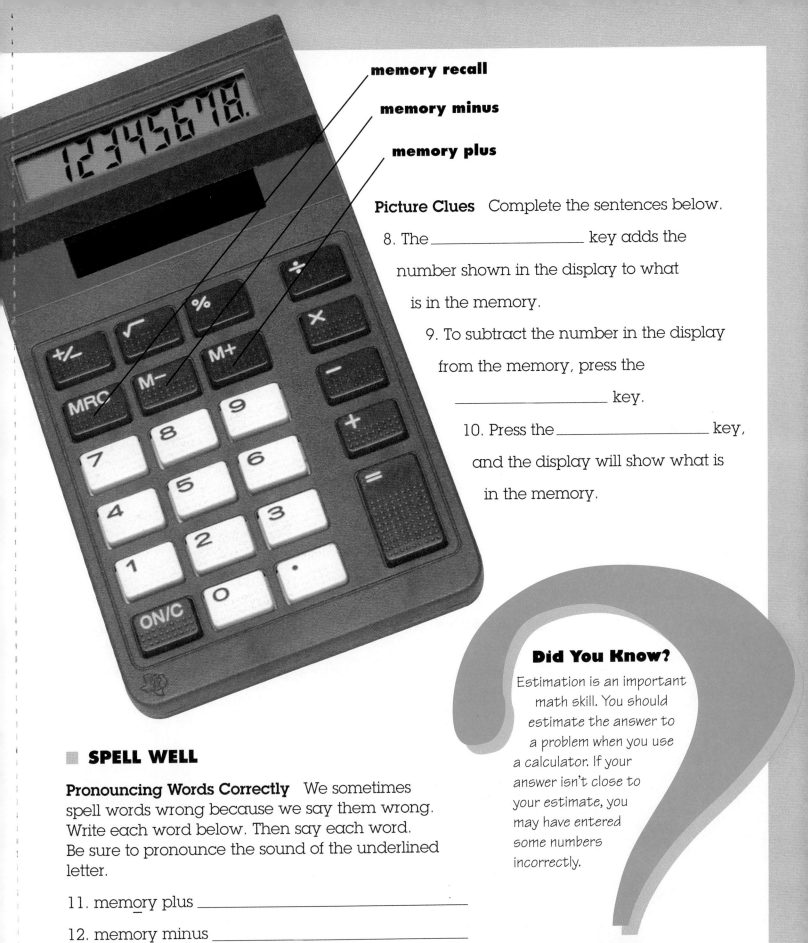

memory recall

memory minus

memory plus

Picture Clues Complete the sentences below.

8. The _____ key adds the number shown in the display to what is in the memory.

9. To subtract the number in the display from the memory, press the _____ key.

10. Press the _____ key, and the display will show what is in the memory.

Did You Know?

Estimation is an important math skill. You should estimate the answer to a problem when you use a calculator. If your answer isn't close to your estimate, you may have entered some numbers incorrectly.

■ SPELL WELL

Pronouncing Words Correctly We sometimes spell words wrong because we say them wrong. Write each word below. Then say each word. Be sure to pronounce the sound of the underlined letter.

11. mem_o_ry plus _____

12. mem_o_ry minus _____

13. mem_o_ry recall _____

length
width
height
weight
capacity
volume
area
perimeter
distance
temperature

_____

_____

1. _____

2. _____

3. _____

4. _____

5. _____

6. _____

7. _____

8. _____

Measurement

How would you describe the size and shape of a soccer field? Words of measurement, like the ones in the word list, help you describe places or objects.

■ GETTING AT MEANING

Context Clues   Complete each sentence with the correct list word from those given in parentheses.

1. In youth soccer, the field is usually 100 yards in length and 50 yards in _____. **(width, length)**

2. The _____ of the field is divided by a halfway line. **(width, length)**

3. The _____ from one goal to the other is 100 yards. **(distance, area)**

4. The entire _____ of the field covers about 5,000 square yards. **(distance, area)**

5. White lines are drawn around the _____ of the field. **(perimeter, volume)**

6. Modern soccer shoes are light in _____ . **(height, weight)**

7. In soccer, the _____ and weight of a player are not as important as the player's speed and fitness. **(height, width)**

8. Soccer can be played outside whether the _____ is warm or cool. **(volume, temperature)**

Understanding Measurements Study the figure to the right.
Complete each sentence with the correct list word.

9. To measure volume, multiply length x width x height.

   The _____ of the box is 27 cubic feet.

10. When the box is filled to its _____

    it holds about ten soccer balls.

3 ft.

volume

capacity

3 ft.

3 ft.

■ **SPELL WELL**

Pronouncing Words Correctly We sometimes
spell words wrong because we say them wrong.
Write each word below. Then say each word.
Be sure to pronounce the sound of the underlined
letter.

11. temperature _____

12. width _____

Measure Up

With a partner, measure the size of your
classroom. Measure to the nearest foot.
On a separate sheet of paper, write your
measurements on a chart like the one
below. Assume the height is 9 feet.

length: _____ feet

width: _____ feet

height: __9__ feet

area (length x width): _____ square feet

volume (length x width x height): _____ cubic feet

Division

Division is one of the four basic math operations. Read the list of words that talk about division and add your own words. Look up unfamiliar words in the Spelling Dictionary.

■ GETTING AT MEANING

Understanding Math Terms When you have 12 tennis balls and want to put them into groups of 3, you **divide** to find the number of groups you can make. You may show the **division** problem in two ways.

$$3 \overline{) 12}^{\,4} \qquad \text{divisor} \overline{)\,\text{dividend}}^{\text{quotient}}$$

$$12 \div 3 = 4 \qquad \text{dividend} \div \text{divisor} = \text{quotient}$$

A **family of facts** can be used to represent the groupings of the tennis balls. Each **number sentence** in a family of facts tells about the **grouping.** Two of the number sentences show related multiplication facts and two of the number sentences show the related division facts.

Write the list word that describes each item.

2. _____

3. _____

4. _____

5. _____

1. _____

6. _____

A number is **divisible** by another if it can be divided by that number with no remainder. When a number cannot be divided exactly by another number, the number left over is called a **remainder.**

Look at the examples below. Complete the sentences with list words.

$$2\overline{)8}^{\,4} \qquad 2\overline{)5}^{\,2R1}$$

7. Eight is _____ by two.

8. One is the _____ in the second problem.

9. When you _____ eight by two, the quotient is four.

10. The symbol ÷ represents the operation of _____ .

■ SPELL WELL

Problem Parts Say the words below. Notice that the last syllables of the two words sound alike but are spelled differently. Write each word and underline the last two letters.

11. divis<u>or</u> _____

12. remaind<u>er</u> _____

Did You Know?
Division is repeated subtraction. To find how many groups of 3 are in 12 you can subtract 3 from 12 until your answer is zero. You can subtract 4 times, so there are 4 groups of 3 in 12.

angle
vertex
endpoint
intersecting
line
parallel
point
ray
segment
perpendicular

_____

_____

Geometry

Geometry is the branch of mathematics that studies and measures lines, angles, and shapes. The words in the list will tell you about geometry. Look up unknown words in the Spelling Dictionary. Add more words.

■ GETTING AT MEANING

Picture Clues Use the illustrations to help you write the list words that complete the sentences.

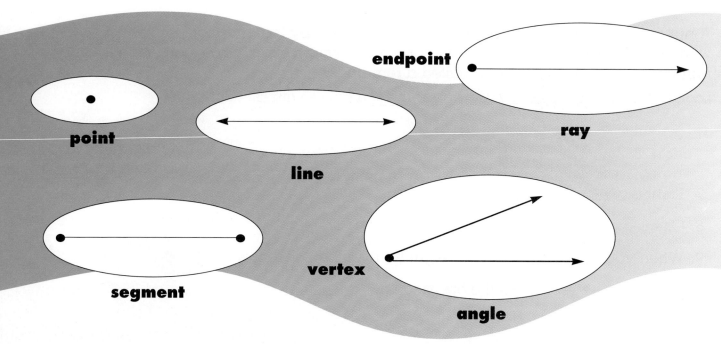

endpoint

point

line

ray

segment

vertex

angle

1. _____

2. _____

3. _____

4. _____

5. _____

6. _____

7. _____

A (1) continues without end in both directions.

A (2) is part of a line. It has two endpoints.

A (3) is part of a line that has one (4) and goes on and on in one direction.

An (5) is formed by two rays with the same endpoint. The endpoint is its (6).

The sharpened end of your pencil could be thought of as a (7).

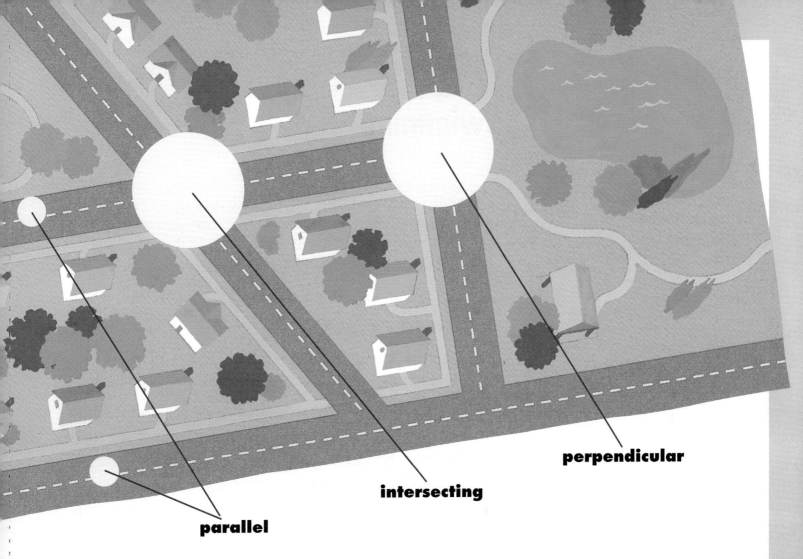

perpendicular

intersecting

parallel

Sometimes lines meet, or intersect. Two lines that cross each other at one point are <u>(8)</u> lines.

Lines that do not meet and remain the same distance apart are called <u>(9)</u> lines.

Intersecting lines that form square corners are called <u>(10)</u> lines.

8. _____

9. _____

10. _____

▣ SPELL WELL

Divide and Conquer Long words are easier to spell when they are divided into syllables. Say the syllables in each word. Then write the words.

11. par • al • lel _____

12. in • ter • sect • ing _____

Did You Know?

The word *geometry* comes from two ancient Greek words that mean "to measure" and "earth." The ancient Egyptians used geometry to figure out the boundaries of their farms every year after the Nile River's flooding washed away or covered landmarks!

kicks
stroke
breathe
floats
treads
dive
dog paddle
backstroke
butterfly
freestyle

_____

_____

1. _____

2. _____

3. _____

4. _____

5. _____

6. _____

Swimming

Swimming is a sport that people of every age enjoy. What swimming skills do you have? Which are you working on? Add your own words about swimming to the list. Check unknown words in the Spelling Dictionary.

■ GETTING AT MEANING

Using Picture Clues Look at the illustration. Complete the sentences using list words.

treads   floats   stroke   kicks   breathe   dog paddle

Jamal is practicing (1), moving his legs and feet.

An instructor shows students a new (2) with his arms.

As Sal raises his arm, he brings his head out of the water to (3).

Mailee does the (4) . Just like a swimming dog, she keeps her head above water and moves her arms in circles.

Robert (5) quietly nearby.

Julie (6) water by moving her feet up and down as if she were walking underwater!

freestyle   dive   butterfly   backstroke

A good (7) will give Alma a super start.

Janice likes the (8) because it's easy to breathe swimming on her back.

Abe works on his (9) stroke. Moving both arms and legs together is tough!

Abe, Janice, and Alma compete in (10) meets. In these races swimmers are free to choose any swimming style.

7. _____

8. _____

9. _____

10. _____

■ SPELL WELL

Double Consonants The double consonants in the words below have only one sound. Remember to include both consonants when you write these words.

11. butterfly _____

12. dog paddle _____

223

Basketball

Basketball is a fun, fast, and entertaining game. Knowing the list words can help you enjoy the game more. Read the sentences below. Add your own related words to the list. Check unknown words in the Spelling Dictionary.

backboard	A **backboard** with a basket hangs over each end of the court.
rim	A basket is made of a net hung from a metal **rim.**
dribble	Players can **dribble** the ball on the floor past an opponent.
rebound	A **rebound** is a ball that bounces off the backboard or rim.
foul	Hitting or pushing another player is a **foul.**
free throw	A player shoots a **free throw** from behind a free throw line.
field goal	A player can score a **field goal** from anywhere on the court.
lay-up	A player close to the basket can shoot a **lay-up** to score.
jump shot	A player jumps straight up to shoot a **jump shot.**
slam-dunk	In a **slam-dunk,** a player slams the ball through the basket from above.

_____   _____

_____   _____

■ GETTING AT MEANING

Rhyming Clues Complete these rhyming basketball cheers with list words.

Just (1) that basketball
down the floor!
Make a (2)
for two points more!

The ball bounces off the (3)
And rolls around the (4).
Get that (5) and put it in!

We'll all howl
If you (6).

1. _____

2. _____

3. _____

4. _____

5. _____

6. _____

Picture Clues   What kind of shot is each player trying to make?
Write the list word that matches each picture.

lay-up   **slam-dunk**   **jump shot**   **free throw**

7. _____

8. _____

9. _____

10. _____

■ **SPELL WELL**

Divide and Conquer   It helps to study some
words piece by piece. Study the words
syllable by syllable. Then cover them and
write them.

11. re • bound _____

12. drib • ble _____

Did You Know?
The first game
of basketball was
played with two
peach baskets and
a soccer ball.

Reporter

articles
headline
deadline
byline
lead
details
interview
verify
sources
editors

_____

_____

Newspapers and magazines employ thousands of reporters. Knowing the list words will help you understand a reporter's job. Use your Spelling Dictionary to learn the exact meanings of the words or to find other words to add to the list.

■ GETTING AT MEANING

Using Picture Clues Look at the illustration below to help you finish each sentence with the correct list word.

1. _____

2. _____

3. _____

Newspapers and magazines contain many (1) about important events and people.

A (2) in big, dark print tells about the article in a few words.

Many articles have a (3) that gives the writer's name.

byline   **headline**   **articles**

WALKER★SCHOOL NEWS

Who's That Shaggy-Looking New Kid?

by Erin Gates

Ms. Maggie Sullivan's kindergarten had an unusual visitor last week. New student Eliot Greenwald's dog Dexter decided to follow him to sch... Dexter ran behind the schoo... bus all the way to Walker S... Then he wouldn't stay outs... on the playground. Ms. Su... kindly allowed Dexter to... in the kindergarten room... Eliot until Mr. Greenwa...

Just Reuse It!

by Jason Nevin

Walker School students have joined the community effort to recycle. First of all, the entire student body has pledged to carry their lunches in reusabl...

bring from home. Also, recyclin... bins have been placed in the cafeteria for collecting used milk cartons, aluminum cans, and aluminum foil.

In addition, recycling bins for paper products have been...

226

Using Definitions Use the definitions to help you complete the news article on the computer screen.

details	the facts of a news story that give more information about the news
editors	people who often write the headlines and add to or rewrite the details of articles
sources	people, places, or written materials where reporters and editors get information
lead	the opening paragraph of a news story
verify	to be sure that a fact is true
interview	to ask people about their activities or opinions
deadline	latest time by which articles must be finished

4. _____

5. _____

6. _____

7. _____

8. _____

9. _____

10. _____

GETTING THE STORY TAKES WORK

Newspaper reporters get their stories from many (4). Some have a regular route called a beat. Some investigate politics or crime. Others report the news from overseas. Reporters sometimes (5) people to get their opinions. Once reporters "get the story," they quickly write it and give it to one of the (6). The most important information goes in the (7), or opening paragraph. The editors must (8) the (9) in the stories. They call people whom reporters have interviewed or check the details in books or magazines or special news services. All this work must be done quickly so that the newspaper can meet its daily (10). At deadline time, a story must go to the printing presses.

Be a Reporter

Grab a pad and pencil and cover your school's beat! Look for something unusual or funny or mysterious that's happening. Interview the people involved to get the details. Be sure to verify them! Then write your story. Have your teacher or another student edit it. Ask if you can read it over your school's P.A. system.

■ SPELL WELL

Problem Parts Sometimes the vowel sound you hear in a word gives you no clue as to its spelling. Pay special attention to the underlined letters below. Then write the words.

11. articles _____

12. editors _____

Photography

camera
film
lens
shutter
focus
portrait
snapshot
develops
negative
print

_____

_____

Photographs surround us everywhere we go. In newspapers, in magazines, on billboards, and in brochures, photographs give us glimpses of people, places, and events. The list words tell about photography. Look up unfamiliar words in the Spelling Dictionary. Add your own related words.

■ GETTING AT MEANING

Diagrams Complete the sentences with words from the labels and captions of the diagram.

film

Load **film** here.

film   shutter   camera   lens   focus

shutter   **lens**

Use the lens to **focus** the picture.

camera

1. A _____ is a photographer's tool.

2. The glass _____ is the camera's "eye." You see your subject through the lens.

3. The lens also helps to _____ the picture so that it will appear sharp and clear.

4. The _____ opens to let light through the lens. The shutter works like an eyelid.

5. As the shutter clicks, a picture is recorded on the _____ inside.

Analogies Use the words in dark type in the following sentences to finish the analogies.

- A special process **develops** the photographs on film.
- A **negative** photograph is developed first. A negative shows dark objects as light and light objects as dark.
- A **print** is made from each negative.
- A **portrait** is a photograph of a person's face.
- A **snapshot** is a photograph taken quickly with a small camera.

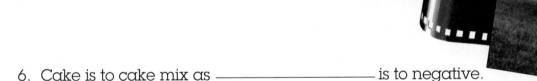

6. Cake is to cake mix as ——————— is to negative.

7. Pattern is to sewing as ——————— is to photograph.

8. Fingerprint is to finger as ——————— is to face.

9. Sketch is to drawing as ——————— is to photography.

10. Bakes is to cake mix as——————— is to film.

■ SPELL WELL

Divide and Conquer Some words are easier to study in smaller parts. Study each word syllable by syllable. Then cover the words and write them.

11. cam • er • a ———————

12. neg • a • tive ———————

Did You Know?
A camera can take a picture faster than you can blink an eye!

Writer's Handbook

INTRODUCTION

You can speak and even read well without knowing how to spell. However, knowing how to spell well is a skill that every good writer needs. This handbook will help you with some of the other skills good writers need.

CONTENTS

The Writing Process

This section answers questions that you might ask about the five steps of the writing process: prewriting, drafting, revising, proofreading, and presenting.

1. PREWRITING

What should I do before I start to write?

Think about and plan your writing before you actually put sentences on paper. Time you spend prewriting is time well spent. Follow these steps and suggestions.

- **Select a topic** by listing ideas; by browsing through books, magazines, or newspapers for ideas; or by reviewing a personal journal or diary.
- **Determine your purpose and audience.** Your purpose may be to express feelings, describe or explain, give or get information, persuade, or tell a story. Your audience could be classmates, your aunt in Tennessee, or a friend.
- **Narrow your topic.** To focus on one specific idea, you might brainstorm questions about the topic, create a word web or cluster, or list and classify key words to explore.
- **Find details** about your topic from a variety of sources and make notes. Make personal observations, interview people, or look up information in books and magazines.
- **Organize your information** to best accomplish your purpose for writing. Use time order, spatial order, or order of importance.

2. DRAFTING

How do I actually begin to write the paper?

Take your writing materials and prewriting notes to a comfortable, well-lighted place. Plan on writing for at least twenty minutes. Try some of these strategies to get started.

- **Ignore** distractions like the telephone and television.
- **Set a goal.** Decide how much that you *will* write now.
- **Review** your notes to find an idea for the first paragraph.
- **Start** with a direct, interesting sentence that states the main idea of the composition. Then let your ideas flow.
- **Push ahead** without worrying about perfect spelling, punctuation, or capitalization.

3. REVISING

How do I start revising?

Revising means to review what you've written and find ways to improve it. To begin, you might do the following:

- **Read your draft to yourself** to catch obvious errors such as unclear sentences.
- **Have a conference** with other students or your teacher.

What kinds of changes should I make?

You might do any or all of the following:

- **Add** words or ideas.
- **Take out** unnecessary words, sentences, or paragraphs.
- **Move** words, sentences, or paragraphs.
- **Substitute** words or ideas to improve your draft.

What kinds of questions should I ask myself?

The questions you'll ask depend on your purpose, audience, and type of writing. Here are some basic questions:

Ask yourself these questions!

- Did I say what I wanted to say?
- Are my details in the best possible order?
- Do I have a clear beginning, middle, and end?
- Does each paragraph have a topic sentence and stick to one idea?
- Can I take out extra words or choose better ones?
- Are all facts and figures correct?

4. PROOFREADING

Why should I proofread, and when and how should I do it?

Proofreading a paper means reading it carefully to find any mistakes in grammar, punctuation, and spelling. Proofread after you have completed revising your first draft to be sure that you have included all corrections. Proofread your final copy too.

Use proofreading symbols such as those at the right to clearly mark the corrections that are needed.

Symbol	Meaning
=	Make a capital.
/	Make a small letter.
∧	Add something.
℮	Take out something.
⊙	Add a period.
¶	New paragraph

What kinds of things should I look for when I proofread?

Use the following questions as a proofreading checklist:

- Do subjects and verbs agree?
- Is each sentence correctly punctuated?
- Have I avoided fragments and run-on sentences?
- Did I capitalize the first word of each sentence?
- Did I capitalize proper nouns and adjectives?
- Did I check spelling and meaning of unfamiliar words?
- Is my handwriting clear and easy to read?

Check for these possible errors!

5. PRESENTING

How should I present my final work?

Publishers have certain guidelines for writers. Teachers do too. The guidelines will vary depending on the assignment.

Here are some suggestions for **regular assignments.**

- Write neatly on the front side only of white lined paper. If you're typing your final copy on a computer, use plain white paper.
- Put your name, the class, and the date in the top right-hand corner of the first page.
- Center the title of your composition on the second line.
- Leave a one-inch margin on the sides of the paper and leave the last line blank.

Special ways to present writing include displaying it on a bulletin board, sharing it in a young author's conference, binding it in an illustrated book, publishing it in a newspaper, and reading it aloud.

Taking Writing Tests

Writing under pressure can be difficult. Improve your performance on writing tests by following these guidelines.

GENERAL GUIDELINES FOR WRITING TESTS

- **Listen carefully to test instructions.** Note how much time you have. Listen for whether to use pen or pencil.
- **Read the assignment and identify the key words.** Be certain that you are writing the correct type of answer. Look for key words like these and know what they mean.

Look for these key words!

Categorize or *Classify:* Sort ideas or facts into groups.
Compare or *Contrast:* Point out similarities (compare) or differences (contrast).
Defend: Give evidence to show why a view is right.
Define: Tell what something is or means.
Describe: Create a word picture with details and examples.
Discuss: State your ideas about what something means.
Evaluate: Give your opinion, with support, on whether an idea is good or bad, right or wrong.
Explain: Make something clear by giving reasons, examples, or steps.
Summarize: State main points, or retell important parts of a story or article.

- **Plan how you'll use your time.** Allow time for prewriting activities, actual writing, and revision.
- **Write a strong opening** to catch your reader's attention. It should address the topic directly.
- **Use specific facts, details, or incidents** to develop your topic.
- **Write an interesting conclusion** that sums up your ideas or brings your story to a satisfying end.

WRITING A PERSONAL NARRATIVE

When you write about something you did or something that happened to you, you are writing a personal narrative.

KEY WORDS IN ASSIGNMENTS

- "Tell **what happened** to you. . ."
- "Write about how you **felt** when. . ."
- "What did you **do** when. . ."

SAMPLE ASSIGNMENTS

- Write about an experience you had when you were a child. Tell what you did and how you felt about your experience.
- Write about something you have done that makes you feel proud of yourself. Be sure to tell where you were when it happened and why it made you feel proud.

A PLAN OF ATTACK

- For both assignments, choose an occasion to write about that will be interesting and entertaining for the reader. If your topic seems too broad, narrow it.
- Jot down the details describing the event you are writing about. Think of strong verbs and colorful adjectives and adverbs to use to relate your story.
- Organize your story in **time order.** Make notes on what happened at the beginning, middle, and end of your experience. Then, when you write, use your time-order notes and list of details as a guide.

FOLLOW-UP CHECKLIST

- Did you tell your story in time order, from beginning to end?
- Did you tell both what happened and how you felt about what happened?
- Did you leave your readers with a clear sense of what kind of person you are?
- Is all capitalization, punctuation, and spelling correct?

WRITING A DESCRIPTION

Descriptive writing allows a reader to experience a scene by appealing to the senses of sight, sound, smell, touch, and taste.

KEY WORDS IN ASSIGNMENTS

- "**Tell** what you **see** (or **hear**, **smell**, **feel**, **taste**). . ."
- "**Describe** what it **looks** (or **sounds**, **smells**, **feels**, **tastes) like**. . ."

SAMPLE ASSIGNMENTS

- Thanksgiving is an American holiday celebrated with a traditional dinner. Describe a Thanksgiving dinner.
- Many people wear uniforms for their jobs. Visualize yourself wearing a uniform for a job you might enjoy. Describe what you are wearing.

A PLAN OF ATTACK

- Know exactly what you must write about. In the first assignment, describe the sights, sounds, smells, and tastes of a Thanksgiving dinner. In the second, tell only about the uniform, not the job itself.
- Jot down specific details that tell about the color, shape, feel, sounds, smells, and tastes. Think of colorful, precise words. What comparisons can you use?
- Choose an order to use to describe details. You might use **time order** for the first assignment, describing the first course through dessert. Many descriptions use **spatial order.** You might describe the uniform from top to bottom.

FOLLOW-UP CHECKLIST

- Does the topic sentence state what you're describing in an interesting way?
- Do all the details focus on your topic?
- Do you follow the order you've decided upon?
- Does your ending tie your description together?
- Is all capitalization, punctuation, and spelling correct?

WRITING INSTRUCTIONS

Instructions tell a reader how to do or make something. Good instructions are written in step-by-step order.

KEY WORDS IN ASSIGNMENTS

- "**Explain how to. . .** "
- "**Describe the steps** you would take to. . ."
- "**Tell how you would**. . ."

SAMPLE ASSIGNMENTS

- Mmmm good! Explain how to make the best-ever ice cream sundae.
- Recycle it! Describe the steps you would take to make a book cover from a brown paper grocery bag.

A PLAN OF ATTACK

- Before you write, list the materials needed and the steps in the process.
- Organize the steps in time order, beginning with the first step and ending with the last.
- When you write, use time-order words like *first, next, then,* and *last* to show the correct order of steps.

FOLLOW-UP CHECKLIST

- Does the topic sentence state what the reader will learn to make or do?
- Are the steps arranged in correct order, and are all the steps there?
- Have you stuck to the topic—or have you put in extra information that you ought to get rid of?
- Are time-order words used to help the reader understand the order of the steps?
- Is all capitalization, punctuation, and spelling correct?

WRITING A FABLE

A fable is a very short story. The characters are usually animals, and the story states a moral, or lesson.

KEY WORDS IN ASSIGNMENTS

- "Write a modern **fable**. . ."
- "Choose a **moral,** or **lesson,** to **illustrate**. . ."

SAMPLE ASSIGNMENTS

- Choose a moral from this list. Then write a modern fable to illustrate it.

    Think how you will get out before you get in.
    Better safe than sorry.
    One good turn deserves another.

- We sometimes think of animals as having human traits—the fox as sly, the owl as wise, and so on. Choose several animals. What morals or lessons might they teach by their actions? Write an original fable that features one or more of these animals.

A PLAN OF ATTACK

- For either assignment, think carefully as you choose or decide upon the moral you will develop into a fable. Visualize animal characters that will teach the lesson well.
- Develop the plot of the fable. List what happens in the beginning, the middle, and the end. Organize the details of the plot in time order.
- Jot down possible dialogue that the animals might use to develop the story and to show character traits.
- End your fable with your moral.

FOLLOW-UP CHECKLIST

- Have you told your story in time order, with a beginning, a middle, and an ending?
- Are the animal characters well chosen to teach the lesson you've chosen to illustrate?
- Does your fable really teach the moral that ends it?
- Is all capitalization, punctuation, and spelling correct?

WRITING COMPARISON/CONTRAST

Comparison tells a reader how two or more people or things are alike. Contrast tells how two or more things are different from each other.

KEY WORDS IN ASSIGNMENTS

- "**Compare** (or **contrast**) these two things (or people, places, ideas, and so on)."
- "Describe the **similarities** (or **differences**) between. . ."
- "How are . . . **alike?** How are . . .**different?**"

SAMPLE ASSIGNMENTS

- Like mother, like daughter. Like father, like son. Write a paragraph explaining how you and one of your family members are alike.
- What's that you're reading? Contrast the differences between reading for pleasure and reading a textbook.

A PLAN OF ATTACK

- Know the purpose of your paragraph. In the first assignment, you will tell about likenesses. In the second, you will tell about differences.
- List the likenesses or differences. Think of vivid, descriptive words to use for the comparison or contrast.
- Decide what order you will use to describe details. You may want to use **order of importance**—from the most important likeness or difference to the least important. If you are making a physical comparison or contrast, you may want to use **spatial order**—from head to toe, for example.

FOLLOW-UP CHECKLIST

- Does the topic sentence state what things are being compared or contrasted?
- Are the points of comparison or contrast arranged in the order you planned?
- Are words like *same* and *different* used to signal comparisons and contrasts?
- Is all capitalization, punctuation, and spelling correct?

WRITING A PERSUASIVE PARAGRAPH

When you write a persuasive paragraph, your goal is to make the reader agree with your opinion. To do this, you must support your opinion with good reasons.

KEY WORDS IN ASSIGNMENTS

- "**Persuade** your parents. . ."
- "Write a paragraph to **convince** your principal. . ."

SAMPLE ASSIGNMENTS

- You have been eyeing the iguana in the pet store for months, and you are sure it would be a perfect pet. Write a paragraph for your parents to persuade them to let you buy it.
- Your hometown's baseball team is playing in a championship game in a nearby town. Convince your teacher to allow your class to watch the championship game, which will be played on a school day.

A PLAN OF ATTACK

- Clearly state the opinion you intend to support.
- List at least three good reasons to support your opinion.
- Organize your reasons in **order of importance.** Usually writers save their strongest reason for last.
- Jot down convincing words to use to persuade your reader.

FOLLOW-UP CHECKLIST

- Does the topic sentence clearly state your opinion?
- Are the supporting reasons organized from least important to most important?
- Are the reasons logical and sensible?
- Does the conclusion summarize the opinion and reasons?
- Is all capitalization, punctuation, and spelling correct?

Models and Guidelines

FRIENDLY LETTER FORM

Study the five parts of the friendly letter below. Notice the capitalization and punctuation in the greeting and the closing. If you know the person you are writing well, omit your address from the heading, but include the date.

21 Juneway Terrace
Glenview, IL 60025
February 13, 20__

Dear Julie,

Thanks for inviting me to your Mardi Gras party! I'm really upset that I can't be there. We're going to be out of town that weekend. Take pictures so I can see all the costumes. Maybe we can get together over summer vacation.

Your friend,

Lizzie

Heading

Greeting

Body

Closing

Signature

State abbreviations:

AL (Alabama)	**LA** (Louisiana)	**OH** (Ohio)
AK (Alaska)	**ME** (Maine)	**OK** (Oklahoma)
AZ (Arizona)	**MD** (Maryland)	**OR** (Oregon)
AR (Arkansas)	**MA** (Massachusetts)	**PA** (Pennsylvania)
CA (California)	**MI** (Michigan)	**RI** (Rhode Island)
CO (Colorado)	**MN** (Minnesota)	**SC** (South Carolina)
CT (Connecticut)	**MS** (Mississippi)	**SD** (South Dakota)
DE (Delaware)	**MO** (Missouri)	**TN** (Tennessee)
FL (Florida)	**MT** (Montana)	**TX** (Texas)
GA (Georgia)	**NE** (Nebraska)	**UT** (Utah)
HI (Hawaii)	**NV** (Nevada)	**VT** (Vermont)
ID (Idaho)	**NH** (New Hampshire)	**VA** (Virginia)
IL (Illinois)	**NJ** (New Jersey)	**WA** (Washington)
IN (Indiana)	**NM** (New Mexico)	**WV** (West Virginia)
IA (Iowa)	**NY** (New York)	**WI** (Wisconsin)
KS (Kansas)	**NC** (North Carolina)	**WY** (Wyoming)
KY (Kentucky)	**ND** (North Dakota)	

CAPITALIZATION

Besides letter parts, capitalize the following:

Names, initials, and titles used with names:

Dr. Martin S. Alvarez, Jr.   Lieutenant Ann Jones

Proper adjectives:

Midwestern values   Canadian bacon   African art

The pronoun *I*:

Laura and I will interview the principal.

Names of cities, states, countries, continents:

Glenview   Utah   Mexico   Australia

Names of lakes, rivers, mountains, structures:

Fish Lake   Po River   Ural Mountain   Navy Pier

Names of streets and street abbreviations:

Fir Street   Locust Ave.   Crown Rd.   East Spruce

Days, months, holidays, special events:

Monday   Wed.   June   Dec.

Labor Day   Olympics

First, last, and all important words in movie, book, story, play, and TV show titles:

Tom Sawyer   The Cat in the Hat   "The Gold Bug"

First word in a sentence:

We'll try harder.

First word inside quotation marks:

Marcus said, "He's allergic to cats."

PUNCTUATION

Use **periods**

- to end declarative and imperative sentences:
    Susan likes sunflowers.   Please listen carefully.

- after most **abbreviations**:
    Ms.   Jan.   Sat.   Jr.   Ave.   P.M.   Dr.

Use **exclamation marks**

- after sentences that show strong feeling:

    We won the championship!

Use **question marks**

- after interrogative sentences:

    Where are the stamps?

Use **commas**

- between the day and the year in a date:

    April 15, 1994

- between the name of a city and state:

    Mendocino, California

- between series of words in a sentence:

    Mr. Lee grows tomatoes, peppers, and beans.

- before the word that joins a compound sentence:

    The sun is out, and the air is warm.

- to separate a noun after a direct address:

    Mom, where's my key?   It's on the desk, Amy.

- before quotation marks or inside the end quotation marks:

    Bob said, "I like soup."   "I prefer salads," said Zoe.

Use **quotation marks**

- around the exact words someone used when speaking:

    Vera asked, "What time is it?"

- around titles of stories, poems, and songs:

    "The Cat's in the Cradle"   "The Pit and the Pendulum"

Underline titles of books and movies:

    Anne of Green Gables   Aladdin

Use **apostrophes**

- to form the possessive of a noun:

    nurse's   brothers'   men's

- in contractions in place of dropped letters:

    wasn't (was not)   don't (do not)   I'm (I am)

Use **colons** between hours and minutes to indicate time:

    2:20   4:45

Spelling Dictionary

Parts of a Dictionary Entry

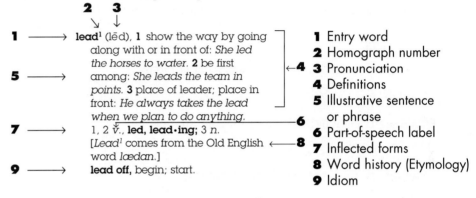

1 ——→ **lead¹** (lēd), **1** show the way by going
along with or in front of: *She led
the horses to water.* **2** be first
5 ——→ among: *She leads the team in
points.* **3** place of leader; place in
front: *He always takes the lead
when we plan to do anything.*
7 ——→ 1, 2 *v.*, **led, lead·ing;** 3 *n.*
[*Lead¹* comes from the Old English
word *lædan.*]
9 ——→ **lead off,** begin; start.

1 Entry word
2 Homograph number
3 Pronunciation
4 Definitions
5 Illustrative sentence
   or phrase
6 Part-of-speech label
7 Inflected forms
8 Word history (Etymology)
9 Idiom

Full Pronunciation Key

a	hat, cap	**i**	it, pin	**p**	paper, cup	**v**	very, save
ā	age, face	**ī**	ice, five	**r**	run, try	**w**	will, woman
ä	father, far			**s**	say, yes	**y**	young, yet
âr	care, hair	**j**	jam, enjoy	**sh**	she, rush	**z**	zero, breeze
		k	kind, seek	**t**	tell, it	**zh**	measure,
b	bad, rob	**l**	land, coal	**th**	thin, both		seizure
ch	child, much	**m**	me, am	**ᴛH**	then, smooth		
d	did, red	**n**	no, in			**ə**	represents:
		ng	long, bring	**u**	cup, butter		a in about
e	let, best			**u̇**	full, put		e in taken
ē	equal, be	**o**	hot, rock	**ü**	rule, move		i in pencil
ėr	term, learn	**ō**	open, go				o in lemon
		ȯ	all, saw				u in circus
f	fat, if	**ô**	order, store				
g	go, bag	**oi**	oil, voice				
h	he, how	**ou**	house, out				

Spellings of English Sounds*

Symbol	Spellings	Symbol	Spellings
a	at, plaid, half, laugh	ng	long, ink, handkerchief, tongue
ā	able, aid, say, age, eight, they, break, vein, gauge, crepe, beret	o	odd, honest
		ō	open, oak, toe, own, home, oh, folk, though, bureau, sew, brooch, soul
ä	father, ah, calm, heart, bazaar, yacht, sergeant		
âr	dare, aerial, fair, prayer, where, pear, their, they're	ȯ	all, author, awful, broad, bought, walk, taught, cough, Utah, Arkansas
b	bad, rabbit		
ch	child, watch, future, question	ô	order, board, floor, tore
		oi	oil, boy
d	did, add, filled	ou	out, owl, bough, hour
e	end, said, any, bread, says, heifer, leopard, friend, bury	p	pay, happy
		r	run, carry, wrong, rhythm
ē	equal, eat, eel, happy, cities, vehicle, ceiling, receive, key, these, believe, machine, liter, people	s	say, miss, cent, scent, dance, tense, sword, pizza, listen
		sh	she, machine, sure, ocean, special, tension, mission, nation
ėr	stern, earth, urge, first, word, journey	t	tell, button, two, Thomas, stopped, doubt, receipt, pizza
f	fat, effort, laugh, phrase		
g	go, egg, guest, ghost, league	th	thin
		TH	then, breathe
gz	example, exhaust	u	up, oven, trouble, does, flood
h	he, who, jai alai, Gila monster		
		u̇	full, good, wolf, should
hw	wheat	ü	food, junior, rule, blue, who, move, threw, soup, through, shoe, two, fruit, lieutenant
i	it, England, ear, hymn, been, sieve, women, busy, build, weird		
ī	I, ice, lie, sky, type, rye, eye, island, high, eider, aisle, height, buy, coyote	v	very, have, of, Stephen
		w	will, quick
		y	yes, opinion
j	jam, gem, exaggerate, schedule, badger, bridge, soldier, large, allegiance	yü	use, few, cue, view, vacuum
		z	zero, has, buzz, scissors, xylophone
k	coat, kind, back, echo, ache, quit, account, antique, excite, acquire	zh	measure, garage, division
		ə	alone, complete, moment, authority, bargain, April, cautious, circus, pageant, physician, oxygen, dungeon, tortoise
l	land, tell		
m	me, common, climb, solemn, palm		
n	no, manner, knife, gnaw, pneumonia		

*Not all English spellings of these sounds are included in this list.

245

A

a·bil·i·ty (ə bil′ə tē), **1** power to do some special thing; skill: *He has great ability in making jewelry.* **2** special natural gift; talent: *Musical ability often shows itself early in life. n., pl.* **a·bil·i·ties.**

a·ble (ā′bəl), having enough power, skill, or means to do something; capable: *A cat is able to see in the dark. adj.*

ac·ci·dent (ak′sə dənt), something harmful or unlucky that happens: *automobile accidents. n., pl.* **ac·ci·dents.**

ac·com·plish·ment (ə kom′plish mənt), something that has been done with knowledge, skill, or ability; achievement: *The teachers were proud of their pupils' accomplishments. n., pl.* **ac·com·plish·ments.**

ac·tion (ak′shən), process of acting; doing something: *The quick action of the firemen saved the building from being burned down. n.*

adobe (definition 3)
an **adobe** village

a·do·be (ə dō′bē), **1** brick made of sun-dried clay. **2** building made of sun-dried clay. **3** built or made of adobe. 1,2 *n.,* 3 *adj.* [*Adobe* was borrowed from Spanish *adobe*, which came from Arabic *at-tūb*, meaning "the brick."]

ad·van·tage (ad van′tij), anything that is in one's favor, or is a benefit; a help in getting something desired: *Good health is always a great advantage. n.*

a·gain (ə gen′), another time; once more: *Come again to play. Say that again. adv.*

air mass (âr′ mas′), a large amount of air with the same temperature and humidity.

aisle (īl), passage between rows of seats in a hall, theater, school, etc.: *The teacher walked down the aisle between the rows of desks. n.*

a·lign (ə līn′), bring into line; arrange in a straight line: *The mechanic aligned the front wheels of our car. v.*

al·ley (al′ē), a narrow back street in a city or town. *n., pl.* **al·leys.**

almond blossom
The **almond blossom**
is the national flower of Israel.

al·low·ance (ə lou′əns), a sum of money given or set aside for expenses: *a household allowance for groceries of $50 a week. My weekly allowance is $1. n.*

al·mond blos·som (ä′mənd blos′əm), flower, especially of a plant that produces a peachlike fruit from a tree growing in Israel. *n.*

al·most (ȯl′mōst), very near to; all but; nearly: *It is almost ten o'clock. I almost missed the train. adv.*

a lot (ə lot′), **1** a great deal; much: *I feel a lot better.* **2** often, a great many: *a great deal: a lot of books.*

al·pha·bet (al′fə bet), the letters of a language arranged in their usual order, not as they are in words. *n.* [*Alphabet* can be traced back to the names of the first two letters of the Greek alphabet: *alpha* A and *beta* B.]

al·ways (ȯl′wāz or ȯl′wiz), at all times; every time: *Night always follows day. adv.*

a·mus·ing (ə myü′zing), causing laughter or smiles: *an amusing joke. adj.*

an·a·con·da (an′ə kon′də), a very large South American snake related to the boa that crushes its prey in its coils. Anacondas live in tropical forests and rivers and are the longest snakes in America, sometimes over 30 feet (9 meters). *n., pl.* **an·a·con·das.**

an·gel (ān′jəl), **1** messenger from God. **2** person as good or as lovely as an angel. **3** a replica used as a statue on a tree. *n.*

an·gle (ang′gəl), **1** the space between two lines or surfaces that meet. **2** the figure formed by two such lines or surfaces. *n.*

an·gry (ang′grē), feeling or showing anger: *I was angrier when you disobeyed me again. adj.,* **an·gri·er, an·gri·est.**

an·i·mal (an′ə məl), any living thing that is not a plant. Most animals move about, feed upon other animals or plants, and have a nervous system. A dog, a bird, a fish, a snake, a fly, and a worm are animals. *n., pl.* **an·i·mals.**

an·nounce (ə nouns′), give public or formal notice of: *The teacher announced that there would be no school tomorrow. v.,* **an·nounced, an·nounc·ing.**

an·nounce·ment (ə nouns′mənt), what is announced or made known: *The principal made two announcements. The announcement was published in the newspapers. n.*

an·oth·er (ə nuŦH′ər), **1** one more: *Have another glass of milk (adj.). I ate a candy bar and then asked for another (pron.).* **2** a different: *Show me another hat.* 1,2 *adj.,* 1 *pron.*

an·ten·na (an ten′ə), one of the long, slender feelers on the head of an insect, scorpion, lobster, etc. *The antennas of the grasshopper can be long or short. n., pl.* **an·ten·nae** (an ten′ē) or **an·ten·nas.**

an·y·way (en′ē wā), in any case; at least: *I am coming anyway, no matter what you say. adv.*

an·y·where (en′ē hwer), in, at, or to any place: *I'll meet you anywhere you say. adv.*

a·pol·o·gize (ə pol′ə jīz), make an apology; say one is sorry; offer an excuse: *I apologized for being late. v.* **a·pol·o·gized, a·pol·o·giz·ing.**

a·pos·tro·phe (ə pos′trə fē), sign (') used: **1** to show the omission of one or more letters in contractions. **2** to show the possessive forms of nouns or indefinite pronouns. **3** to form plurals of letters and numbers. *n.*

ap·pear·ance (ə pir′əns), outward look: *a pleasing appearance. n.*

ap·point·ment (ə point′mənt), meeting with someone at a certain time and place; engagement: *an appointment to see the doctor at four o'clock. n.*

ap·pre·ci·ate (ə prē′shē āt), think highly of; recognize the worth or quality of; value; enjoy: *Almost everyone appreciates good food. v.* **ap·pre·ci·at·ed, ap·pre·ci·at·ing.**

A·pril (ā′prəl), the fourth month of the year. It has 30 days. *n.*

are (är; *unstressed* ər), form of the verb **be** used with *we, you,* and *they* and any plural noun to indicate the present tense. *We are ready. You are next. They are waiting. v.*

ar·e·a (âr′ē ə), amount of surface; extent of surface: *The area of this floor is 600 square feet. n., pl.* **ar·e·as.**

ar·gue (är′gyü), discuss with someone who disagrees: *He argued with his sister about who should wash the dishes. v.* **ar·gued, ar·gu·ing.**

ar·rive (ə rīv′), come to; reach: *You should arrive at school before nine o'clock. v.* **ar·rived, ar·riv·ing.**

ar·thri·tis (är thrī′tis), inflammation of a joint or joints of the body. *n.*

ar·ti·cle (är′tə kəl), a written composition on a special subject, complete in itself, but forming part of a magazine, newspaper, or book: *This newspaper has a good article on gardening. n., pl.* **ar·ti·cles.**

art·ist (är′tist), person who is skilled in any of the fine arts, such as sculpture, music, or literature. *n.*

ash·es (ash′iz), what remains of a thing after it has thoroughly burned: *Ashes have to be removed from the fireplace to make room for more wood. n. pl.*

ask (ask), try to find out by words; inquire: *Why don't you ask? She asked about our health. Ask the way. v.*

antenna
Snails have slender
antennae.

a	hat	ī	ice	u̇	put	ə *stands for*	
ā	age	o	not	ü	rule	a	in about
ä	far, calm	ō	open	ch	child	e	in taken
âr	care	ȯ	saw	ng	long	i	in pencil
e	let	ô	order	sh	she	o	in lemon
ē	equal	oi	oil	th	thin	u	in circus
ėr	term	ou	out	ŦH	then		
i	it	u	cup	zh	measure		

astronaut

An **astronaut** is trained
to travel in space.

barometer

A **barometer** predicts
changes in weather.

as·sign (ə sīn′), **1** appoint (to a post or duty): *We were assigned to decorate the room for the party.* **2** name definitely; fix; set: *The judge assigned a day for the trial. v.*

as·sign·ment (ə sīn′mənt), something assigned, especially a piece of work to be done: *Today's assignment in arithmetic consists of ten examples. n., pl.* **as·sign·ments.**

as·tro·naut (as′trə nôt), pilot or member of the crew of a spacecraft. *n.*

At·lan·tic O·cean (at lan′tik ō′shən), ocean east of North and South America, west of Europe and Africa.

at·tack (ə tak′), **1** use force or weapons against; set upon to hurt; begin fighting: *The dog attacked the cat. The enemy attacked at dawn.* **2** act harmfully on: *Locusts attacked the crops. v.*

Au·gust (ô′gəst), the eighth month of the year. It has 31 days. *n.*

aunt (ant), **1** sister of one's father or mother. **2** wife of one's uncle. *My aunt's name is Sarah. n.*

au·to·graph (ô′tə graf), **1** a person's signature: *Many people collect the autographs of celebrities.* **2** write one's name in or on: *The movie star autographed my program.* **1** *n.,* **2** *v.*

Ave. or **ave.,** Avenue; avenue.

a·while (ə hwīl′), for a short time: *Stay awhile. adv.*

B

ba·by (bā′bē), **1** child too young to walk or speak; infant: *The babies' mothers took them to the park.* **2** the youngest of a family or group. *n., pl.* **ba·bies.**

back·board (bak′bôrd′), (in basketball) the upright, rectangular surface of wood, glass, or plastic, to which the basket is fastened. *n.*

back·pack (bak′pak·), a pack, often supported by a frame, that is worn on the back by hikers and campers to carry food, clothes, and equipment. *n.*

back·stroke (bak′strōk′), a swimming stroke made by a swimmer lying on his back. *n.*

ba·con (bā′kən), salted and smoked meat from the back and sides of a hog. *n.* **bring home the bacon,** succeed; win; earn a living.

band (band), group of musicians performing together, especially on wind and percussion instruments: *The school band played several marches. n.*

bare·foot (bâr′fut′), without shoes and stockings on: *A barefoot child played in the puddles (adj.). If you go barefoot, watch out for broken glass (adv.). adj., adv.*

ba·rom·e·ter (bə rom′ə tər), instrument for measuring the pressure of air, used in determining height above sea level and in predicting probable changes in the weather. *n.*

bar·rel (bar′əl), container with a round, flat top and bottom and sides that curve out slightly. Barrels are usually made of boards held together by hoops. *n.*

base·ball (bās′bôl′), **1** game played with bat and ball by two teams of nine players each, on a field with four bases. A player who touches all the bases, under the rules, scores a run. **2** ball used in this game. *n.*

bas·ket·ball (bas′kit bôl′), **1** game played with a large, round ball by two teams of five players each. The players try to toss the ball through a ring into a net shaped like a basket but open at the bottom. **2** ball used in this game. *n.*

beach (bēch), an almost flat shore of sand or pebbles over which water washes when high. *n., pl.* **beach·es.**

beat (bēt), **1** stroke or blow made again and again: *the beat of a drum.* **2** get the better of; defeat; overcome: *Their team beat ours by a huge score.* **3** mix by stirring rapidly with a fork, spoon, or other utensil: *I helped make the cake by beating the eggs.* 1 *n.,* 2,3 *v.,* **beat, beat·en** (bēt′n) or **beat, beat·ing.**

beau·ti·ful (byü′tə fəl), very pleasing to see or hear; delighting the mind or senses. *adj.*

be·cause (bi kòz′), for the reason that; since: *Because we were late, we ran the whole way home. conj.*

beet (bēt), the thick, fleshy root of a garden plant. Red beets and their green leaves are eaten as vegetables. Sugar is made from white beets. *n.*

be·gin (bi gin′), do the first part; make a start: *begin on one's work. When shall we begin? Begin at the third chapter. v.,* **be·gan** (bi gan′), **be·gun** (bi gun′), **be·gin·ning.**

be·go·nia (bi gō′nyə), a tropical plant often grown for its large, richly colored leaves and waxy flowers. *n., pl.* **be·go·nias.** [*The begonia was named after Michel Bégon, 1638-1710, a French patron of botany.*]

be·hav·ior (bi hā′vyər), manner of behaving; way of acting: *Her sullen behavior showed that she was angry. n.*

be·hind (bi hīnd′), **1** not on time; late: *The class is behind in its work.* **2** farther back: *The rest of the bikers are still behind. adv.*

be·lieve (bi lēv′), **1** think (somebody) tells the truth: *Her friends believe her.* **2** think; suppose: *I believe I will go. v.,* **be·lieved, be·liev·ing.**

bev·y (bev′ē), a small group or flock: *a bevy of quail. n., pl.* **bev·ies.**

bib (bib), cloth worn under the chin, especially by babies and small children, to protect clothing during meals. *n.*

bi·cus·pid (bī kus′pid), a double-pointed tooth that tears and grinds food. Adult human beings have eight bicuspids. *n.*

bi·cy·cle (bī′sik əl), a lightweight vehicle with two wheels, one behind the other, that support a metal frame on which there is a seat. The rider pushes two pedals and steers with handlebars. *n.*

big (big), great in amount or size; large: *a big room, a big book. Making automobiles is a big business. An elephant is a big animal. adj.* **big·ger, big·gest.**

blan·ket (blang′kit), a soft, heavy covering woven from wool, cotton, nylon, or other material, used to keep people or animals warm. *n.*

bleach·ers (blē′chərz), section of wooden or plastic benches for spectators at baseball or other outdoor events. Bleachers are not roofed, and are the lowest priced seats. *n. pl.*

bliss·ful (blis′fəl), very happy; joyful: *blissful memories of a summer vacation. adj.*

block (blok), space in a city or town enclosed by four streets; square. *n.*

bloom·ers (blü′mərz), loose trousers, gathered at the knee, formerly worn by women and girls for physical training: *In the old days girls wore bloomers when playing sports. n. pl.* [*Bloomers were named for Amelia J. Bloomer, 1818-1894, an American magazine publisher who popularized their use.*]

blub·ber (blub′ər), fat of whales and some other sea animals. The oil obtained from whale blubber was formerly burned in lamps. *n.*

bicycle
riding **bicycles** in
the park

a	hat	ī	ice	ù	put	ə *stands for*	
ā	age	o	not	ü	rule	a	in about
ä	far, calm	ō	open	ch	child	e	in taken
âr	care	ò	saw	ng	long	i	in pencil
e	let	ô	order	sh	she	o	in lemon
ē	equal	oi	oil	th	thin	u	in circus
ėr	term	ou	out	ŦH	then		
i	it	u	cup	zh	measure		

bridge

a **bridge** over the bay

broccoli

two stalks of **broccoli**

Blvd., boulevard.

bo·lo·gna (bə lōʹnē), a large sausage usually made of beef, veal, and pork. n., pl. **bo·lo·gnas.** [*Bologna* was named for *Bologna,* Italy, where it was first made.]

boom (büm), a deep hollow sound like the roar of cannon or of big waves: *The big bell tolled with a loud boom. n.*

bor·row (borʹō), get (something) from another person with the understanding that it must be returned: *I borrowed his book and promised to return it in a week. v.*

boss (bȯs), person who hires workers or watches over or directs them; foreman; manager: *It was the boss's decision to hire the new construction worker. n., pl.* **boss·es.**

bot·tle (botʹl), container for holding liquids, made of glass, plastic, etc. Bottles often have narrow necks fitted with caps or stoppers: *drink a bottle of milk. n.*

bow¹ (bou), **1** to stoop; bend: *The old man was bowed by age.* **2** submit; yield: *She bowed to her parents' wishes. v.* **bow out,** withdraw. **take a bow,** accept praise or applause for something done.

bow² (bō), **1** weapon for shooting arrows. A bow usually consists of a strip of flexible wood bent by a string. **2** a slender rod with horsehairs stretched on it, for playing a violin, cello, etc. *n.*

bow³ (bou), the forward part of a ship, boat, or aircraft. *n.*

boy (boi), a male child from birth to about eighteen. *n.*

brain·storm (brānʹstôrmʹ), INFORMAL. a sudden idea or inspiration. *n.*

brake¹ (brāk), **1** anything used to slow or stop the motion of a wheel or vehicle by pressing or scraping or by rubbing against. **2** slow or stop by using a brake: *The driver braked the speeding car and it slid to a stop.* **1** *n.,* **2** *v.,* **braked, brak·ing.**

brake² (brāk), a thick growth of bushes; thicket. *n.*

break (brāk), **1** come apart or make come apart; smash: *The plate broke into pieces when it fell on the floor.* **2** fail to keep; act against: *to break a promise. People who break the law are punished. v.,* **broke, bro·ken, break·ing.**

breathe (brēᴛH), stop for breath; rest; allow to rest and breathe. *v.,* **breathed, breath·ing.**

breath·less (brethʹlis), out of breath: *Running upstairs very fast made me breathless. adj.*

bridge (brij), something built over a river, road, railroad, or other obstacle, so that people, cars, trains, etc., can get across. *n.*

bright (brīt), lively or cheerful: *There was a bright smile on his face. adj.* —**brightʹly,** *adv.* —**brightʹness,** *n.*

bring (bring), come with or carry (a thing or person) from another place; take along to a place or person: *The bus brought us home. Bring me a clean plate. v.,* **brought, bring·ing.**

broad·leaf (brȯdʹlēfʹ), of or about a type of tree with broad, flat leaves. An oak is a broadleaf tree. *adj.*

broc·co·li (brokʹə lē), vegetable with green branching stems and flower heads. It belongs to the cabbage family. *n., pl.* **broc·co·li.** [*Broccoli* comes from Italian *broccoli,* meaning "sprouts."]

broke (brōk), See **break.** *I broke my watch. v.*

bro·ken (brōʹkən), separated into parts by a break; in pieces: *a broken leg, a broken cup. adj.*

brook (brůk), a small stream; creek. *n.*

broth·er (bruᴛHʹər), son of the same parents. A boy is a brother to the other children of his parents. *I knocked on my brother's door. n.*

brought (brȯt), See **bring.** *I brought my lunch yesterday. They were brought to school in a bus. v.*

bruise (brüz), injury to the body, caused by a fall or a blow, that breaks blood vessels without breaking the skin: *The bruise on my arm turned black and blue. n.*

bub·ble (bub'əl), **1** a thin, round film of liquid enclosing air or gas. The surface of boiling water is covered with bubbles. **2** plan or idea that looks good, but soon falls apart. *n.*

buf·fa·lo (buf'ə lō), the bison of North America. *n., pl.* **buf·fa·loes, buf·fa·los,** or **buf·fa·lo.**

build (bild), make by putting materials together; construct: *People build houses, bridges, and machines. Birds build nests. v.,* **built** (bilt), **build·ing.**

bunch (bunch), group of things of the same kind growing, fastened, placed, or thought of together: *a bunch of grapes, a bunch of flowers, a bunch of sheep. n., pl.* **bunch·es.**

bush (bush), a woody plant smaller than a tree, often with many separate branches starting from or near the ground. *n., pl.* **bush·es.**

busi·ness (biz'nis), thing that one is busy at; work; occupation: *A carpenter's business is building. n.*

bus·y (biz'ē), having plenty to do; working; active; not idle: *a busy person. adj.,* **bus·i·er, bus·i·est.**

butch·er (buch'ər), person who cuts up and sells meat. *n.*

but·ter·fly (but'ər flī'), **1** an insect with a slender body and two pairs of large, often brightly colored, overlapping wings. **2** a swimming stroke, a type of breast stroke, in which both arms are pulled upward out of the water and forward while the feet are kicking up and down. *n., pl.* **but·ter·flies.**

but·ton (but'n), **1** a round, flat piece of metal, bone, glass, or plastic, fastened on garments to hold them closed or to decorate them. **2** fasten the buttons of; close with buttons: *Button your coat.* 1 *n.,* 2 *v.*

by-line (bī'līn'), line at the beginning of a newspaper or magazine article giving the name of the writer. *n.*

C

cab·i·net (kab'ə nit), piece of furniture with shelves or drawers, used to hold articles for use or display: *a medicine cabinet, a filing cabinet for letters. We keep our very best dishes in the china cabinet. n.*

ca·ble (kā'bəl), an insulated bundle of wires which carries an electric current. *n.*

cac·tus (kak'təs), plant with a thick, fleshy stem that usually has spines but no leaves. Most cactuses grow in very hot, dry regions of America and often have brightly colored flowers. *n., pl.* **cac·tus·es, cac·ti** (kak'tī).

caf·e·ter·i·a (kaf'ə tir'ē ə), restaurant where people serve themselves. *n., pl.* **caf·e·ter·i·as.**

cam·er·a (kam'ər ə), machine for taking photographs or motion pictures. A camera lens focuses light rays through the dark inside part of the camera onto film which is sensitive to light. *n.*

Can·a·da (kan'ə də), country in the N part of North America, consisting of ten provinces and two territories and extending from the Atlantic to the Pacific. *Capital:* Ottawa. *n.*

ca·nal (kə nal'), waterway dug across land for ships or small boats to go through or to carry water to places that need it. *n.*

ca·noe (kə nü'), **1** a light boat pointed at both ends and moved with a paddle. **2** paddle a canoe; go in a canoe. 1 *n.,* 2 *v.,* **ca·noed, ca·noe·ing.**

butterfly (definition 1)
three colorful
butterflies

a	hat	ī	ice	u̇	put	ə *stands for*	
ā	age	o	not	ü	rule	a	in about
ä	far, calm	ō	open	ch	child	e	in taken
âr	care	ȯ	saw	ng	long	i	in pencil
e	let	ô	order	sh	she	o	in lemon
ē	equal	oi	oil	th	thin	u	in circus
ėr	term	ou	out	ŦH	then		
i	it	u	cup	zh	measure		

catcher

a **catcher** kneeling

behind home plate

ca·pac·i·ty (kə pas′ə tē), amount of room or space inside; largest amount that can be held by a container. *n., pl.* **ca·pac·i·ties.**

care (kâr), **1** a troubled state of mind because of fear of what may happen; worry: *Few people are completely free from care.* **2** be concerned; feel interest. **1** *n.,* **2** *v.,* **cared, car·ing.**
take care of, watch over; be careful with: *Take care of your money.*

care·ful (kâr′fəl), showing care; done with thought or effort; exact; thorough: *Arithmetic requires careful work. adj.* —**care′ful·ly,** *adv.*

care·less (kâr′lis), not thinking what one says; not watching what one does; not careful: *I was careless and broke the cup. adj.*

car·i·bou (kar′ə bü), the North American reindeer. *n., pl.* **car·i·bous** or **car·i·bou.**

car·ni·vore (kär′nə vôr), any animal that feeds chiefly on flesh. Carnivores have large, strong teeth with sharp cutting edges. *n.*

cash (kash) money in the form of coins and bills. *n.*

cat (kat), a small, furry, flesh-eating mammal, often kept as a pet or for catching mice and rats: *The cat meowed for food. n.*

catch (kach), **1** grab or seize (something in flight): *Catch the ball with both hands.* **2** come upon suddenly; surprise; *Mother caught me just as I was hiding her birthday present. v.,* **caught, catch·ing.**

catch·er (kach′ər), a baseball player positioned behind the batter to catch the ball thrown by the pitcher. *n.*

ca·the·dral (kə thē′drəl), a large or important church. *n.*

cat·tle·ya or·chid (kat′lē ə ôr′kid), a tropical South American plant with showy flowers. [The *cattleya orchid* was named for William *Cattley,* died 1832, English patron of botany.]

cattleya orchid

The **cattleya orchid** is

the national flower of

Costa Rica.

caught (kot), See **catch.** *I caught the ball. v.*

cause (koz), **1** person, thing, or event that makes something happen: *The flood was the cause of much damage.* **2** make happen; make do; bring about: *The fire caused much damage.* **1** *n.,* **2** *v.,* **caused, caus·ing.**

cel·e·brat·ed (sel′ə brā′tid), much talked about; famous; well-known: *a celebrated author. adj.*

cel·er·y (sel′ər ē), vegetable related to parsley, with long, crisp stalks. Celery is eaten either raw or cooked. *n.*

Cel·si·us (sel′sē əs), of, based on, or according to the Celsius scale; centigrade. *adj.* [The *Celsius* scale was named for Anders *Celsius,* 1701-1744, a Swedish astronomer who invented it in 1742.]

ce·ment (sə ment′), a fine, gray powder made by burning clay and limestone. Cement is used to make concrete and mortar. *n.*

cer·e·mo·ny (ser′ə mō′nē), a special act or set of acts to be done on special occasions such as weddings, funerals, graduations, or holidays: *The graduation ceremony was held in the gymnasium. n., pl.* **cer·e·mo·nies.**

cer·tain (sėrt′n) without a doubt; sure: *It is certain that 2 and 3 do not make 6. I am certain that these are the facts. adj.*

chalk·board (chok′bôrd′), a smooth, hard surface, used for writing or drawing on with crayon or chalk. *n.*

cham·pi·on (cham′pē ən), person, animal, or thing that wins first place in a game or contest: *He is the swimming champion of our school. n.*

change (chānj), **1** make or become different: *She changed the room by painting the walls green. The wind changed from east to west.* **2** change one's clothes; *After swimming we went to the cabin and changed. v.,* **changed, chang·ing.**

Cha·nu·kah (hä′nə kə), Hanukkah. *n.*

chap·ter (chap′tər), main division of a book or other writing, dealing with a particular part of the story or subject. *n.*

charge (chärj), **1** put down as a debt to be paid: *We charged the entire dinner, so the restaurant will send a bill for it.* **2** a task, a responsibility: *The charge of the baby was given to my sister.* 1 *v.*, **charged, charg·ing;** 2 *n.*

Char·tres (shär′trə), city in N France. Its Gothic cathedral is more than 700 years old. *n.*

chase (chās), run or follow after to catch or kill: *The cat chased the mouse.* *v.*, **chased, chas·ing.**

check (chek), stop suddenly. *v.*

cheer·ful (chir′fəl), full of cheer; joyful; glad: *She is a smiling, cheerful girl.* *adj.*

child (chīld), **1** a young boy or girl: *games for children.* **2** son or daughter: *Parents love their children.* *n.*, *pl.* **chil·dren** (chil′drən).

child·hood (chīld′hud), time during which one is a child. *n.*

Chi·nese New Year (chī′nēz nü′ yir′), a yearly event that begins between the dates of January 21 and February 19. It lasts four days, and on the last day people dress as dragons.

choc·o·late (chok′lit *or* chok′ə lit), **1** candy made of chocolate. **2** made of or flavored with chocolate: *chocolate cake.* 1 *n.*, 2 *adj.*

chop (chop), cut by hitting with something sharp: *You can chop wood with an ax. We chopped down the dead tree.* *v.*, **chopped, chop·ping.**

chore (chôr), an odd job; small task: *Feeding the dog is my daily chore.* *n.*, *pl.* **chores.**

Christ·mas (kris′məs), the yearly celebration of the birth of Christ; December 25. *n.*, *pl.* **Christ·mas·es.**

church (chėrch), building for public Christian worship. *n.*

cin·na·mon (sin′ə mən), spice made from the dried inner bark of a small tree of the East Indies: *Put cinnamon into the apple cider and heat it up.* *n.*

cir·cus (sėr′kəs), a traveling show of acrobats, clowns, horses, riders, and wild animals. The performers who give the show and the performances they give are both called the circus. *n.*, *pl.* **cir·cus·es.**

cit·i·zen (sit′ə zən), person who by birth or by choice is a member of a nation. A citizen owes loyalty to that nation and is given certain rights by it. *Many immigrants have become citizens of the United States.* *n.*

class (klas), group of students taught together: *The art class meets in room 202.* *n.*, *pl.* **class·es.**

class·mate (klas′māt′), member of the same class in school. *n.*

class·room (klas′rüm′), room in which classes are held. *n.*

clat·ter (klat′ər), a confused noise like that of many plates being struck together: *The clatter in the cafeteria made it hard for us to hear one another talk.* *n.*

clear key (klir′ kē′), the calculator key that enables the user to remove the number in the display window from the calculator's memory.

climb (klīm), **1** go up, especially by using the hands or feet, or both; ascend: *She climbed the stairs quickly.* **2** go in any direction, especially with the help of hands: *climb over a fence, climb down a ladder.* *v.*

cinnamon
different forms of the
spice **cinnamon**

a	hat	**ī**	ice	**u̇**	put	**ə** stands for	
ā	age	**o**	not	**ü**	rule	**a**	in about
ä	far, calm	**ō**	open	**ch**	child	**e**	in taken
âr	care	**ȯ**	saw	**ng**	long	**i**	in pencil
e	let	**ô**	order	**sh**	she	**o**	in lemon
ē	equal	**oi**	oil	**th**	thin	**u**	in circus
ėr	term	**ou**	out	**ᴛʜ**	then		
i	it	**u**	cup	**zh**	measure		

collection

a baseball card

collection

compass

Compasses show

directions.

close¹ (klōz), bring together or move the parts of so as to leave no opening; shut: *Close the door. The sleepy child's eyes are closing.* v., **closed, clos·ing.**

close² (klōs), intimate; dear: *We are close friends.* adj., **clos·er, clos·est.**

clos·et (kloz′it), a small room for storing clothes or household supplies. n.

clothes (klōz or klōŦHz), coverings for a person's body: *I bought some new clothes for my trip.* n. pl.

cloud (kloud), 1 mass of tiny drops of water, water vapor, or ice particles floating in the air high above the earth. Clouds may be white, rounded heaps, streamers, or dark, almost black, masses. 2 mass of smoke or dust in the air. n.

coal (kōl), a black mineral that burns and gives off heat, composed mostly of carbon. It is formed from partly decayed vegetable matter under great pressure in the earth. Anthracite and bituminous coal are two kinds of coal. n.

col·lapse (kə laps′), fall in; shrink together suddenly: *Sticking a pin into the balloon made it collapse.* v., **col·lapsed, col·laps·ing.**

col·lec·tion (kə lek′shən), group of things gathered from many places and belonging together: *Our library has large collections of books.* n., pl. **col·lec·tions.**

co·logne (kə lōn′), a fragrant liquid, not so strong as perfume. n.

col·o·ny (kol′ə nē), group of animals or plants of the same kind, living or growing together: *a colony of ants. Coral grows in colonies.* n., pl. **col·o·nies.**

col·or (kul′ər), any color except black, white, or gray; red, yellow, blue, or any combination of them. The color green is a mixture of yellow and blue. n.

comb (kōm), take out tangles with a comb. v.

come (kum), move toward: *Come this way.* v., **came** (kām), **come, com·ing.**

com·mer·cial (kə mėr′shəl), 1 having to do with trade or business: *a store or other commercial establishment.* 2 an advertising message on radio or television, broadcast between or during programs. 1 adj., 2 n.

com·mon (kom′ən), 1 from all; by all; to all; general: *By common consent of the class, she was chosen president.* 2 often met with; ordinary; usual. adj.

com·mute (kə myüt′), 1 travel regularly to and from work by train, bus, automobile, etc. 2 the distance or trip ordinarily traveled by a commuter: *a long commute, an easy commute.* 1 v., **com·mut·ed, com·mut·ing;** 2 n.

com·pass (kum′pəs), instrument for showing directions, especially one consisting of a needle that points to the North Magnetic Pole. n., pl. **com·pass·es.**

com·pas·sion·ate (kəm pash′ə nit), wishing to help those that suffer; sympathetic; pitying. adj.

com·plete (kəm plēt′), 1 with all the parts; whole; entire: *We have a complete set of garden tools.* 2 make whole or entire; make up the full number or amount of: *I completed the set of dishes by buying the cups and saucers.* 1 adj., 2 v., **com·plet·ed, com·plet·ing.** —**com·plete′ly,** adv.

com·pose (kəm pōz′), 1 make up; form: *The ocean is composed of salt water.* 2 put together. To compose a story or poem is to construct it from words. To compose a piece of music is to invent the tune and write down the notes. v., **com·posed, com·pos·ing.**

com·po·si·tion (kom′pə zish′ən), thing composed. A symphony, poem, a school exercise, or painting is a composition. n.

con·cert (kon′sərt), a musical performance in which several musicians or singers take part: *The school orchestra gave a concert last night.* n.

con·duct (kən dukt′), transmit; be a channel for: *Those pipes conduct steam to the radiators upstairs.* v.

con·fes·sion (kən fesh′ən), act of confessing; owning up; telling one's mistakes or sins. *n.*

con·fi·dence (kon′fə dəns), firm belief in oneself; self-confidence: *Years of work at school have given her great confidence. n.*

con·fuse (kən fyüz′), **1** throw into disorder; mix up; bewilder: *So many people talking to me at once confused me.* **2** be unable to tell apart; mistake (one thing or person for another): *People often confuse this girl with her twin sister. v.,* **con·fused, con·fus·ing.**

con·i·fer (kon′ə fər *or* kō′nə fər), plant that bears cones. The pine, fir, spruce, hemlock, and larch are conifers. *n., pl.* **con·i·fers.**

con·scious·ness (kon′shəs nis), condition of being conscious; awareness: *The injured woman did not regain consciousness for two hours. n.*

con·sti·tu·tion (kon′stə tü′shən *or* kon′stə tyü′shən), **1** way in which a person or thing is organized; nature; makeup: *A person with a good constitution is strong and healthy.* **2** system of fundamental principles according to which a nation, state, or group is governed: *The United States has a written constitution.* **3** the Constitution, the written set of fundamental principles by which the United States is governed. *n.*

con·sum·er (kən sü′mər), a living thing that has to eat to stay alive. Animals are consumers, but plants make their own food. *n., pl.* **con·sum·ers.**

con·test (kon′test *for 1,2;* kən test′ *for 3*), **1** trial of skill to see which can win. A game or race is a contest.

2 a fight, struggle, or dispute. **3** argue against; dispute about: *The decision was not contested.* 1,2 *n.,* 3 *v.*

con·test·ant (kən tes′tənt), person who takes part in a contest: *My sister was a contestant in the 100-yard dash. n.*

cool (kül), somewhat cold; more cold than hot: *a cool, cloudy day. adj.*

co·or·di·nate (kō ôrd′n it), any of a set of numbers that give the position of a point by reference to fixed lines or axes. *n., pl.* **co·or·di·nates.**

corn (kôrn), kind of grain that grows on large ears; Indian corn. *n.*

cor·rect (kə rekt′), **1** free from mistakes; right: *give the correct answer.* **2** change to what is right; remove mistakes or faults from: *Correct any misspellings that you find.* 1 *adj.,* 2 *v.*

cor·rec·tion (kə rek′shən), a change to correct an error or mistake: *Write in your corrections neatly. n.*

couch (kouch), a long seat, usually upholstered and having a back and arms; sofa: *She sat on the couch and read the newspaper. n., pl.* **couch·es.**

could've (kud′əv), could have.

coun·se·lor *or* **coun·sel·lor** (koun′sə lər), person who gives advice; adviser. *The counselor helped my brother select some courses for college. n.*

cou·ple (kup′əl), **1** INFORMAL. a small number; a few: *Give me a couple of those apples—about four of them.* **2** man and woman who are married, engaged, partners in a dance, etc. *n.*

constitution
(definition 3)
the **Constitution** of
the United States

						ə stands for	
a	hat	**ī**	ice	**u̇**	put		
ā	age	**o**	not	**ü**	rule	**a**	in about
ä	far, calm	**ō**	open	**ch**	child	**e**	in taken
âr	care	**ȯ**	saw	**ng**	long	**i**	in pencil
e	let	**ô**	order	**sh**	she	**o**	in lemon
ē	equal	**oi**	oil	**th**	thin	**u**	in circus
ėr	term	**ou**	out	**ᵺ**	then		
i	it	**u**	cup	**zh**	measure		

cou·ra·geous (kə rā′jəs), full of courage; brave; fearless. *adj.*

course (kôrs), **1** regular order: *the course of nature.* **2** a series of studies in a school, college, or university. A student must complete a certain course in order to graduate: *Biology is the course I will take to become a science teacher. n.*

court (kôrt), place marked off for a game: *a tennis court, a basketball court. n.*

court·room (kôrt′rüm′), room where a court of law is held. *n.*

cous·in (kuz′n), son or daughter of one's uncle or aunt. First cousins have the same grandparents; second cousins have the same great-grandparents. *n.*

cov·er (kuv′ər), **1** put something over: *I covered the child with a blanket.* **2** anything that covers. Books have covers. A box, can, or jar usually has a cover. A blanket is a cover. **3** be enough for; provide for: *My allowance covers my lunch at school.* 1,3 *v.*, 2 *n.*

cov·er·let (kuv′ər lit), a covering, especially a covering for a bed. *n.*

cov·ey (kuv′ē), a small flock of partridges, quail, etc. *n., pl.* **cov·eys.**

cow·ard (kou′ərd), person who lacks courage or is easily made afraid; person who runs from danger, trouble, etc. *n.*

crash (krash) a sudden, loud noise like many dishes falling and breaking: *The lightning was followed by a crash of thunder. n., pl.* **crash·es.**

cra·zy (krā′zē), unwise or senseless; foolish: *It was a crazy idea to jump out of such a high tree. adj.,* **cra·zi·er, cra·zi·est.**

cred·it (kred′it), a trust in a person's ability and intention to pay: *This store will extend credit to you by opening a charge account in your name. n.*

cried (krīd), See **cry.** *The baby cried until its mother picked it up. v.*

croc·o·dile (krok′ə dīl), a large, lizardlike reptile with thick skin, similar to the alligator, but having a long narrow head and webbed feet. Crocodiles live in the rivers and marshes of the warm parts of Africa, Asia, Australia, and America. *n.*

cross·walk (kros′wok′), area marked with lines, used by pedestrians in crossing a street. *n., pl.* **cross·walks.**

crowd (kroud) a large number of people together: *A crowd gathered at the scene of the fire. n.*

cruise (krüz), **1** sail about from place to place on pleasure or business; sail over or about: *Freighters and tankers cruise the oceans of the world.* **2** a voyage from place to place for pleasure: *We went for a cruise on the Great Lakes last summer.* 1 *v.,* **cruised, cruis·ing;** 2 *n.*

crumb (krum), a very small piece of bread, cake, etc., broken from a larger piece: *I fed crumbs to the birds. n.*

crum·ble (krum′bəl), fall to pieces; decay: *The old wall was crumbling away at the edges. v.,* **crum·bled, crum·bling.**

crutch (kruch), a support to help a lame or injured person walk. It is a stick with a padded crosspiece at the top that fits under a person's arm and supports part of the weight in walking. *n., pl.* **crutch·es.**

cry (krī), call loudly; shout: *"Wait!" she cried from behind me. v.,* **cried, cry·ing.**

cuck·oo clock (kü′kü klok′), clock with a little toy bird that makes a sound like that of the European cuckoo to mark intervals of time.

cue card (kyü′ kärd′), words written out as to what to do or when to act: *He held up the cue cards to the actor so he could continue the play. n., pl.* **cue cards.**

cur·few (kėr′fyü), rule requiring certain persons to be off the streets or at home before a fixed time: *There is a 10 p.m. curfew for children in our city. n.*

courtroom

hearing a case in the

courtroom

crocodile

A **crocodile** is a large reptile.

cur·rent (kėr′ənt), **1** flow of electricity through a wire, etc.: *The current went off when lightning hit the power lines.* **2** of the present time: *We discuss current events in social studies class.* 1 n., 2 adj.

cur·tain (kėrt′n), drapery that separates a stage from where an audience sits. n., pl. **cur·tains.**

cush·ion (kush′ən), a soft pillow or pad used to sit, lie, or kneel on: *I rested my head on a cushion.* n.

cuspid (kus′pid), the kind of tooth with a sharp point used to tear food. Adults have four cuspids. n.

cute (kyüt), pretty and dear: *a cute baby.* adj., **cut·er, cut·est.**

D

dad (dad), INFORMAL. father: *Dad's new car is green.* n.

dahl·ia (dal′yə), a tall plant with large, showy flowers of many colors and varieties that bloom in autumn. It is related to the aster. n., pl. **dahl·ias.** [The *dahlia* was named for Anders *Dahl*, 1751-1789, a Swedish botanist.]

dai·ly (dā′lē), done, happening, or appearing every day, or every day but Sunday, day by day: *a daily newspaper, a daily visit.* adj.

dair·y (dâr′ē), room or building where milk and cream are kept and made into butter and cheese. n., pl. **dair·ies.**

dance (dans), move in rhythm, usually in time with music: *She can dance very well.* v., **danced, danc·ing.**

dan·ger (dān′jer), chance of harm; nearness to harm; risk; peril: *The trip through the jungle was full of danger.* n.

dark (därk), **1** absence of light; darkness: *Don't be afraid of the dark.* **2** night; nightfall: *The dark comes on early in the winter.* n. —**dark′ness,** n.

dead·line (ded′līn′), the latest possible time to do something: *The teacher made Friday afternoon the deadline for handing in all book reports.* n.

deal (dēl), distribute playing cards: *It's your turn to deal.* v., **dealt, deal·ing.**

dealt (delt), See **deal.** *The cards have been dealt.* v.

de·bris (də brē′), scattered fragments; ruins; rubbish: *The street was covered with debris from the explosion.* n.

Dec., December.

De·cem·ber (di sem′bər), the 12th and last month of the year. It has 31 days. n.

de·cide (di sīd′), make up one's mind; resolve: *She decided to be a scientist.* v., **de·cid·ed, de·cid·ing.**

de·ci·sion (di sizh′ən), **1** a making up of one's mind; deciding: *I have not yet come to a decision about buying the property.* **2** judgment reached or given: *The jury brought in a decision of not guilty.* n.

de·com·pos·er (dē′kəm pō′zər), any living thing that puts materials from dead plants and animals back into soil, air, and water. n.

deed (dēd), thing done; act; action: *a good deed. Deeds, not words, are needed.* n.

deep (dēp), **1** going a long way down from the top or surface: *the deepest well. The pond is deeper in the middle.* **2** in depth: *a tank 8 feet deep.* adj., **deep·er, deep·est.**

dance
dancing in a ballet

a	hat	ī	ice	u̇	put	ə *stands for*	
ā	age	o	not	ü	rule	a	in about
ä	far, calm	ō	open	ch	child	e	in taken
âr	care	ȯ	saw	ng	long	i	in pencil
e	let	ô	order	sh	she	o	in lemon
ē	equal	oi	oil	th	thin	u	in circus
ėr	term	ou	out	∓H	then		
i	it	u	cup	zh	measure		

desert¹

exploring the dry

desert

de·gree (di grē′), **1** unit for measuring temperature: *The freezing point of water is 32 degrees (32°) Fahrenheit, or 0 degrees (0°) Celsius.* **2** unit for measuring an angle or an arc of a circle. A degree is 1/90 of a right angle or 1/360 of the circumference of a circle. 45 degrees (45°) is half a right angle. *n., pl.* **de·grees.**

de·lay (di lā′), **1** put off till a later time: *We will delay the party for a week and hold it next Saturday.* **2** a putting off till a later time: *The delay upset our plans.* **3** be late; go slowly; stop along the way: *Do not delay on this errand.* *1,3 v., 2 n., pl.* **de·lays.**

de·liv·er·y (di liv′ər ē), a carrying and giving out of letters, goods, etc.: *There is one delivery of mail a day in our city.* *n., pl.* **de·liv·er·ies.**

dem·o·crat·ic (dem′ə krat′ik), of a democracy; like a government run by the people who live under it. *adj.*

dem·on·stra·tion (dem′ən strā′shən), a showing or explaining something by carrying out experiments or by using samples: *A compass was used in a demonstration of the earth's magnetism.* *n., pl.* **dem·on·stra·tions.**

den·im (den′əm), a heavy, coarse cotton cloth with a diagonal weave, used for overalls, sports clothes, etc. *n.* [*Denim* comes from French *serge de Nimes,* meaning "serge from Nimes," a town in France where the fabric was made.]

der·mis (dėr′mis), the sensitive layer of skin beneath the outer skin; derma. *n.*

de·scrip·tion (di skrip′shən) a telling in words how a person, place, thing, or an event looks or behaves; describing: *The reporter's description of the hotel fire made me feel as if I were right at the scene.* *n.*

des·ert¹ (dez′ərt), a dry, barren region that is usually sandy and without trees. The Sahara Desert is a great desert in northern Africa. *n.*

de·sert² (di zert′), go away and leave a person or a place, especially one that should not be left; forsake: *She deserted her old friends when she became famous.* *v.*

de·sign (di zīn′), **1** arrangement of details, form, and color in painting, weaving, building, etc.: *a wallpaper design in tan and brown.* **2** make a first sketch of; arrange form and color of; draw in outline: *design a dress.* *1 n., 2 v.*

de·tail (di tāl′ or dē′tāl), a small or unimportant part: *Her report was complete: it didn't leave out a single detail.* *n., pl.* **de·tails.**

de·ter·mi·na·tion (di tėr′mə nā′shən), great firmness in carrying out a purpose; fixed purpose: *His determination was not weakened by the difficulties he met.* *n.*

de·ter·mine (di tėr′mən), make up one's mind very firmly; resolve: *He determined to become the best player on the team.* *v.*

dev·as·tate (dev′ə stāt), lay waste; destroy; ravage: *A long war devastated the country.* *v.,* **dev·as·tat·ed, dev·as·tat·ing.**

de·vel·op (di vel′əp), **1** come into being or activity; grow: *Plants develop from seeds.* **2** treat (a photographic film or plate) with chemicals to bring out the picture: *A photographer develops film and makes prints.* **3** make or become known: *The lawyer's investigation did not develop any new facts.* *v.*

di·a·ry (dī′ər ē), a book for writing down each day of what has happened to one, or what one has done or thought, during that day. *n., pl.* **di·a·ries.**

dic·tion·ar·y (dik′shə ner′ē), book that explains the words of a language or of some special subject. It is arranged alphabetically. You can use this dictionary to find out the meaning, spelling, or pronunciation of a word. *n., pl.* **dic·tion·ar·ies.**

did·n't (did′nt), did not: *I didn't hear you.*

diary

A **diary** is for writing personal thoughts.

dif·fer·ent (dif′ər ənt), **1** not alike; not like: *People have different names. A boat is different from an automobile.* **2** not like others or most others; unusual. *adj.*

di·rect (də rekt′ or dī rekt′), have authority or control over; manage or guide: *The teacher directs the work of the class. v.*

di·rec·tion (də rek′shən or dī rek′shən), a directing; managing or guiding: *the direction of a play or movie. The school is under the direction of the principal. n.*

dirt·y (dėr′tē), soiled by dirt; not clean: *Children playing in the mud get dirty. adj.*

dis·a·gree (dis′ə grē′), have unlike opinions; differ: *Doctors sometimes disagree about the proper method of treating a patient. Your account of the accident disagrees with hers. v.*, **dis·a·greed, dis·a·gree·ing.**

dis·ap·pear (dis′ə pir′), pass from sight; from existence; stop being seen: *The dog disappeared around the corner. When spring comes, the snow disappears. v.*

dis·ap·point·ment (dis′ə point′mənt), a being disappointed; the feeling you have when you do not get what you expected or hoped for: *When she did not get a new bicycle, her disappointment was very great. n.*

dis·cov·er (dis kuv′ər), see or learn of for the first time; find out: *discover a new drug, discover a secret. v.*

dis·hon·est (dis on′ist), ready to cheat; not upright: *A person who lies or steals is dishonest. adj.*

dis·like (dis līk′), not like; object to; have a feeling against: *He dislikes studying and would rather play football. v.*, **dis·liked, dis·lik·ing.**

dis·o·be·di·ence (dis′ə bē′dē əns), refusal to obey; failure to obey: *The child was punished for disobedience. n.*

dis·play (dis plā′), a showing of information in visual form, as on the screen of a computer or calculator. *n.*

dis·tance (dis′təns), space in between: *The distance from the farm to the town is five miles. n.*

dis·trust (dis trust′), have no confidence in; not trust; be suspicious of; doubt: *Many people distrust statements made in advertisements. v.*

dive (dīv), **1** plunge headfirst into water. **2** act of diving: *The crowd applauded the girl's graceful dive.* **1** *v.*, **dived** or **dove** (dōv), **dived, div·ing;** **2** *n.*

di·vide (də vid′), to find how a total amount can be separated into an equal number of groups, or into groups of equal size. *v.*, **di·vid·ed, di·vid·ing.**

div·i·dend (div′ə dend), number or quantity to be divided by another: *In 728 ÷ 16, 728 is the dividend. n.*

di·vis·i·ble (də viz′ə bəl), able to be divided without leaving a remainder: *12 is divisible by 1, 2, 3, 4, 6, and 12. adj.*

di·vi·sion (də vizh′ən), operation of dividing one number by another: *26 ÷ 2 = 13 is a simple division. n.*

di·vi·sor (də vī′zər), number or quantity by which another is to be divided: *In 728 ÷ 16, 16 is the divisor. n.*

doc·tor (dok′tər), person trained in treating diseases or injuries. *Physicians, surgeons, dentists, and veterinarians are doctors. n.*

does·n't (duz′nt), does not.

dive (definition 1)

a	hat	**ī**	ice	**u̇**	put	**ə** stands for	
ā	age	**o**	not	**ü**	rule	**a**	in about
ä	far, calm	**ō**	open	**ch**	child	**e**	in taken
âr	care	**ȯ**	saw	**ng**	long	**i**	in pencil
e	let	**ô**	order	**sh**	she	**o**	in lemon
ē	equal	**oi**	oil	**th**	thin	**u**	in circus
ėr	term	**ou**	out	**ᵀH**	then		
i	it	**u**	cup	**zh**	measure		

dog pad·dle (dȯg′ pad′l), a downward swimming stroke in which the arms and legs stay under the water and each limb paddles by turns, first one and then the other: *The child did the dog paddle in the pool.*

dol·phin (dol′fən), a sea mammal related to the whale, but smaller. It has a beaklike snout and remarkable intelligence. *n.*

don·key (dong′kē), a small animal somewhat like a horse but with longer ears and a shorter mane. *n., pl.* **don·keys.**

door·bell (dôr′bel′), bell that a caller may ring by pressing a button or pulling a handle on the outside of a door to a house. *n.*

down·stairs (doun′stârz′), on or to a lower floor: *Look downstairs for my glasses (adv.) The downstairs rooms are dark (adj.).*

Dr., Doctor.

drib·ble (drib′əl), **1** move (a ball) along by bouncing it or giving it short kicks: *dribble a basketball, dribble a soccer ball.* **2** act of dribbling a ball. 1 *v.,* **drib·bled, drib·bling;** 2 *n.*

dried (drīd), See **dry.** *I dried my hands. The dishes have already been dried. v.*

drive (drīv), **1** go or carry in an automobile or carriage: *We want to drive through the mountains on the way home. She drove us to the station.* **2** (in sports) hit very hard and fast: *drive a golf ball.* **3** make by drilling, boring: *drive a well. v.,* **drove, driv·en** (driv′ən), **driv·ing.**

drive·way (drīv′wā′), a privately owned road to drive on, usually leading from a house or garage to the road. *n.*

drove (drōv), See **drive.** *We drove two hundred miles today. v.*

drown (droun), die under water or other liquid because of lack of air to breathe: *We almost drowned when our sailboat suddenly overturned. v.,* **drowned, drown·ing.**

dolphin

a **dolphin** enjoying

the water

dry (drī), make or become dry: *We washed and dried the dishes after dinner. Clothes dry in the sun. v.,* **dried, dry·ing.**

dry cleaner (drī′ klē′nər), person or business that does dry cleaning. *n.*

dry dock (drī′ dok′), dock built watertight so that the water may be pumped out or kept high. Dry docks are used for building or repairing ships. *n.*

dry run (drī′ run′), a practice test or session. *n.*

dud (dud), shell or bomb that fails to explode. *n.*

dune (dün or dyün), mound or ridge of loose sand heaped up by the wind. *n.*

dur·ing (dur′ing or dyur′ing), through the whole time of; throughout: *The children played inside during the storm. prep.*

E

ear (ir), part of the body by which people and animals hear. It consists of the external ear, the middle ear, and the inner ear. *n.*
be all ears, INFORMAL. listen eagerly; pay careful attention: *The children were all ears while their teacher read them the exciting story.*
play by ear, play (a piece of music or a musical instrument) without using written music: *She can't read notes but she can play any tune on the piano by ear.*

ear ca·nal (ir′ kə nal′), tunnel sound travels through to the eardrum. *n.*

ear·drum (ir′drum′), a thin membrane across the middle ear that vibrates when sound waves strike it. *n.*

ear·ring (ir′ring′), ornament for the ear. *n., pl.* **ear·rings.**

earth·quake (ėrth′kwāk′), a shaking or sliding of a portion of the earth's crust. It is caused by the sudden movement of masses of rock far beneath the earth's surface. Earthquakes are often related to volcanic activity. *n.*

e·del·weiss (ā′dl vīs), a small plant that grows in high places, such as the mountains in Austria and Switzerland. It has heads of very small, white flowers in the center of star-shaped leaf clusters. *n., pl.* **e·del·weiss** or **e·del·weiss·es.**

edge (ej), **1** line or place where something ends or begins; side: *This page has four edges. We walked to the edge of the water.* **2** rim; brink: *The stag stood on the edge of the cliff. n.*

ed·i·tor (ed′ə tər), person who edits: *She is the editor of our school paper. n., pl.* **ed·i·tors.**

e·lect (i lekt′), choose or select for an office by voting: *We elect our class officers every autumn. v.,* **elect·ed, elect·ing.**

e·lec·tion (i lek′shən), a choosing or selecting for an office by vote: *In our city we have an election for mayor every four years. n.*

e·lec·tric·i·ty (i lek′tris′ə tē), form of energy which can produce light, heat, motion, and magnetic force. Electricity makes light bulbs shine, televisions play, and cars start. *n.*

el·e·phant (el′ə fənt), a huge, heavy mammal, the largest living land animal, with ivory tusks and a long, muscular snout called a trunk. *n.*

e·lev·en (i lev′ən), **1** one more than ten; 11. **2** a football or cricket team. *1,2 n., 1 adj.*

e·mer·gen·cy (i mėr′jən sē), **1** a sudden need for immediate action: *I keep a box of tools in my car for use in an emergency.* **2** for a time of sudden need: *The surgeon did an emergency operation. 1 n., pl.* **e·mer·gen·cies;** *2 adj.*

e·nam·el (i nam′əl), the smooth, hard, glossy outer layer of the teeth. *n.*

end·point (end′point′), the point at the end of a line segment or ray. *n., pl.* **end·points.**

en·e·my (en′ə mē), a force, nation, army, fleet, or air force that opposes another; person, ship, etc., of a hostile nation. *n., pl.* **en·e·mies.**

en·er·gy (en′ər jē), capacity for doing work, such as lifting or moving an object. Light, heat, and electricity are different forms of energy: *A steam engine changes heat into mechanical energy. n., pl.* **en·er·gies.**

en·er·vate (en′ər vāt), lessen the vigor or strength of; weaken: *A hot, damp climate enervates people who are not used to it. v.,* **en·er·vat·ed, en·er·vat·ing.**

en·gine (en′jən), machine that changes energy from fuel, steam, water pressure, etc., into motion and power. An engine is used to apply power to some work, such as a car engine. *n.*

Eng·lish (ing′glish), the language of England. English is also spoken in the United States, Canada, Australia, New Zealand, the Republic of South Africa, and many other countries. *n. sing.*

e·nough (i nuf′), quantity or number needed or wanted; sufficient amount: *I had enough to eat. n.*

ep·i·der·mis (ep′ə dėr′mis), the outer layer of the skin. *n.*

ep·i·gram (ep′ə gram), a short, pointed or witty saying. EXAMPLE: "Speech is silver, but silence is golden." *n.*

e·qual (ē′kwəl), **1** the same in amount, size, number, value, or rank: *Ten dimes are equal to one dollar. All persons are considered equal before the law.* **2** the same throughout; even; uniform: *equal pieces. adj.*

edelweiss
The **edelweiss** is the national flower of Austria.

elephant
The **elephant** is the largest four-footed animal.

a	hat	ī	ice	u̇	put	ə *stands for*	
ā	age	o	not	ü	rule	a	in about
ä	far, calm	ō	open	ch	child	e	in taken
âr	care	ȯ	saw	ng	long	i	in pencil
e	let	ô	order	sh	she	o	in lemon
ē	equal	oi	oil	th	thin	u	in circus
ėr	term	ou	out	₮H	then		
i	it	u	cup	zh	measure		

evergreen

the majestic **evergreen**

experiment

working on an

experiment with light

e·qual·ly (ē′kwə lē), in equal shares; in an equal manner: *Divide the pie equally. My sister and brother are equally talented. adv.*

e·quals key (ē′kwəlz kē′), key that supplies a result of a calculator's next calculation.

e·qua·tion (i kwā′zhən), statement of the equality of two quantities. EXAMPLES: $(4 \times 8) + 12 = 44$. $C = 2\pi r$. *n.*

e·qua·tor (i kwā′tər), an imaginary circle around the middle of the earth, halfway between the North Pole and the South Pole. The United States is north of the equator; Australia is south of it. *n.*

Er·ie (ir′ē), **Lake,** one of the five Great Lakes; it borders Ohio, Pennsylvania, New York, and Canada. *n.*

er·ror (er′ər), a message that appears on a calculator when more digits are generated than can be displayed. *n.*

e·rup·tion (i rup′shən) a bursting or throwing forth: *There was an eruption of glowing melted rock from the mountain top. n.*

es·cape (e skāp′), get out and away; get free: *The bird escaped from its cage. v.,* **es·caped, es·cap·ing.**

es·pe·cial·ly (e spesh′ə lē), more than others; specially; particularly; principally; chiefly. *adv.*

etc., et cetera. *Etc.* is usually read "and so forth." *Etc.* shows that the definition applies to many similar items in addition to the ones mentioned.

eve (ēv), the evening or day before a holiday or some other special day: *New Year's Eve, Christmas Eve, the eve of my birthday. n.*

eve·ning (ēv′ning), the last part of day and early part of night; time between sunset and bedtime. *n.*

ev·er·green (ev′ər grēn′), a plant that has green leaves or needles all year round. *n., pl.* **ev·er·greens.**

eve·ry·bod·y (ev′rē bud′ē or ev′rē bod′ē), every person; everyone: *Everybody likes the principal. pron.*

eve·ry·one (ev′rē wun or ev′rē wən), each one; everybody: *Everyone in the class is here. pron.*

ex·act·ly (eg zakt′lē), accurately; precisely; just so; quite right. *adv.*

ex·cel·lent (ek′sə lənt), of unusually good quality; better than others; superior: *Excellent work deserves high praise. adj.*

ex·cept (ek sept′) leaving out; other than: *He works every day except Sunday. prep.*

ex·cess (ek ses′ or ek′ses), part that is too much; more than enough: *The tailor trimmed off the excess from the cloth being measured for the two sleeves. n.*

ex·cite (ek sīt′), **1** stir up the feelings of: *News of the wedding excited the entire family.* **2** arouse: *Plans for a field trip excited the students' interest. v.,* **ex·cit·ed, ex·cit·ing.**

ex·cuse (ek skyūs′), reason, real or pretended, that is given; explanation: *Sickness was his excuse for being absent from school. n.*

ex·hib·it (eg zib′it), an exhibiting; public showing: *The village art exhibit drew 10,000 visitors. n.*

ex·pect (ek spekt′), think something will probably come or happen; look forward to: *I expect to take a vacation in May. v.*

ex·per·i·ment (ek sper′ə mənt), trial or test to find out something: *a chemistry experiment. Scientists test out theories by experiments. n.*

ex·pert (ek′spėrt′), a very skillful person; person who knows a great deal about some special thing: *She is an expert at fishing. n.*

ex·plain (ek splān′), make plain or clear; tell the meaning of: *The teacher explained long division to the class. Will you explain this poem to me? v.*

ex·plo·sion (ek splō′zhən), a bursting with a loud noise; a blowing up: *The explosion shook the whole neighborhood. n.*

ex·tra (ek′strə), beyond what is usual, expected, or needed; additional: *extra fare, extra pay, extra favors.* *adj.* [*Extra* was probably shortened from *extraordinary.*]

ex·traor·di·nar·y (ek strôr′də ner′ē), beyond what is ordinary; very unusual; very remarkable: *Eight feet is an extraordinary height for a person. adj.*

eye (ī), the organ of the body by which people and animals see. *n.*
an eye for an eye, punishment as severe as the injury.
catch one's eye, attract one's attention: *The bright red sign caught my eye.*
see eye to eye, agree entirely: *My parents and I do not see eye to eye on my weekly allowance.*

eye·lash (ī′lash′), 1 one of the hairs on the edge of the eyelid. 2 fringe of such hairs. *n., pl.* **eye·lash·es.**

F

Fahr·en·heit (far′ən hīt), a scale for measuring temperature on which 32 degrees marks the freezing point of water and 212 degrees marks the boiling point. *adj.* [The *Fahrenheit* scale was named for Gabriel D. *Fahrenheit,* 1686-1736, the German physicist who introduced it.]

fair·ness (fâr′nis), a being fair: *Our teacher is known for fairness in grading pupils. n.*

fam·i·ly (fam′ə lē), 1 a father, mother, and their children: *Our town has about a thousand families.* 2 all of a person's relatives: *His family's reunion is an annual event. n., pl.* **fam·i·lies.**

family of facts, (fakts), related number sentences for addition and subtraction (or multiplication and division) that contain all the same numbers.

fat (fat), 1 having much flesh; fleshy; plump; well-fed: *a fat baby, a fat pig.* 2 large or larger than usual: *a fat contract, a fat salary. adj.,* **fat·ter, fat·test.**

fa·ther (fä′ᴛʜər), a male parent. *n.*

fault (fȯlt), a break in the earth's crust, with the mass of rock on one side of the break pushed up, down, or sideways. *n., pl.* **faults.**

fa·vor·ite (fā′vər it), liked better than others. *adj.*

fear·less (fir′lis), without fear; afraid of nothing; brave; daring. *adj.*

Feb., February.

Feb·ru·ar·y (feb′rü er′ē or feb′yü er′ē), the second month of the year. It has 28 days except in leap years, when it has 29. *n.*

fed·er·al (fed′ər əl), formed by an agreement between states establishing a central government to handle their business while the states keep separate their own affairs: *Switzerland and the United States both became nations by federal union. adj.*

feel·ing (fē′ling), 1 emotion. Joy, sorrow, fear, and anger are feelings. *The loss of the ball game stirred up much feeling.* 2 feelings, *pl.* tender or sensitive side of one's nature: *You hurt my feelings when you yelled at me. n., pl.* **feel·ings.**

fence (fens), railing, wall, put around a yard, garden, field, farm, etc., to show where it ends or to keep people or animals out or in. Most fences are made of wood, wire, or metal. *n.*

Fahrenheit
The **Fahrenheit** scale is used on these thermometers.

a	hat	**ī**	ice	**u̇**	put	**ə** stands for	
ā	age	**o**	not	**ü**	rule	**a**	in about
ä	far, calm	**ō**	open	**ch**	child	**e**	in taken
âr	care	**ȯ**	saw	**ng**	long	**i**	in pencil
e	let	**ô**	order	**sh**	she	**o**	in lemon
ē	equal	**oi**	oil	**th**	thin	**u**	in circus
ėr	term	**ou**	out	**ᴛʜ**	then		
i	it	**u**	cup	**zh**	measure		

fern
two Boston **ferns**

fern (fèrn), kind of plant that has roots, stems, and feathery leaves, but does not have flowers or seeds. The plant reproduces by means of spores which grow in little brown clusters on the backs of the leaves. *n., pl.* **ferns.**

fer·ti·lize (fèr′tl īz), unite with (an egg cell) in fertilization; impregnate. *v.,* **fer·ti·lized, fer·ti·liz·ing.**

few (fyü), not many: *Few people attended the meeting. adj.*

field (fēld), piece of land used for crops or for pasture. *n.*

field goal (fēld′ gōl′), (in basketball) a basket scored while the ball is in play, counting two points.

fil·i·gree (fil′ə grē), very delicate, lacelike, ornamental work of gold or silver wire. *n.*

film (film), roll or sheet of thin, flexible material covered with a coating that is sensitive to light, used in taking photographs. *n.*

fi·nal·ly (fī′nl ē), at the end; at last. *adv.*

fin·ger (fing′gər), one of the five slender divisions that end the hand, especially the four besides the thumb. *n.*
put one's finger on, point out exactly: *The inspector was able to put his finger on the weak point in the suspect's alibi.*

fire·proof (fīr′prüf′), very resistant to fire; almost impossible to burn: *A building made entirely of steel and concrete is fireproof. adj.*

first (fèrst), **1** coming before all others: *She is first in her class.* **2** person, thing, place, etc., that is first: *We were the first to get here.* **1** *adj.,* **2** *n.*

first aid (fèrst′ ād′), emergency treatment given to an injured or sick person before a doctor sees the person.

flash·light (flash′līt′), a portable electric light, operated by batteries. *n.*

flaw (flȯ), defective area: *There is a flaw in this shirt. n.*

football (definition 2)

flawed (flȯd), having a defect: *a flawed diamond. adj.*

float (flōt), stay on top of or be held up by air, water, or other liquid. *A cork will float, but a stone sinks. v.*

Flo·ri·da (flôr′ə də), one of the southeastern states of the United States. *Abbreviation:* Fla. or FL *Capital:* Tallahassee. *n.*

flow·er (flou′ər), part of a plant that produces the seed; blossom. It has modified leaves called petals. Flowers are often beautifully colored or shaped. *n., pl.* **flow·ers.**

fly (flī), any of a large group of insects that have two wings and make a buzzing sound, especially the housefly. *n., pl.* **flies.**

fo·cus (fō′kəs), bring (rays of light, heat, etc.) to a focus: *The lens focused the sun's rays on a piece of paper. v.* **fo·cused, fo·cus·ing,** or **fo·cussed, fo·cus·sing.**

food chain (füd′ chān′), several kinds of living things that are linked because each uses another as food. Cats, birds, caterpillars, and plants eat the one named next.

food web (füd′ web′), the flow of energy and materials through connected food chains. *n.*

foot (füt), the end part of a leg; part that a person, animal, or thing stands on. *n., pl.* **feet** (fēt).
put one's best foot forward, INFORMAL. do one's best.

foot·ball (füt′bȯl′), **1** game played with an inflated leather ball by two teams of eleven players each, on a field with a goal at each end. A player scores by carrying the ball over the goal line by a run or pass, or by kicking it through the goal posts. **2** ball used in this game. *n.*

fore·cast (fôr′kast′), what is coming; prophecy; prediction: *What is the forecast for the weather today? n.* **—fore′cast′er,** *n.*

fo·rest (fôr′ist), a large piece of land covered with trees; thick woods. *n.*

for·get (fər get′), fail to think of; fail to do, take, notice, etc.: *I forgot to call the dentist. v.,* **for·got, for·got·ten** (fər got′n) or **for·got, for·get·ting.**

for·got (fər got′), See **forget**. *She was so busy that she forgot to eat her lunch.* *v.*

form (fôrm), **1** be formed; take shape: *Clouds form in the sky.* **2** piece of printed paper with blank spaces to be filled in: *We filled out a form to get a license for our dog.* 1 *v.*, 2 *n.*

foul (foul), **1** (in football, basketball, etc.) an unfair play; thing done against the rules. **2** make an unfair play against. 1 *n.*, 2 *v.*

four·teen (fôr′tēn′), four more than ten; 14. *n.*, *adj.*

fourth (fôrth), next after the third; last in a series of 4. *adj.*, *n.*

Fourth of July, Independence Day.

fran·tic (fran′tik), very much excited; wild with rage, fear, pain, or grief. *adj.*

freck·le (frek′əl), a small, light-brown spot on the skin, often caused by exposure to the sun. *n.*, *pl.* **freck·les.**

free·style (frē′stīl′), a freestyle race or figure-skating contest. *n.*

free throw (frē′ thrō′), (in basketball) an unblocked shot from a line **(free-throw line)** about 15 feet (4.5 meters) away from the basket, awarded to a player fouled by a member of the opposing team, and worth one point.

friend (frend), **1** person who knows and likes another. *My friend's companionship is priceless.* **2** person who favors and supports: *She was a generous friend to the poor.* *n.*

front (frunt), the line where two air masses meet. *n.*

fruit (früt), a juicy or fleshy product of a tree, bush, shrub, or vine which consists of the seed and its covering and is usually sweet and good to eat. Apples and pears are fruits. *n.*

fuch·sia (fyü′shə), shrub with handsome pink, red, or purple flowers that droop from the stems. *n.*, *pl.* **fuch·sias.** [The *fuchsia* was named for Leonhard *Fuchs*, 1501-1566, a German botanist.]

fudge (fuj), a soft candy made of sugar, milk, chocolate, butter, etc. *n.*

fu·el (fyü′əl), **1** anything that can be burned to produce useful heat or power. Coal, wood, and oil are fuels. **2** supply with fuel. **3** get fuel: *The ship will have to fuel at the nearest port.* 1 *n.*, *pl.* **fu·els,** 2,3 *v.*

fun·ny (fun′ē), **1** causing laughter; amusing: *The clown's funny jokes and antics kept us laughing.* **2** INFORMAL. strange; queer; odd. *adj.*, **fun·ni·er, fun·ni·est.**

fur (fėr), **1** the soft hair covering the skin of many animals. **2** skin with such hair on it. Fur is used to make, cover, trim, or line clothing. *n.*

fur·ni·ture (fėr′nə chər), movable articles needed in a room or house. Beds, chairs, tables, and desks are furniture. *n.*

fruit
Fresh **fruit** is good for your health.

G

gag (gag), **1** something put in a person's mouth to prevent talking or crying out. **2** INFORMAL. joke; amusing remark or trick. *n.*

gal·lant (gal′ənt), noble in spirit or in conduct; brave: *King Arthur was a gallant knight.* *adj.*

gal·lon (gal′ən), measure for liquids equal to 4 quarts. *n.*

gang (gang), group of people acting or going around together: *A whole gang of us went swimming.* *n.*

gallon
a **gallon** of milk

a	hat	ī	ice	u̇	put	ə stands for	
ā	age	o	not	ü	rule	a	in about
ä	far, calm	ō	open	ch	child	e	in taken
âr	care	ȯ	saw	ng	long	i	in pencil
e	let	ô	order	sh	she	o	in lemon
ē	equal	oi	oil	th	thin	u	in circus
ėr	term	ou	out	ᴛʜ	then		
i	it	u	cup	zh	measure		

gas·o·line (gas′ə lēn′ *or* gas′ə lēn′), a colorless, liquid mixture of hydrocarbons that evaporates and burns very easily. It is made from petroleum or from gas formed in the earth and is used as a fuel to run automobiles, airplanes, etc. *n.*

gen·tle (jen′tl), not severe, rough, or violent; mild and soft: *a gentle tap. a gentle sound. adj.*, **gen·tler, gen·tlest.**

ghost (gōst), spirit of a dead person, supposed to appear to living people as a pale, dim, shadowy form: *A ghost was said to haunt the house. n.*

gi·ant (jī′ənt), like a giant; huge: *a giant potato. adj.*

gi·gan·tic (jī gan′tik), very large; huge: *a gigantic elephant. adj.*

gi·raffe (jə raf′), a large African mammal that chews its cud and has hoofs, a very long neck, long legs, and a spotted skin. Giraffes are the tallest living animals. *n.*

girl (gėrl), **1** a female child from birth to about eighteen: *The girl's face was young and pretty.* **2** a young, unmarried woman. *n.*

girl·friend (gėrl′frend′), INFORMAL. **1** boy's sweetheart or steady female companion. **2** a female friend. *n.*

glass (glas), **1** container to drink from made of glass: *I filled the glass with water.* **2 glasses,** *pl.* eyeglasses. *n., pl.* **glass·es.**

go (gō), move along. *v.* **went, gone** (gon), **going.**

good·ness (gùd′nis), a being good; kindness. *n.*

grand·ma (grand′mä′ *or* gram′ə), INFORMAL. grandmother: *My grandma's cookies are delicious. n.*

grand·pa (grand′pä′ *or* gram′pə), INFORMAL. grandfather: *My grandpa's stories are very funny. n.*

grand·par·ent (grand′pâr′ent *or* grand′par′ent), grandfather or grandmother: *Both sets of grandparents' letters arrived today. n.*

grass·hop·per (gras′hop′ər), a winged insect with strong hind legs for jumping. Locusts and katydids are grasshoppers. *n.*

grate·ful (grāt′fəl), feeling kindly because of a favor received; wanting to do a favor in return: *I am grateful for your help. adj.*

great·ness (grāt′nis), great mind or character. *n.*

group (grüp), number of persons or things together: *A group of children were playing tag. n.*

group·ing (grü′ping), putting a known number of objects into each group and making as many groups as you can. *v.*

guess (ges), form an opinion of something without really knowing. *v.*, **guessed, guess·ing.**

guest (gest), person who is received and entertained at another's home or staying at a hotel or motel. *n.*

H

ham·burg·er (ham′bėr′gər), ground beef, usually shaped into round, flat cakes and then fried or broiled and placed in a roll or bun. *n.* [*Hamburger* comes from a German word meaning "of Hamburg."]

ham·mer (ham′ər), hit again and again. *v.*

ham·ster (ham′stər), a small rodent with a short tail and large cheek pouches. Hamsters are used in scientific research and are often kept as pets. *n.*

hand (hand), the end part of the arm, below the wrist, which takes and holds objects. Each hand has four fingers and a thumb. *n.*
at first hand, from direct knowledge or experience.
by hand, by using the hands, not machinery: *embroidered by hand.*
lend a hand, help.
wash one's hands of, have no more to do with; refuse to be responsible for: *I washed my hands of that job when I discovered what I had done.*

giraffe
Giraffes are the tallest animals in the world.

grasshopper
a **grasshopper** and its surroundings

hand·sig·nal (hand′ sig′nəl), hand held to give a sign, notice, or warning, or to point out something: *The girl gave a hand signal when she turned. n.*

Ha·nuk·kah (hä′nə kə), a yearly Jewish festival celebrated in November or December. Candles are lighted on each of the eight days of Hanukkah. *n.* Also, **Chanukah.**

hap·pen (hap′ən), **1** come about; take place; occur: *What happened at the party yesterday?* **2** be or take place by chance: *Accidents will happen. v.,* **hap·pened, hap·pen·ing.**

hap·pen·ing (hap′ə ning), something that happens; event; occurrence: *The evening newscast reviewed the happenings of the day. n.*

hap·py (hap′ē), feeling as you do when you are well and are having a good time; glad; pleased; contented: *She is happy in her new work. adj.,* **hap·pi·er, hap·pi·est.**

head (hed), the top part of the human body containing the brain, eyes, nose, ears, and mouth. *n.* **lose one's head,** get excited; lose one's self-control.

head·line (hed′līn′), words printed in heavy type at the top of a newspaper article telling what it is about. *n.*

head·phone (hed′fōn′), earphone held against one or both ears by a band over the head. *n., pl.* **head·phones.**

heal (hēl), **1** make whole, sound, or well; bring back to health; cure. **2** become whole or sound; get well; return to health; be cured: *My cut healed in a few days. v.*

health (helth), condition of body or mind: *be in excellent health. n.*

hear (hir), **1** take in a sound or sounds through the ear: *We couldn't hear in the back row.* **2** receive news or information: *I heard from my parents. v.,* **heard** (hėrd), **hear·ing.**

heart (härt), **1** the part of the body that pumps the blood. **2** the part that feels, loves, hates, and desires: *a heavy heart, a kind heart.* **3** figure shaped like this: ♥ *n.*

heart·bro·ken (härt′brō′kən), crushed by sorrow or grief. *adj.*

he'd (hēd), **1** he had: *He'd had an accident.* **2** he would: *He'd come if he could.*

height (hīt), measurement from top to bottom; how tall a person is; how high a thing is; how far up a thing goes: *the height of a mountain. n.*

he'll (hēl), he will: *He'll tell us the story tomorrow afternoon.*

hel·met (hel′mit), covering made of steel, leather, plastic, or some other sturdy material, worn to protect the head. *n.*

help·less (help′lis), not able to help oneself: *A baby is helpless. adj.*

hem·i·sphere (hem′ə sfir), half of a sphere or globe, half of the earth's surface. The earth has four hemispheres: western, eastern, northern, and southern. *n., pl.* **hem·i·spheres.**

her·bi·vore (hėr′bə vôr), any animal that feeds mainly on plants. *n.*

her·self (hər self′), form of *she* or *her* used to make a statement stronger: *She did it herself. pron.*

hide (hīd), put or keep out of sight; conceal: *Hide it where no one else will find it. v.,* **hid** (hid), **hid·den** (hid′n) or **hid, hid·ing.**

high·way (hī′wā′), a main public road or route. *n.*

headphone
listening to music
through the
headphones

herbivore
A rabbit is a
herbivore.

a	hat	**ī**	ice	**u̇**	put	**ə** stands for
ā	age	**o**	not	**ü**	rule	**a** in about
ä	far, calm	**ō**	open	**ch**	child	**e** in taken
âr	care	**ȯ**	saw	**ng**	long	**i** in pencil
e	let	**ô**	order	**sh**	she	**o** in lemon
ē	equal	**oi**	oil	**th**	thin	**u** in circus
ėr	term	**ou**	out	**ᵺ**	then	
i	it	**u**	cup	**zh**	measure	

hippopotamus

hip·po·pot·a·mus (hip/ə pot/ə məs), a huge, thick-skinned, almost hairless mammal found in and near the rivers of Africa that eats plants and can stay under water for a long time. *n., pl.* **hip·po·pot·a·mus·es, hip·po·pot·a·mi** (hip/ə pot/ə mī).

hob·by (hob/ē), something a person especially likes to work at or study which is not the person's main business or occupation; favorite pastime. *n., pl.* **hob·bies.**

hock·ey (hok/ē), game played by two teams on ice or on a field. The players hit a puck or ball with curved sticks to drive it across a goal. *n.*

ho·gan (hō/gän/), dwelling used by the Navajos. Hogans are built with logs and covered with earth. *n., pl.* **ho·gans.** [*Hogan* was borrowed from a Navajo word.]

hol·i·day (hol/ə dā), **1** day when one does not work; day of pleasure and enjoyment: *Labor Day and the Fourth of July are holidays in the United States.* **2** Often, **holidays,** *pl.* vacation. *n.*

home (hōm), place where a person or family lives; one's own house; where a person was born or brought up. *Her home is at 25 South Street. n.*

hogan
A **hogan** is a type of house.

home·less (hōm/lis), without a home: *a stray, homeless dog. adj.* **—home/less·ness,** *n.*

hon·ey (hun/ē), a thick, sweet, yellow or golden liquid that bees make out of the nectar they collect from flowers. *n.*

hon·or (on/ər), great respect; high regard; *held in honor. n.*

hope·ful (hōp/fəl), feeling and giving or showing hope; expecting to receive what one desires: *a hopeful attitude. adj.* **—hope/ful·ly,** *adv.*

hope·less (hōp/lis), feeling or giving no hope: *He was disappointed so often that he became hopeless. adj.*

horn (hôrn), a hard, hollow, permanent growth, usually curved and pointed and in pairs, on the heads of cattle, sheep, goats, and certain other animals. *n.*
blow one's own horn or **toot one's own horn,** INFORMAL, praise oneself; boast.

hos·pi·tal (hos/pi təl), place for the care of the sick or injured. *n.*

hot (hot), having much heat; very warm: *Fire is hot. The sun is hot today. adj.,* **hot·ter, hot·test.**

ho·tel (hō tel/), house or large building that supplies rooms and food for pay to travelers and others. *n.*

house (hous), building in which people live. *n., pl.* **hous·es** (hou/ziz).

how·ev·er (hou ev/ər), in spite of that; nevertheless; yet: *We were very late for dinner; however, there was plenty left for us. adv.*

huge (hyüj), very big; extremely large or great: *A whale is a huge animal. adj.*

hu·mid·i·ty (hyü mid/ə tē), moisture in the air: *On a hot, sultry day, the humidity is high. The humidity today is worse than the heat. n.*

hu·mor (hyü/mər), funny or amusing quality: *I see no humor in your tricks. n.*

hu·mor·ous (hyü/mər əs), full of humor; funny: *We all laughed at the humorous story. adj.*

Hur·on (hyür/ən), **Lake,** one of the five Great Lakes; it borders Michigan and Canada. *n.*

hy·dro·e·lec·tric (hī/drō i lek/trik), developing electricity from water power. *adj.*

I

I'd (īd), **1** I would: *I'd enjoy a vacation right now.* **2** I had: *I'd just finished dinner when she called.*

ig·nore (ig nôr/), pay no attention to; disregard: *The driver ignored the traffic light and almost hit another car. v.,* **ig·nored, ig·nor·ing.**

i·gua·na (i gwä/nə), a large tropical American lizard having a spiny crest along its back. *n., pl.* **i·gua·nas.**

I'll (īl), I will: *I'll call you tomorrow.*

I'm (īm), I am: *I'm going to the concert tonight.*

i·mag·ine (i maj′ən), suppose; guess: *I cannot imagine what you mean.* v., **i·mag·ined, i·mag·in·ing.** —**i·mag·i·na·ble,** *adj.*

im·pos·si·ble (im pos′ə bəl), not capable of being, being done, or happening; not possible: *It is impossible for two and two to be six. adj.*

in·ac·tive (in ak′tiv), not active; idle; slow: *Bears are inactive during the winter. adj.*

in·ci·sor (in sī′zər), tooth having a sharp edge for cutting; one of the front teeth between the canine teeth in either jaw. Humans have eight incisors. *n.*

in·com·plete (in′kəm plēt′), not complete; lacking some part; unfinished. *adj.*

in·con·ven·ient (in′kən vē′nyənt), not convenient; causing trouble, difficulty, or bother; troublesome: *Shelves that are too high to reach easily are inconvenient. adj.*

in·cor·rect (in′kə rekt′), containing errors or mistakes; not correct; wrong: *Today's local newspaper gave an incorrect account of the accident. adj.*

in·cred·i·ble (in kred′ə bəl), hard to believe; seeming too extraordinary to be possible; unbelievable: *The racing car rounded the curve with incredible speed. adj.*

in·de·pend·ent (in′di pen′dənt), **1** not influenced by others; thinking or acting for oneself: *an independent voter, an independent thinker.* **2** person who is independent in thought or behavior. 1 *adj.* 2 *n.*

in·jur·y (in′jər ē), hurt or loss caused to or endured by a person or thing; harm; damage: *She escaped from the train wreck without injury. n., pl.* **in·jur·ies.**

inner ear (in′ər ir′), the fluid-filled part of the ear that sends messages to the brain.

in·stru·ment (in′strə mənt), **1** a mechanical device that is portable, and usually operated by hand; tool: *a dentist's instruments.* **2** device for producing musical sounds: *wind instruments. n.*

in·su·late (in′sə lāt), keep from losing or transferring electricity, heat, sound, etc., especially by covering, packing, or surrounding with a material that does not conduct electricity, heat, etc.: *Telephone wires are often insulated by a covering of rubber. v.,* **in·su·lat·ed, in·su·lat·ing.**

in·ten·si·ty (in ten′sə tē), extreme degree; great vigor; violence: *intensity of thought, intensity of feeling. n., pl.* **in·ten·si·ties.**

in·ter·est·ing (in′tər ə sting *or* in′tə res′ting), arousing interest; holding one's attention: *Stories about travel and adventure are interesting. adj.*

in·ter·sect·ing (in′tər sekt′ing), crossing each other at a point: *intersecting lines. adj.*

in·ter·view (in′tər vyü), a meeting between a reporter and a person from whom information is sought for publication or broadcast. *n.*

in·to (in′tü; *before consonants often* in′tə), to the inside of; toward and inside: *Come into the house. We drove into the city. I will look into the matter. prep.*

In·u·it (in′ü it *or* in′yü it), the people living mainly in the arctic regions of the world; the Eskimo people. *n.*

instrument
(definition 2)
types of brass
instruments

a	hat	**ī**	ice	**u̇**	put	**ə** *stands for*	
ā	age	**o**	not	**ü**	rule	**a**	in about
ä	far, calm	**ō**	open	**ch**	child	**e**	in taken
âr	care	**ȯ**	saw	**ng**	long	**i**	in pencil
e	let	**ô**	order	**sh**	she	**o**	in lemon
ē	equal	**oi**	oil	**th**	thin	**u**	in circus
ėr	term	**ou**	out	**ŦH**	then		
i	it	**u**	cup	**zh**	measure		

jai alai

playing the game of
jai alai

in·vade (in vād/), enter with force or as an enemy; attack: *Soldiers invaded the country to conquer it.* v., **in·vad·ed, in·vad·ing.**

in·va·sion (in vā/zhən), an invading; entering by force or as an enemy; attack. n.

in·ven·tion (in ven/shən), something new, thing invented: *Television is a modern invention.* n.

in·vis·i·ble (in viz/ə bəl), not visible; not capable of being seen: *Thought is invisible. Germs are invisible to the naked eye.* adj.

in·vite (in vīt/), ask (someone) politely to come to some place or to do something: *I invited some friends to a party. We invited them to join our club.* v., **in·vit·ed, in·vit·ing.**

i·ris (ī/ris), the colored part of the eye around the pupil. n., pl. **i·ris·es.**

i·ron (ī/ərn), **1** an implement with a flat surface that is heated and used to press clothing. **2** smooth or press (cloth, etc.) with a heated iron. 1 n., 2 v.

is·land (ī/lənd), body of land smaller than a continent and completely surrounded by water: *Cuba is a large island.* n.

is·sue (ish/ü), send out; put forth: *This magazine is issued every week.* v., **is·sued, is·su·ing.**

it'll (it/l), it will: *It'll be better soon.*

it's (its), **1** it is: *It's my turn.* **2** it has: *It's been a beautiful day.*

J

jai a·lai (hī/ lī/), game similar to handball, played on a walled court with a hard ball. The ball is caught and thrown with a kind of curved wicker basket fastened to the arm.

James (jāmz), a boy's name. *James's house is next door to mine.* n.

Jan·u·ar·y (jan/yü er/ē), the first month of the year. It has 31 days. n.

jewel

This **jewel** is a sapphire.

jay·walk (jā/wok/), walk across a street without paying attention to traffic rules. v. —**jay·walk·ing,** n.

jer·sey (jėr/zē), a close-fitting, pullover sweater made of a machine-woven cloth with a tight weave. n. [*Jersey* gets its name from the island of *Jersey,* where this cloth had been made for a long time.]

jew·el (jü/əl), a precious stone; gem. n., pl. **jew·els.**

juice (jüs), the liquid part of fruits, vegetables, and meats: *the juice of a lemon, meat juice.* n.

Ju·ly (jù lī/), the seventh month of the year. It has 31 days. n.

jum·bo (jum/bō), INFORMAL. a big person, animal, or thing; something unusually large of its kind: *a jumbo ice-cream cone.* adj. [*Jumbo* comes from the name of a large circus elephant.]

jump shot (jump/ shot/), (in basketball) shot made while jumping, especially at the highest point of the jump. n.

June (jün), the sixth month of the year. It has 30 days. n.

jur·y (jùr/ē), group of persons chosen to give a judgment in a court of law or to decide who is the winner in a contest: *The jury gave her poem the first prize.* n., pl. **jur·ies.**

K

Kan·sas (kan/zəs), one of the midwestern states of the United States. *Abbreviation:* Kans. or KS *Capital:* Topeka. n.

kay·ak (kī/ak), an Eskimo canoe made of skins stretched over a light frame of wood or bone with an opening in the middle for a person. n. Also, **kaiak.**

key se·quence (kē/ sē/kwəns), a connected series of keys on a calculator used in order to obtain a result.

kick (kik), strike out with the foot: *The boy kicked the soccer ball.* v.

kin·der·gar·ten (kin′dər gärt′n), school or class for children from about 4 to 6 years old that educates them by games, toys, and pleasant occupations. *n.* [*Kindergarten* is from German *Kindergarten*, which comes from *Kinder*, meaning "children," and *Garten*, meaning "garden."]

kitch·en (kich′ən), room or area where food is cooked. *n.* [*Kitchen* comes from Old English *cycene*, and can be traced back to Latin *coquere*, meaning "to cook."]

knee (nē), the joint between the thigh and the lower leg. *n.*

kneel (nēl), go down on one's knee or knees: *She knelt down to pull a weed. He kneels in prayer. v.,* **knelt** (nelt) or **kneeled, kneel·ing.**

knit (nit), make (cloth or an article of clothing) by looping yarn or thread together with long needles, or by machinery which forms loops instead of weaving: *knit a pair of socks. v.,* **knit·ted** or **knit, knit·ting.**

knob (nob), handle on a door, drawer, etc.: *the knob on the dial of a television set. n.*

knot (not), **1** a fastening made by tying or twining together pieces of one or more ropes, cords, strings, etc.: *a square knot, a slip knot.* **2** tie or twine together in a knot: *He knotted two ropes together.* **3** group; cluster: *A knot of students stood talking outside the classroom.* 1,3 *n.,* 2 *v.,* **knot·ted, knot·ting.**

know (nō), have knowledge, have facts: *I know from experience how to drive on icy roads. She knows the poem. v.,* **knew** (nü), **known, know·ing.**

known (nōn), See **know.** *George Washington is known as the father of his country. v.*

Kwan·zaa or **Kwan·za** (kwän′zə), a yearly African American celebration celebrating various African festivals. It lasts from December 26 to January 1. *n.* [*Kwanzaa* is from Swahili *Kwanza*, originally meaning "first (fruits)," which comes from *kuanza*, meaning "to begin."]

L

la·crosse (lə kròs′), game played on a field with a ball and long-handled, loosely strung rackets by two teams, usually of 10 players each. The players carry the ball in the rackets, trying to send it into the other team's goal. *n.*

la·dy (lā′dē), **1** woman of good family and high social position: *a lady by birth.* **2** a well-bred woman: *I borrowed the lady's umbrella.* **3** a polite term for any woman. "Ladies" is often used in speaking or writing to a group of women: *Ladies, please be seated.* **4** woman who has the rights and authority of a lord. *n., pl.* **la·dies.**

lamb (lam), a young sheep. *n.*

land·form (land′fôrm′), a physical feature of the earth's surface. Plains, plateaus, hills, and mountains are landforms. *n., pl.* **land·forms.**

large (lärj), of more than the usual size, amount, or number; big: *America is a large country. A hundred thousand dollars is a large sum of money. adj.,* **larg·er, larg·est.**

la·sa·gna (lə zä′nyə), dish consisting of chopped meat, cheese, and tomato sauce, baked with layers of wide noodles. *n.*

Kwanzaa
a family celebrating
Kwanzaa

lasagna
lasagna topped with
grated cheese

a	hat	**ī**	ice	**u̇**	put	**ə** *stands for*	
ā	age	**o**	not	**ü**	rule	**a**	in about
ä	far, calm	**ō**	open	**ch**	child	**e**	in taken
âr	care	**ȯ**	saw	**ng**	long	**i**	in pencil
e	let	**ô**	order	**sh**	she	**o**	in lemon
ē	equal	**oi**	oil	**th**	thin	**u**	in circus
ėr	term	**ou**	out	**ᴛʜ**	then		
i	it	**u**	cup	**zh**	measure		

library (definition 2)
gathering information at
the **library**

lion
A **lion** can be 3 feet
high at the shoulder.

late·ly (lāt′lē), a little while ago; not long ago; recently: *He has not been looking well lately. adv.*

lat·i·tude (lat′ə tüd *or* lat′ə tyüd), distance north or south of the equator, measured in degrees. A degree of latitude is about 69 miles (111 kilometers). *n.*

laugh (laf), make the sounds and movements of the face and body that show one is happy or amused: *We all laughed at the joke. v.,* **laughed, laugh·ing.**

lay-up (lā′up′), (in basketball) a shot from close under the basket. *n.*

la·zy (lā′zē), not willing to work or be active: *He lost his job because he was lazy. adj.,* **la·zi·er, la·zi·est.**

lead (lēd), the opening paragraph in a newspaper or magazine article. A lead often summarizes the information in the body of the article. *n.*

lead·er (lē′dər), person who leads, or is well fitted to lead: *an orchestra leader. That girl is a born leader. n., pl.* **lead·ers.**

least (lēst), less than any other; smallest; slightest: *Ten cents is a little money; five cents is less; one cent is least. I have the least work. adj.*

leg (leg), one of the limbs on which people and animals stand and walk. *n.*
on one's last legs, about to fail, collapse, or die.
pull one's leg, INFORMAL. fool, trick, or make fun of one.
shake a leg, hurry up.

length (lengkth *or* length), how long a thing is; what a thing measures from end to end; the longest way a thing can be measured: *the length of a room, an animal eight inches in length. n.*

lens (lenz), **1** a curved piece of glass which brings closer together or sends wider apart the rays of light passing through it. The lens of a camera forms images on film. **2** the part of the eye that focuses light rays upon the retina. *n., pl.* **lens·es.**

let's (lets), let us: *Let's go for a walk.*

let·tuce (let′is), the large, crisp, green leaves of a garden plant, used in salad. *n.*

lev·el (lev′əl), **1** having the same height everywhere; flat; even: *a level floor.* **2** an instrument for showing whether a surface is level. 1 *adj.,* 2 *n.*

li·brar·i·an (lī brer′ē ən), person in charge of a library. *n.*

li·brar·y (lī′brer′ē), **1** collection of books, magazines, films, recordings, etc. **2** room or building where such a collection is kept for public use and borrowing. *n., pl.* **li·brar·ies.**

limb (lim), a large branch: *They sawed the dead limb off the tree. n.*

line (līn), a set of points continuing without end in both directions. *n.*

li·on (lī′ən), a large, strong, flesh-eating cat, with a dull-yellowish coat, and a loud roar. It is found in Africa and southern Asia. The male has a full, flowing mane of coarse hair. *n.*

liq·uid (lik′wid), **1** substance that is not a solid or a gas; substance that flows freely like water. **2** In the form of a liquid; melted: *liquid soap, butter heated until it is liquid.* 1 *n.,* 2 *adj.*

lo·cal (lō′kəl), of a place; of a certain place or places: *the local doctor, local self-government, local news. adj.*

lo·cate (lō′kāt), establish in a place: *They located their new store on Second Avenue. v.,* **lo·cat·ed, lo·cat·ing.**

lo·ca·tion (lō kā′shən), position or place: *The camp was in a bad location as there was no water near it. n.*

lock (lok), an enclosed section of a canal or dock in which the level of the water can be changed by letting water in or out, to raise or lower ships. *n., pl.* **locks.**

lon·gi·tude (lon′jə tüd *or* lon′jə tyüd), distance east or west on the earth's surface, measured in degrees from Greenwich, England. *n.*

loose (lüs), **1** not tight: *loose clothing.* **2** not firmly set or fastened in: *a loose tooth.* 1,2 *adj.,* **loos·er, loos·est.**

lose (lüz), **1** not have any longer; have taken away from one by accident, carelessness, parting, death, etc.: *lose a finger, lose a friend, lose one's life.* **2** fail to win: *lose the prize. v.,* **lost** (lòst), **los·ing.**

lo·tus (lō′təs), kind of water lily that grows in Egypt, India, and Asia. *n., pl.* **lo·tus·es.**

loud (loud), **1** making a great sound; not quiet or soft: *a loud voice, a loud noise.* **2** in a loud manner: *The hunter called long and loud. adj.*

love (luv), have such a warm liking or deep feeling for: *We love our parents. I love my country. v.,* **loved, lov·ing.**

lux·ur·i·ate (lug zhùr′ē āt or luk shùr′ē āt), **1** indulge in luxury. **2** take great delight: *The campers planned to luxuriate in hot baths when they came home.* **3** grow very abundantly. *v.,* **lux·ur·i·at·ed, lux·ur·i·at·ing.**

M

ma·chine (mə shēn′), arrangement of fixed and moving parts for doing work, each part having some special function: *Sewing machines and washing machines make housework easier. n.*

mag·net (mag′nit), stone or piece of metal that has the property of attracting iron or steel. A lodestone is a natural magnet. *n.*

mag·net·ic field (mag net′ik fēld′), space around a magnet or electric current in which its magnetic force is felt. *n.*

mag·net·ism (mag′nə tiz′əm), properties or qualities of a magnet; the showing of magnetic properties. *n.*

mar·ble (mär′bəl), **1** a hard rock formed from limestone by heat and pressure. It may be white or colored and can be polished to a smooth gloss. Marble is used for statues and in buildings. **2** made of marble. 1 *n.,* 2 *adj.*

March (märch), the third month of the year. It has 31 days. *n.*

mat·ter (mat′ər), importance; significance: *Let it go since it is of no matter. n.*

maul (mòl), beat and pull about; handle roughly. *v.,* **mauled, maul·ing.**

max·im (mak′səm), a short rule of conduct; proverb: *"Look before you leap" is a maxim. n.*

may (mā), be permitted or allowed to: *May I have an apple? v., past tense* **might.**

May (mā), the fifth month of the year. It has 31 days. *n.*

mean[1] (mēn), have as a purpose; have in mind. *v.,* **meant, mean·ing.**

mean[2] (mēn), not noble; petty; unkind; small-minded: *It is mean to spread gossip about your friends. adj.*

meant (ment), See **mean[1]**. *She explained what she meant. v.*

meet[1] (mēt), **1** come face to face (with something or someone coming from the other direction): *Our car met another car on a narrow bridge.* **2** fulfill; put an end to; satisfy: *The campers took along enough food to meet their needs for a week.* **3** a meeting; a gathering: *an athletic meet.* 1,2 *v.,* **met** (met), **meet·ing;** 3 *n.* —**meet′er,** *n.*

lotus
The **lotus** is the national flower of India.

magnet
A **magnet** attracts iron or steel.

a	hat	ī	ice	ù	put	ə *stands for*	
ā	age	o	not	ü	rule	a	in about
ä	far, calm	ō	open	ch	child	e	in taken
âr	care	ò	saw	ng	long	i	in pencil
e	let	ô	order	sh	she	o	in lemon
ē	equal	oi	oil	th	thin	u	in circus
ėr	term	ou	out	ŦH	then		
i	it	u	cup	zh	measure		

meet² (mēt), OLD USE. suitable; proper; fitting: *It is meet that you should help your friends. adj.*

Mem·or·i·al Day (mə môr′ē əl dā′), holiday for remembering and honoring members of the United States armed services who have died. In most states, it is observed on the last Monday in May.

mem·or·y (mem′ər ē), person, thing, or event that is remembered: *I was so young when we moved that our old house is only a vague memory. n., pl.* **mem·or·ies.**

memory mi·nus (mem′ər ē mī′nəs), the calculator key that enables the user to subtract the display from what is in the memory.

memory plus (mem′ər ē plus′), the calculator key that enables the user to add the display to what is in the memory.

memory re·call (mem′ər ē rē′kȯl′), the calculator key that enables the user to display what is in memory.

men·u (men′yü), list of the food served at a meal; bill of fare. *n.*

me·rid·i·an (mə rid′ē ən), an imaginary circle passing through any place on the earth's surface and through the North and South Poles. Meridians mark longitude. *n., pl.* **me·rid·i·ans.**

me·te·o·rol·o·gist (mē′tē ə rol′ə jist), a person who studies weather. *n.*

me·ter¹ (mē′tər), the basic unit of length in the metric system. A meter is equal to 39.37 inches. *n.* Also, **metre.**

me·ter² (mē′tər), 1 any kind of poetic rhythm; the arrangement of beats or accents in a line of poetry. 2 musical rhythm; the arrangement of beats in music: *Three-fourths meter is waltz time. n.*

met·ric (met′rik), of the meter or the metric system. *adj.*

Mich·i·gan (mish′ə gən), **Lake,** one of the five Great Lakes. It lies entirely within the United States. *n.*

middle ear (mid′l ir′), the three tiny bones that carry sound waves from the eardrum to the inner ear. *n.*

model (definition 1)
painting a **model** of the space shuttle

Middle English (mid′l ing′glish), period in the development of the English language between Old English and Modern English, lasting from 1100 to about 1500.

might (mīt), See **may.** *Mother said that we might play in the barn. v.*

might·'ve (mīt′əv), might have: *He might've been outdoors when you called.*

mis·be·have (mis′bi hāv′), behave badly. *v.,* **mis·be·haved, mis·be·hav·ing.**

mis·for·tune (mis fôr′chən), bad luck; unlucky accident. *She had the misfortune to break her arm. n.*

mis·lead (mis lēd′), cause to go in the wrong direction; lead astray: *Our guide misled us and we got lost. v.,* **mis·led, mis·lead·ing.**

mis·led (mis led′), See **mislead.** *We were misled on our hike by a careless guide. v.*

mis·place (mis plās′), put in a place and then forget where it is; mislay: *I have misplaced my pencil. v.,* **mis·placed, mis·plac·ing.**

miss (mis), 1 fail to hit: *I swung at the ball and missed it.* 2 fail to catch: *miss the train.* 3 notice the absence of; feel keenly the absence of: *I missed you while you were away. v.,* **missed, miss·ing.**

mis·sion (mish′ən), a sending or being sent on some special work; errand. An operation by one or more aircraft against the enemy is called a mission. *n.*

Mis·sis·sip·pi (mis′ə sip′ē), 1 large river in the United States. It flows south from N Minnesota to the Gulf of Mexico. 2 one of the south central states of the United States. *Abbreviation:* Miss. or MS. *Capital:* Jackson. *n.*

mis·spell (mis spel′), spell incorrectly. *v.*

mis·treat (mis trēt′), treat badly. *v.*

mod·el (mod′l), 1 a small copy: *a model of a ship or an engine.* 2 thing or person to be copied or imitated: *Your mother is a fine person; make her your model. n.*

mois·ture (mois′chər), slight wetness; water or other liquid suspended in drops in the air or spread on a surface. *n.*

mo·lar (mō′lər), tooth with a broad surface for grinding. A person's back teeth are molars. *n.*

mo·ment (mō′mənt), a very short space of time; instant. *n.*

mon·ey (mun′ē), coins of gold, silver, or other metal, or paper notes which represent these metals, issued by a government for use in buying and selling. *n., pl.* **mon·eys** or **mon·ies.**

mon·key (mung′kē), **1** animal of the group most like human beings. **2** person, especially a child, who is full of mischief. *n., pl.* **mon·keys.**

mood (müd), state of mind or feeling: *I am in the mood to play now; I don't want to study. n.*

morn·ing (môr′ning), the early part of the day, ending at noon. *n.*

moth·er (muŦH′ər), a female parent. *I'll have to ask my mother. n.*

mo·tor (mō′tər), an engine, such as a gasoline or diesel engine, that makes a machine go. *n.*

mo·tor·cy·cle (mō′tər sī′kəl), a two-wheeled motor vehicle which resembles a bicycle but is heavier and larger. *n.*

moun·tain (moun′tən), a very high hill. *n.*

mouth (mouth), the opening through which a person or animal takes in food; space containing the tongue and teeth. *n.*
down in the mouth, INFORMAL. in low spirits; discouraged.

move·ment (müv′mənt), **1** act or fact of moving: *We run by movements of the legs.* **2** the moving parts of a machine; special group of connected parts that move together. The movement of a watch consists of many little wheels. *n.*

Mr. or **Mr** (mis′tər), Mister, a title put in front of a man's name or the name of his position: *Mr. Stern, Mr. President. pl.* **Messrs.**

Mrs. or **Mrs** (mis′iz), a title put in front of a married woman's name: *Mrs. Weiss. pl.* **Mmes.**

Ms. (miz), a title put in front of a woman's name: *Ms. Karen Hansen. pl.* **Mses.**

muf·fin (muf′ən), a small, round cake made of wheat flour, corn meal, or the like, often without sugar. *n.*

mul·ti·pli·ca·tion (mul′tə plə kā′shən), operation of multiplying one number by another. *n.*

mu·sic (myü′zik), beautiful, pleasing, or interesting arrangements of sounds. *n.*

music box (myü′zik boks′), box or case containing apparatus for producing music mechanically. *n.*

music hall (myü′zik hȯl′), hall for musical performances. *n.*

music vid·e·o (myü′zik vid′ē ō), a short musical film or videotape or videodisc. *pl.* **music vid·e·os.**

mus·tard (mus′tərd), a yellow powder or paste made from the seeds of the mustard plant, used as seasoning. *n.*

must·n't (mus′nt), must not: *You mustn't wake the baby.*

my·self (mī self′), form used instead of *me* or *I* in cases like: *I can cook for myself. I hurt myself. pron.*

mys·ter·y (mis′tər ē), something that is hidden or unknown; secret. *n., pl.* **mys·ter·ies.**

monkey (definition 1)

mountain

a	hat	ī	ice	u̇	put	ə stands for	
ā	age	o	not	ü	rule	a	in about
ä	far, calm	ō	open	ch	child	e	in taken
âr	care	ȯ	saw	ng	long	i	in pencil
e	let	ô	order	sh	she	o	in lemon
ē	equal	oi	oil	th	thin	u	in circus
ėr	term	ou	out	ŦH	then		
i	it	u	cup	zh	measure		

N

na·tion (nā′shən), people occupying the same country, united under the same government, and usually speaking the same language. *n.*

na·tion·al (nash′ə nəl), of a nation; belonging to a whole nation: *national laws, a national disaster. adj.*

na·tur·al gas (nach′ər əl gas′), a combustible gas formed naturally in the earth, consisting primarily of methane. It is used as a fuel.

Nav·a·jo (nav′ə hō), member of a tribe of American Indians living mainly in New Mexico, Arizona, and Utah. *n., pl.* **Nav·a·jo, Nav·a·jos,** or **Nav·a·joes.**

nee·dle·leaf (nē′dl lēf′), of or about a type of tree with thin, sharp needles. A pine is a needleleaf tree. *adj.*

neg·a·tive (neg′ə tiv), a photographic image in which the lights and shadows are reversed. Prints are made from it. *n.*

neigh·bor (nā′bər), someone who lives in the next house or nearby. *n.*

neph·ew (nef′yü), son of one's brother or sister; son of one's brother-in-law or sister-in-law. *n.*

nerve (nėrv), **1** mental strength; courage: *nerves of steel.* **2** INFORMAL. rude boldness; impudence. *n.*

net (net), an open fabric made of string, cord, or thread, knotted together in such a way as to leave holes regularly arranged. *n.*

news·cast·er (nüz′kas′tər or nyüz′kas′tər), person or commentator who gives the news on a newscast. *n.*

newspaper
We read **newspapers**
for information.

news·pa·per (nüz′pā′pər or nyüz′pā′pər), a daily or weekly publication printed on large sheets of paper folded together, telling the news, carrying advertisements, and having stories, pictures, articles, and useful information. *n.*

nic·o·tine (nik′ə tēn′), poison contained in the leaves, roots, and seeds of tobacco. *n.* [*Nicotine* comes from Jean *Nicot,* about 1530-1600, a Frenchman who introduced tobacco to France in about 1560.]

night (nīt), **1** the time between evening and morning, especially when it is dark. **2** the darkness of night; the dark. *n.*

night crawl·er (nīt′ krol′ər), a large earthworm that comes to the surface of the ground at night.

night·gown (nīt′goun′), a long, loose garment worn by a woman or child in bed. *n.*

night·mare (nīt′mâr′), a very distressing dream or experience: *The hurricane was a nightmare. n.*

night·time (nīt′tīm′), time between evening and morning. *n.*

non·sense (non′sens), worthless stuff; junk: *a drawer full of useless gadgets and other nonsense. n.*

noon (nün), 12 o'clock in the daytime; middle of the day. *n.*

nose (nōz), the part of the face or head just above the mouth. The nose has openings for breathing and smelling. *n.*
lead by the nose, have complete control over.

No·vem·ber (nō vem′bər), the 11th month of the year. It has 30 days. *n.*

num·ber (num′bər), **1** the count or sum of a group of things or persons; amount: *The number of students in our class is twenty.* **2** figure or mark that stands for a number; numeral. *n.*

number key (num′bər kē′), a key on a calculator that shows one of the numbers 0 through 9. *n., pl.* **number keys.**

number sen·tence (num′bər sen′təns), a way to write a relationship between numbers. 18 + 27 = 45 and 9 > 6 are number sentences.

o

oak (ōk), several kinds of trees or shrubs found in most parts of the world, with strong, hard, durable wood and nuts called acorns. *n.*

oc·cur (ə kėr′), take place; happen: *Storms often occur in winter. v.*, **oc·curred, oc·cur·ring.**

o·cean (ō′shən), the great body of salt water that covers almost three-fourths of the earth's surface; the sea. *n.*

oc·e·lot (os′ə lot *or* ō′sə lot), a spotted cat somewhat like a leopard, but smaller, found from Texas through Mexico and into parts of South America. *n.*

o'clock (ə klok′), of the clock; by the clock: *It is one o'clock. adv.*

Oc·to·ber (ok tō′bər), the tenth month of the year. It has 31 days. *n.*

odd (od), strange; peculiar; unusual: *What an odd house; it has no windows. adj.*

of (ov *or* uv; *unstressed* əv),
1 belonging to: *a friend of my childhood, the news of the day, the driver of the car.* **2** in regard to; concerning; about: *think well of somebody. prep.*

off (ȯf), so as to stop or lessen: *Turn the water off. adv.*

of·fer (ȯ′fər), hold out to be taken or refused; present: *offer one's hand. She offered us her help. v.*

of·fice (ȯ′fis), place in which the work of a business or profession is done; room in which to work: *The doctor's office is closed. n.*

of·ten (ȯ′fən), in many cases; many times; frequently: *Blame is often misdirected. We come here often. adv.*

oil (oil), any of several kinds of thick, fatty or greasy liquids that are lighter than water, burn easily, and are soluble in alcohol, but not in water, such as mineral oils, kerosene, vegetable and animal oils, olive oils. *n.*

oil gland (oil′ gland′), gland of the skin that secretes oil. *n.*

Old Eng·lish (ōld′ ing′glish), period in the history of the English language before 1100.

om·niv·ore (om′nə vôr), a consumer that eats producers and consumers. *n.*

on·ly (ōn′lē), merely; just: *only on weekends. adv.*

On·tar·io (on ter′ē ō), **Lake,** one of the five Great Lakes; it borders New York and Canada. The water from Niagara Falls flows from Lake Erie to Lake Ontario. It is the smallest of the five Great Lakes. *n.*

o·pen (ō′pən), **1** not shut; not closed; letting (anyone or anything) in or out: *Open windows let in the fresh air.* **2** make or become open: *He is opening the window. The door opened.* **3** spread out or unfold: *open a book, open a letter.* 1 *adj.*, 2,3 *v.*, **o·pened, o·pen·ing.**

op·er·a·tion (op′ə rā′shən), the way a thing works: *The operation of this machine is simple. n.*

operation key (op′ə rā′shən kē′), the key which tells the calculator what to perform. The symbols +, −, ×, and ÷ appear on the operation keys. *n., pl.* **operation keys.**

op·tic (op′tik), of the eye; of the sense of sight. The **optic nerve** goes from the eye to the brain. *adj.*

or·ches·tra (or′kə strə), group of musicians playing together on various stringed, wind, and percussion instruments. *n., pl.* **or·ches·tras.**

ocelot
An **ocelot** can be up to 3 feet long without the tail.

a	hat	**ī**	ice	**u̇**	put	**ə** *stands for*	
ā	age	**o**	not	**ü**	rule	**a**	in about
ä	far, calm	**ō**	open	**ch**	child	**e**	in taken
âr	care	**ȯ**	saw	**ng**	long	**i**	in pencil
e	let	**ô**	order	**sh**	she	**o**	in lemon
ē	equal	**oi**	oil	**th**	thin	**u**	in circus
ėr	term	**ou**	out	**ŦH**	then		
i	it	**u**	cup	**zh**	measure		

parallel (definition 1)
parallel stripes on a
piece of fabric

oth·er (uŦH′ər), **1** additional or further: *I have no other place to go.* **2** other person or thing. 1 *adj.*, 2 *pron.*

our (our), of us; belonging to us: *We need our coats now. adj.*

our·selves (our selvz′), form used instead of *we* or *us* in cases like: *We cook for ourselves. pron. pl.*

out·cast (out′kast′), person or animal cast out from home and friends. *n.*

out·er ear (ou′tər ir′), the part of the ear outside of the head and the ear canal.

out·look (out′lùk′), way of thinking about things; attitude of mind; point of view: *a cheerful outlook on life. n.*

out·side (out′sīd′), **1** the side or surface that is out; outer part: *polish the outside of a car, the outside of a house.* **2** on or to the outside; outdoors: *Run outside and play.* 1 *n.*, 2 *adv.*

o·ven (uv′ən), an enclosed space, usually in a stove, for baking, roasting, and sometimes broiling food. *n.*

P

pack·age (pak′ij), bundle of things packed or wrapped together; box with things packed in it; parcel. *n.*

pad·dle (pad′l), row (a boat or canoe) with a paddle or paddles. *v.*, **pad·dled, pad·dling.**

pain·ful (pān′fəl), causing pain; unpleasant; hurting: *a painful illness, a painful duty. adj.*

pan·ic (pan′ik), a fear spreading through a multitude of people so that they lose control of themselves; unreasoning fear: *When the theater caught fire, there was a panic. n.*

Parthenon
the ancient **Parthenon**
in Greece

par·al·lel (par′ə lel), **1** straight lines or planes, lying or extending alongside of one another, always equidistant, but never meeting. **2** any of the imaginary circles around the earth parallel to the equator, marking degrees of latitude that run east and west. 1 *adj.*, 2 *n.*, *pl.* **par·al·lels.**

par·al·lel cir·cuit (par′ə ləl sėr′kit), a circuit that connects several objects in a way that the current for each object has its own path.

par·ent (pâr′ənt *or* par′ənt), father or mother. *n.*, *pl.* **par·ents.**

Par·the·non (pär′thə non), temple of Athena on the Acropolis in Athens, regarded as the finest example of Doric architecture. *n.*

par·tic·i·pate (pär tis′ə pāt), have a share; take part. *v.*, **par·tic·i·pat·ed, par·tic·i·pat·ing.**

pave·ment (pāv′mənt), a covering or surface for streets, sidewalks, etc., made of asphalt, concrete, gravel, stones, etc. *n.*

pay·ment (pā′mənt), amount paid: *a monthly payment of $10. n.*

peace (pēs), freedom from war: *work for world peace. n.*

peace·ful (pēs′fəl), **1** full of peace; quiet; calm: *It was peaceful in the mountains.* **2** free from trouble or disturbance. *adj.*

ped·al (ped′l), **1** lever worked by the foot; the part on which the foot is placed to move any kind of machinery. **2** move by pedals: *He pedaled his bicycle slowly up the hill.* 1 *n.*, 2 *v.*, **ped·aled, ped·al·ing** or **ped·alled, ped·al·ling.**

pe·des·tri·an (pə des′trē ən), person who goes on foot; walker. *n.*, *pl.* **pe·des·tri·ans.**

peep (pēp), **1** the cry of a young bird or chicken; a sound like a chirp or squeak. **2** make such a sound; chirp. 1 *n.*, 2 *v.*

pe·o·ny (pē′ə nē), garden plant with large, showy red, pink, or white flowers. *n.*, *pl.* **pe·o·nies.** [The *peony* was named by the Greeks for Paeon, physician of the gods (because the plant was used in medicine).]

peo·ple (pē′pəl), men, women, and children; persons. *n. pl.*

per·fect (pėr′fikt), without defect; not spoiled at any point; faultless: *a perfect spelling paper. adj.*

pe·rim·e·ter (pə rim′ə tər), the outer boundary of a figure or area: *the perimeter of a circle, the perimeter of a garden. n.*

per·pen·dic·u·lar (pėr′pən dik′ yə lər), at right angles to. Perpendicular lines intersect to form right angles. *adj.*

per·son·al (pėr′sə nəl), of a person; individual; private: *a personal letter, a personal matter. adj.*

per·son·al·i·ty (pėr′sə nal′ə tē), the personal or individual quality that makes one person be different or act differently from another. *n., pl.* **per·son·al·i·ties.**

pet·al (pet′l), one of the parts of a flower that are usually colored. A daisy has many petals. *n.*

pho·to (fō′tō), picture made with a camera. A photograph is made by the action of light rays from the thing pictured passing through the lens of the camera onto the film. *n.*

pick·le (pik′əl), cucumber preserved in salt water, vinegar, or other liquid. *n.*

piece (pēs), **1** one of the parts into which a thing is divided or broken; bit. **2** portion; limited part; small quantity: *a piece of bread. n.*

pig·eon (pij′ən), any of a group of birds with thick bodies, short tails and legs, which makes a cooing sound, including doves and many varieties of domestic pigeons. *n.*

Pil·grim (pil′grəm), one of the Puritan settlers of Plymouth Colony in 1620. *n., pl.* **Pil·grims.**

pint (pīnt), unit of measure for liquids and dry things, equal to ½ quart; 2 cups; 16 fluid ounces. *n.*

pis·til (pis′tl), the part of a flower that produces seeds. It consists, when complete, of an ovary, a style, and a stigma. *n.*

pitch·er[1] (pich′ər), container for holding and pouring liquids, with a lip on one side and a handle on the other. *n.*

pitch·er[2] (pich′ər), a baseball player who pitches the ball to the batter. *n.*

piz·za (pēt′sə), a spicy Italian dish made by baking a large flat layer of bread dough covered with cheese, tomato sauce, herbs, etc. *n., pl.* **piz·zas.**

plain (plān), a flat stretch of land; prairie: *Cattle and horses wandered over the plains. n., pl.* **plains.**

plate (plāt), a large section of rock that makes up part of the earth's crust. *n., pl.* **plates.**

pla·teau (pla tō′), plain in the mountains or at a height considerably above sea level; large, high plain. *n., pl.* **pla·teaus** (pla tōz′).

play (plā), **1** something done to amuse oneself; fun; sport; recreation: *The children are happy at play.* **2** have fun; do something in sport. *The kitten plays with its tail. He played a joke on his sister.* 1 *n.*, 2 *v.*

pledge (plej), **1** a solemn promise: *they made a pledge to give money to charity.* **2** promise solemnly: *We pledge allegiance to the flag.* 1 *n.*, 2 *v.*, **pledged, pledg·ing.**

pluck·y (pluk′ē), having or showing courage: *a plucky dog. adj.*, **pluck·i·er, pluck·i·est.**

pock·et (pok′it), a small bag or pouch sewed into clothing for carrying money or other small articles. *n.*

pod (pod), a small herd of whales or seals. *n.*

po·et·ry (pō′i trē), poems: *a collection of poetry. n.*

point (point), (in mathematics) something that has position without length or width. *n.*

pitcher[1]
a **pitcher** of milk

a	hat	ī	ice	u̇	put	ə *stands for*	
ā	age	o	not	ü	rule	a	in about
ä	far, calm	ō	open	ch	child	e	in taken
âr	care	ȯ	saw	ng	long	i	in pencil
e	let	ô	order	sh	she	o	in lemon
ē	equal	oi	oil	th	thin	u	in circus
ėr	term	ou	out	ᵺ	then		
i	it	u	cup	zh	measure		

polar bear

po·lar bear (pō′lər bâr′) a large, white bear of the arctic regions.

pole (pōl), either of two parts where opposite forces are strongest. A magnet or battery has both a positive pole and a negative pole. *n., pl.* **poles.**

pol·len (pol′ən), tiny grains that make seeds when combined with a flower's eggs. *n.*

pol·lu·tion (pə lü′shən), anything that dirties the environment, especially waste material: *pollution in the air. n.*

pond (pond), body of still water, smaller than a lake. *n.*

pop (pop), make a short, quick, explosive sound. *v.,* **popped, pop·ping.**

pore (pôr), a very small opening. Sweat comes through the pores in the skin. *n.*

por·trait (pôr′trit *or* pôr′trāt), picture of a person, especially of the face. *n.*

pot·ter·y (pot′ər ē), pots, dishes, vases, etc., made from clay and hardened by heat. *n., pl.* **pot·ter·ies.**

pour (pôr), flow or cause to flow in a steady stream: *I poured the milk from the bottle. The rain poured down on the field. v.*

pow·er (pou′ər), **1** strength or force; might. **2** authority; influence; control; right: *Congress has power to declare war. n.*

pottery

ancient **pottery** made by North American Indians

pow·er·ful (pou′ər fəl), having great power or force; mighty; strong: *a powerful person, a powerful medicine, a powerful argument. adj.*

pred·a·tor (pred′ə tər), a consumer that hunts and eats animals. *n.*

pres·sure (presh′ər), a state of trouble or strain: *She has been working under pressure. n.*

prey (prā), animal hunted and killed for food by another animal: *Mice and birds are the prey of cats. n.*

prime me·rid·i·an (prīm′ mə rid′ē ən), meridian from which the longitude east and west is measured. It passes through Greenwich, England, and its longitude is 0 degrees.

print (print), **1** photograph produced from a negative. **2** produce a photograph by transmission of light through a negative. 1 *n.,* 2 *v.*

pri·vate (prī′vit), not for the public; for just a few special people or for one: *a private road, a private house. adj.*

prob·a·bly (prob′ə blē), more likely than not. *adv.*

pro·duc·er (prə dü′sər), a living thing that can use sunlight to make sugars. *n., pl.* **pro·duc·ers.**

prod·uct (prod′əkt), **1** that which is produced; result of work or of growth: *factory products, farm products.* **2** number resulting from multiplying two or more numbers together: *40 is the product of 8 and 5. n., pl.* **prod·ucts.**

proud (proud), feeling or thinking well of, showing satisfaction: *I am proud to call him my friend. adj.*

psy·chol·o·gist (sī kol′ə jist), an expert who is trained to help people with feelings, especially troubled feelings that last a long time. *n.*

pud·ding (pùd′ing), a soft cooked food, usually sweet: *rice pudding. n.*

pueb·lo (pweb′lō), an Indian village built of adobe and stone. *n., pl.* **pueb·los.**

pun·ish (pun′ish), cause pain, loss, or discomfort to for some fault or offense: *punish criminals for wrongdoing. v.* [*Punish* is from Old French *puniss-,* a form of *punir,* meaning "punish," which came from Latin *punire,* meaning "penalty."]

pun·ish·ment (pun′ish mənt), pain, suffering, or loss: *Her punishment for lying was not being allowed to watch TV. n.*

pup (pup), a young dog; puppy. *n.*

pu·pil¹ (pyü′pəl), person who is learning in school or being taught by someone. *n.*

pu·pil² (pyü′pəl), the opening in the center of the iris of the eye which looks like a black spot and where light can enter the eye. *n.*

pur·suit (pər süt′), a chase: *The dog is in pursuit of the cat. n.*

Q

quart (kwôrt), measure of capacity for liquids, equal to one-fourth of a gallon: *a quart of milk. n.*

queen (kwēn), woman who rules a country and its people. *n.*

ques·tion (kwes′chən), thing asked in order to get information; inquiry: *The teacher answered the children's questions. n.*

quick (kwik), fast and sudden; swift: *The cat made a quick jump. Many weeds have a quick growth. adj.*

qui·et (kwī′ət), making no sound; with little or no noise: *quiet footsteps, a quiet room. adj.*

quilt (kwilt), cover for a bed, usually made of two pieces of cloth with a soft pad between, held in place by stitching. *n.*

quit (kwit), **1** stop: *They quit work at five.* **2** leave: *quit one's job. v.,* **quit** or **quit·ted, quit·ting.**

quite (kwīt), **1** completely; entirely: *a hat quite out of fashion. I am quite alone.* **2** actually; really; positively: *quite the thing. adv.*

quo·tient (kwō′shənt), number arrived at by dividing one number by another. In 26 ÷ 2 = 13, 13 is the quotient. *n.*

R

rain gauge (rān′ gāj′), a tool that measures precipitation. *n.*

rat·tle (rat′l), toy, instrument, etc., that makes a noise when it is shaken. *n.*

ray (rā), a set of points that has one endpoint and that extends without end in one direction. *n.*

Rd., Road.

re·act (rē akt′), act in response: *Dogs react to affection. v.*

re·al·ly (rē′ə lē), actually; truly; in fact. *adv.*

rea·son (rē′zn), **1** justification; explanation: *What is your reason for being so late?* **2** think logically; think things out: *Most animals can't reason. 1 n., 2 v.*

re·bound (rē′bound′), (in basketball) a ball that bounds back off the backboard or the rim of the basket after a shot has been made. *n.*

re·build (rē bild′), build again or anew. *v.,* **re·built** (rē bilt′), **re·build·ing.**

re·call (ri kȯl′), call back to mind; remember: *I can recall stories told to me when I was a small child. v.*

re·ceiv·er (ri sē′vər), thing that receives: *Public telephones have coin receivers for change. n.*

re·cent (rē′snt), done or made not long ago: *recent events. adj.*

re·cess (rē′ses or ri ses′), time during which work stops: *There will be a short recess before the next meeting. n.*

rec·og·nize (rek′əg nīz), **1** know again: *You have grown so much that I scarcely recognized you.* **2** identify: *recognize a person from a description. v.,* **rec·og·nized, rec·og·niz·ing.**

quilt
a sampler **quilt**

							ə stands for	
a	hat	ī	ice	u̇	put		ə stands for	
ā	age	o	not	ü	rule	a	in about
ä	far, calm	ō	open	ch	child	e	in taken
âr	care	ȯ	saw	ng	long	i	in pencil
e	let	ô	order	sh	she	o	in lemon
ē	equal	oi	oil	th	thin	u	in circus
ėr	term	ou	out	ᴛʜ	then		
i	it	u	cup	zh	measure		

re·cord (rek′ərd), a thin, flat disk, usually of vinyl or other plastic, with narrow grooves on its surface, used on a phonograph. *n.*

record

re·cov·er (ri kuv′ər), 1 get back (something lost, taken away, or stolen): *recover one's health, recover a lost purse.* 2 get well; get back to a normal condition: *She is recovering from a cold.* *v.*

rec·tan·gle (rek′tang′gəl), a four-sided plane figure with four right angles. *n.*

re·cy·cle (rē sī′kəl), to process or treat (something) in order that it may be used again. Paper, aluminum, and glass products are commonly recycled. *v.,* **re·cy·cled, re·cy·cling.**

red (red), the color of blood or of a ruby: *The jewel is redder than the sun at sunset.* *n., adj.,* **red·der, red·dest.**

re·flec·tor (ri flek′tər), a piece of glass or metal for reflecting light: *The motorist saw the reflector on the girl's bike and slowed down.* *n.*

re·late (ri lāt′), 1 give an account of; tell: *The traveler related her adventures.* 2 be connected in any way: *We are interested in what relates to ourselves.* *v.,* **re·lat·ed, re·lat·ing.**

recycle

children **recycling**

paper, cans, and bottles

rel·a·tive (rel′ə tiv), person who belongs to the same family as another, such as father, brother, aunt, nephew, or cousin. *n., pl.* **rel·a·tives.**

re·lax (ri laks′), loosen up; make or become less stiff or firm: *Relax when you dance.* *v.*

re·main·der (ri mān′dər), 1 number left over after subtracting one number from another. In 9 – 2, the remainder is 7. 2 number left over after dividing one number by another. In 14 ÷ 3, the quotient is 4 with a remainder of 2. *n.*

re·mem·ber (ri mem′bər), call back to mind: *I can't remember that man's name.* *v.*

re·mote (ri mōt′), out of the way; secluded. *adj.*

re·place (ri plās′), fill or take the place of: *A substitute replaced our teacher.* *v.,* **re·placed, re·plac·ing.**

re·ply (ri plī′), answer by words or action; respond: *She replied with a shout. The washing machine replied with a bang.* *v.,* **re·plied, re·ply·ing.**

rep·re·sent (rep′ri zent′), act in place of; speak and act for: *We chose a committee to represent us.* *v.*

re·pro·duce (rē′prə düs′ or rē′prə dyüs′), produce offspring: *Most plants reproduce by seeds.* *v.,* **re·pro·duced, re·pro·duc·ing.**

re·pub·lic (ri pub′lik), nation or state in which the citizens elect representatives to manage the government, which is usually headed by a president. The United States and Mexico are republics. *n.*

res·cue (res′kyü), a saving or freeing from danger, capture, harm, etc.: *A dog was chasing our cat when your sister came to the rescue.* *n.*

re·search (ri sėrch′ or rē′sėrch′), 1 a careful hunting for facts or truth; inquiry; investigation: *cancer research.* 2 to hunt for facts or truth; inquire; investigate. 1 *n., pl.* **re·search·es;** 2 *v.*

re·sent (ri zent′), feel injured and angry at; feel indignation at: *I resented being called lazy.* *v.*

res·er·va·tion (rez′ər vā′shən), land set aside by the government for a special purpose: *an Indian reservation.* *n.*

re·source (ri sôrs′ or rē′sôrs′), 1 any supply that will meet a need. We have resources of money, of knowledge, of strength, etc. 2 **resources,** *pl.* the actual and potential wealth of a country: *natural resources, human resources.* *n., pl.* **re·sourc·es.**

re·sult (ri zult′), good or useful effect: *The new medicine got results.* *n.*

ret·i·na (ret′n ə), layer of cells at the back of the eyeball that is sensitive to light and receives the images of things looked at. *n., pl.* **ret·i·nas, ret·i·nae** (ret′n ē′).

re·un·ion (rē yü′nyən), a coming together again: *the reunion of parted friends. n.*

re·use (rē yüz′), use again: *reuse the papers. v.,* **re·used, re·us·ing.**

Rhode Is·land (rōd′ ī′lənd), one of the northeastern states of the United States. Rhode Island is the smallest state. *Abbreviation:* R.I. or RI *Capital:* Providence.

Rich·ter scale (rik′tər skāl′), a scale for indicating the force or magnitude of earthquakes. On this scale, light tremors register 1.5, while highly destructive earthquakes measure 8.3.

rid·den (rid′n), See **ride.** *I had ridden my horse all day. v.*

ride (rīd), sit on a horse and make it go. *v.,* **rode** (rōd), **rid·den, rid·ing.**

rim (rim), an edge, border, or margin on or around anything: *the rim of a wheel, the rim of a basketball net. n.*

riv·er (riv′ər), **1** a large, natural stream of water that flows into a lake, ocean, etc. **2** any abundant stream or flow: *rivers of lava. n.*

rob (rob), take away from by force or threats; steal from; plunder; pillage: *Bandits robbed the bank of thousands of dollars. v.,* **robbed, rob·bing.**

rough (ruf), **1** not smooth; not level; not even: *rough boards, the rough bark of an oak tree, a rough, rocky hill.* **2** INFORMAL. unpleasant; hard; severe: *She had a rough time in the hospital. adj.*

run·way (run′wā′), **1** a paved strip at an airport on which aircraft land and take off. **2** way, track, groove, trough, etc., along which something moves, slides, etc. *n.*

s

sad (sad), not happy; full of sorrow: *You feel sad if your best friend goes away. adj.,* **sad·der, sad·dest.**

safe (sāf), free from harm or danger: *Keep money in a safe place. adj.,* **saf·er, saf·est. —safe′ly,** *adv.*

sage·brush (sāj′brush′), a grayish shrub that smells like sage, common on the dry plains of western North America. *n.*

said (sed), See **say.** *He said he would come. They had said "No" every time. v.*

salm·on (sam′ən), a large saltwater and freshwater food fish with silvery scales and yellowish-pink flesh. It appears in the northern Atlantic and northern Pacific, and it swims up rivers in order to spawn. *n., pl.* **salm·on.**

say (sā), speak; utter: *What did you say? "Thank you," she said. v.,* **said, say·ing.**

scar·y (skâr′ē), INFORMAL. **1** causing fright or alarm: *scary sounds, a scary movie.* **2** easily frightened. *adj.,* **scar·i·er, scar·i·est.**

school¹ (skül), place for teaching and learning. *n.*

school² (skül), a large number of the same kind of fish or water animals swimming together: *a school of mackerel. n.*

scis·sors (siz′ərz), tool or instrument for cutting that has two sharp blades so fastened that their edges slide against each other. *n. pl. or sing.*

scrap·book (skrap′bůk′), book in which pictures or clippings are pasted and kept. *n.*

a	hat	ī	ice	ů	put	ə	stands for
ā	age	o	not	ü	rule	a	in about
ä	far, calm	ō	open	ch	child	e	in taken
âr	care	ȯ	saw	ng	long	i	in pencil
e	let	ô	order	sh	she	o	in lemon
ē	equal	oi	oil	th	thin	u	in circus
ėr	term	ou	out	ŦH	then		
i	it	u	cup	zh	measure		

scratch (skrach), **1** rub or scrape to relieve itching: *Don't scratch your mosquito bites.* **2** a mark made by scratching: *He had a large scratch on his arm.* 1 *v.,* 2 *n., pl.* **scratch·es.**
from scratch, with no advantages; without help; without prepackaged ingredients.

scream (skrēm), a loud, sharp, piercing cry. *n.*

screen (skrēn), **1** wire woven together with small openings in between. **2** a glass surface on which television pictures, computer information, radar images, etc., appear. *n.*

scrub (skrub), **1** rub hard; wash or clean by rubbing: *I scrubbed the floor with a brush and soap.* **2** a scrubbing: *Give your hands a good scrub.* 1 *v.,* **scrubbed, scrub·bing;** 2 *n.*

seal
Seals usually live in cold areas.

seal (sēl), a flesh-eating sea mammal with large flippers, living usually in cold regions. *n., pl.* **seals** or **seal.**

sea·son (sē′zn), **1** one of the four periods of the year; spring, summer, autumn, or winter. **2** any period of time marked by something special: *a holiday season, the harvest season. n.*

see (sē), be aware of by using the eyes; look at: *See that black cloud. v.,* **saw** (sò), **seen, see·ing.**

seed (sēd), the part of a plant from which another plant like it can grow. A seed has an outer skin or coat which encloses the embryo that will become the new plant and a supply of food for its growth. *n., pl.* **seeds** or **seed.**

seen (sēn), See **see.** *Have you seen Father? v.*

seg·ment (seg′mənt), two points and the part of a line between them. *n.*

seismograph
A **seismograph**
records sudden movements of the earth's crust.

seis·mo·graph (sīz′mə graf), instrument for recording the direction, strength and length of earthquakes. *n.* [*Seismograph* comes from Greek *seismos,* meaning "earthquake," and the combining form *-graph.*]

sep·a·rate (sep′ə rāt′), **1** keep apart; be between; divide: *The Atlantic Ocean separates America from Europe.* **2** divide into parts or groups: *separate a tangle of yarn. v.,* **sep·a·rat·ed, sep·a·rat·ing.**

sep·a·ra·tion (sep′ə rā′shən), a being apart; being separated: *The friends were glad to meet after so long a separation. n.*

Sep·tem·ber (sep tem′bər), the ninth month of the year. It has 30 days. *n.*

ser·ies cir·cuit (sir′ēz sèr′kit), a circuit that connects several objects one after the other so that the current flows in a single path.

ser·i·ous (sir′ē əs), showing deep thought or purpose; thoughtful; grave: *a serious manner, a serious face. adj.*

serve (sèrv), **1** put (food or drink) on the table. **2** in tennis, a player's turn to start the play by hitting the ball. 1 *v.,* **served, serv·ing;** 2 *n.*

set (set), **1** put in the right place, position, or condition; put in proper order; arrange: *The doctor set my broken leg. Set the clock. Set the table for dinner.* **2** number of things or persons belonging together; group; outfit: *a set of dishes.* 1 *v.,* **set, set·ting;** 2 *n.*

sev·er·al (sev′ər əl), more than two or three but not many; some; a few: *gain several pounds (adj.). Several have given their consent (n.)*

sham·poo (sham pü′), **1** wash (the hair, the scalp, a rug, etc.) with a soapy or oily preparation. **2** a washing of the hair, the scalp, a rug, etc., with such a preparation. **3** the preparation used in this way. 1 *v.,* **sham·pooed, sham·poo·ing;** 2,3 *n., pl.* **sham·poos.**

share (shâr), use together; enjoy together; have in common: *The sisters share the same room. v.,* **shared, shar·ing.**

she (shē), anything thought of as female and spoken about or mentioned before: *She was my sister. She was a fine old ship. pron.*

sheep (shēp), mammal with a thick coat and hoofs that chews its cud, and makes a baaing sound. Sheep are related to goats and are raised for wool, meat, and skin. *n., pl.* **sheep.**

she'll (shēl), she will: *She'll help you with your problem.*

shel·ter (shel′tər), **1** something that covers or protects from weather, danger, or attack. **2** protection; refuge. *n.*

sher·iff (sher′if), the most important law-enforcing officer of a county. A sheriff appoints deputies who help to keep order in the county. *n.*

shoot (shüt), **1** send swiftly: *A bow shoots an arrow. She shot question after question at us.* **2** move suddenly and swiftly: *A car shot by us. Flames shot up from the burning house.* **3** take (a picture) with a camera; photograph. **4** send (a ball, puck, marble, etc.) toward the goal, pocket, etc. *v.,* **shot** (shot), **shoot·ing.**

short (shôrt), not long; of small extent from end to end. *adj.*

should·n't (shůd′nt), should not: *You shouldn't cross the street without looking both ways.*

show (shō), **1** make clear to; explain to: *Show us how to do the problem.* **2** a play, motion picture, etc., or a performance of one of these: *The show starts at 6:00.* **1** *v.,* **showed, shown** or **showed, show·ing;** **2** *n.*

show·er (shou′ər), bath in which water pours down on the body from an overhead nozzle. *n.*

shown (shōn), See **show.** *We were shown many tricks by the magician.* *v.*

shud·der (shud′ər), tremble with horror, fear, cold. *v.*

shut·ter (shut′ər), a movable cover, slide, etc., for closing an opening. The device that opens and closes in front of the lens of a camera is the shutter. *n.*

sign (sīn), **1** write: *Sign your initials here.* **2** an inscribed board, space, etc., serving for advertisement, information, regulations, etc.: *See the sign over the door. The stop sign is used by the crossing guard.* **3** motion or gesture used to mean, represent, or point out something: *talk to a deaf person by signs.* **1** *v.,* **2,3** *n.*

sig·nal (sig′nəl), **1** a sign giving notice, warning, or pointing out something. **2** make a signal or signals to: *She signaled the car to stop by raising her hand.* **1** *n.,* **2** *v.,* **sig·naled, sig·nal·ing** or **sig·nalled, sig·nal·ling.**

sil·ver (sil′vər), **1** a shiny, white, precious metal. **2** made of silver: *a silver spoon.* **1** *n.,* **2** *adj.*

sim·ple (sim′pəl), easy to do or understand: *a simple problem.* *adj.,* **sim·pler, sim·plest.**

si·ren (sī′rən), kind of whistle that makes a loud, piercing sound: *We heard the fire engine's siren.* *n.*

sis (sis), INFORMAL. sister. *n.*

sit (sit), rest on the lower part of the body with the weight off the feet: *She sat in a chair.* *v.,* **sat** (sat), **sit·ting.**

skate·board (skāt′bôrd′), **1** a narrow board resembling a surfboard, with roller-skate wheels attached to each end, used for gliding or moving on any hard surface. **2** to ride a skateboard: *The neighborhood children love to skateboard in the summer.* **1** *n.,* **2** *v.*

skate·board·ing (skāt′bôr′ding), the sport of riding a skateboard. *n.*

sheep
a **sheep** and its young

silver
a **silver** table setting

a	hat	**ī**	ice	**ů**	put	**ə** stands for	
ā	age	**o**	not	**ü**	rule	**a**	in about
ä	far, calm	**ō**	open	**ch**	child	**e**	in taken
âr	care	**ȯ**	saw	**ng**	long	**i**	in pencil
e	let	**ô**	order	**sh**	she	**o**	in lemon
ē	equal	**oi**	oil	**th**	thin	**u**	in circus
ėr	term	**ou**	out	**ŦH**	then		
i	it	**u**	cup	**zh**	measure		

ski (definition 1)

skis and ski poles

ski (skē), **1** one of a pair of long, slender pieces of hard wood, plastic, or metal, that can be fastened to the shoes or boots to enable a person to glide over snow. **2** glide over the snow on skis. 1 *n.,* *pl.* **skis** or **ski;** 2 *v.,* **skied, ski·ing.**

skirt (skėrt), **1** a woman's or girl's garment that hangs from the waist. **2** something like a skirt: *A skirt covered the legs of the chair. n.*

skulk (skulk), a group of animals that prey on game, as the fox or weasel. *n.*

sky·scrap·er (skī/skrā/pər), a very tall building. *n.*

slam-dunk (slam/dungk/), (in basketball) a shot made by leaping so that the hands are above the rim of the basket, and throwing the ball down through the netting. *n.*

slap (slap), put, dash, or cast with force. *v.,* **slapped, slap·ping.**

slip (slip), slide suddenly without wanting to: *He slipped on the icy sidewalk. v.,* **slipped, slip·ping.**

slip·per (slip/ər), a light, low shoe that is slipped on easily: *dancing slippers, bedroom slippers. n., pl.* **slip·pers.**

slow (slō), not fast: *Traffic is very slow during rush hour. I walked slowly home. adj.* —**slow/ly,** *adv.*

small (smȯl), **1** not large; little; not large as compared with other things of the same kind: *A cottage is smaller than a house.* **2** not great in amount, value: *The cent is our smallest coin. adj.,* **small·er, small·est.**

smoke (smōk), the mixture of gases and particles of carbon that can be seen rising in a cloud from anything burning. *n.*

smug·gle (smug/əl), bring, take, put, etc., secretly: *I tried to smuggle my puppy into the house. v.,* **smug·gled, smug·gling.**

snack (snak), **1** a light meal, especially one eaten between regular meals. **2** to eat a light meal. *We snacked on fruit after school.* 1 *n.,* 2 *v.*

snail (snāl), a small, soft-bodied animal that crawls very slowly. Most snails have spiral shells on their backs into which they can move for protection. *n.*

snap·shot (snap/shot/), photograph taken quickly with a small camera. *n.*

snore (snôr), a harsh rough sound made in sleeping. *n.*

soc·cer (sok/ər), game played with a round ball between two teams of eleven players each. The players may strike the ball with any part of the body except the hands and arms. Only the goalkeeper may touch the ball with the hands and arms. Players score by knocking the ball into a net cage at either end of the field. *n.*

soft (sȯft), **1** not hard; not stiff; yielding easily to touch: *a soft pillow.* **2** not loud: *a soft voice.* 1,2 *adj.* —**soft/ness,** *n.*

soft·ball (sȯft/bȯl/), **1** a kind of baseball that is played on a smaller field, with a larger and softer ball, and lighter bats. Softball must be pitched underhand. **2** the ball used in this game. *n.*

soft-boiled (sȯft/boild/), (of an egg) boiled only a little so that the yolk is still soft. *adj.*

soft drink (sȯft/ dringk/), drink that does not contain alcohol.

soft·en (sȯf/ən), make or become soft: *Hand lotion softens the skin. Soap softens in water. v.*

soft soap (sȯft/ sōp/), a liquid or semiliquid soap.

some·one (sum/wun), some person; somebody: *Someone is coming. pron.*

some·thing (sum/thing), some thing; a particular thing not named or known: *I'm sure I've forgotten something. n.*

some·times (sum/tīmz), now and then; at times. *adv.*

some·where (sum/hwâr), in or to some place; in or to one place or another: *She lives somewhere in the area. adv.*

soccer

playing the game of

soccer

source (sôrs), person or place from which anything comes or is obtained: *The newspaper gets news from many sources. Mines are the chief source of diamonds.* n., pl. **sourc·es.**

south·ern (suᴛн′ərn), 1 toward the south: *a southern view.* 2 from the south: *a southern breeze.* adj.

speak (spēk), 1 say words; talk: *speak clearly.* 2 use (a language): *Do you speak French?* v., **spoke** (spōk), **spo·ken** (spō′kən), **speak·ing.**

spe·cial (spesh′əl), more than ordinary; unusual; exceptional. adj.

speech (spēch), what is said; the words spoken: *We made the usual farewell speeches.* n., pl. **speech·es.**

spi·der (spī′dər), a small animal with eight legs, no wings, and a body divided into two parts. Spiders are arachnids that spin webs to catch insects for food. n.

spider web (spī′dər web′), the delicate, silken threads spun by a spider.

spore (spôr), a single cell capable of growing into a new plant or animal. Spores are produced by plants that do not have flowers, such as ferns or molds. n., pl. **spores.**

spot·less (spot′lis), without a spot: *a spotless white shirt.* adj.

square (skwâr), 1 a plane figure with four equal sides and four right angles. 2 having this shape: *a square box. A block of stone is usually square.* 1 n., 2 adj., **squar·er, squar·est.**

squash (skwäsh), press or be pressed until soft or flat; crush: *She squashed the bug. Carry the cream puffs carefully, for they squash easily.* v.

squeak (skwēk), make a short, sharp, shrill sound: *A mouse squeaks.* v.

squeal (skwēl), 1 make a long, sharp, shrill cry: *A pig squeals when it is hurt.* 2 such a cry. 1 v., 2 n.

squeeze (skwēz), 1 press hard; compress: *Don't squeeze the kitten; you'll hurt it.* 2 force out by pressure: *squeeze juice from a lemon.* 3 crush; crowd: *Six people squeezed into the little car.* v., **squeezed, squeez·ing. —squeez′a·ble,** adj.

squirm (skwėrm), turn and twist; writhe: *The restless boy squirmed in his chair.* v.

squir·rel (skwėr′əl), a small, bushy-tailed rodent that usually lives in trees. n.

squirt (skwėrt), force out (liquid) through a narrow opening: *squirt water through a tube, squirt water at the statue.* v.

sta·men (stā′mən), the part of a flower that contains the pollen. The stamens are surrounded by the petals. n., pl. **sta·mens, stam·i·na** (stam′ə nə).

stand (stand), be set upright; be placed; be located: *The box stands over there. Some food stood on the table.* v., **stood, stand·ing.**

state (stāt), of a state: *a state road, state police, state government.* adj.

state·ment (stāt′mənt), something stated; report; account: *Her statement was correct.* n.

sta·tion (stā′shən), a regular stopping place: *She met her at the bus station.* n.

steal (stēl), 1 take (something) that does not belong to one; take dishonestly. 2 move secretly or quietly: *She stole softly out of the house.* 3 (in baseball) run to (second base, third base, or home plate) as the pitcher throws the ball to the catcher. v., **stole, sto·len** (stō′lən), **steal·ing.**

spider

a crab **spider**

a	hat	ī	ice	u̇	put	ə stands for	
ā	age	o	not	ü	rule	a	in about
ä	far, calm	ō	open	ch	child	e	in taken
âr	care	ȯ	saw	ng	long	i	in pencil
e	let	ô	order	sh	she	o	in lemon
ē	equal	oi	oil	th	thin	u	in circus
ėr	term	ou	out	ᴛн	then		
i	it	u	cup	zh	measure		

steam (stēm), give off steam: *The cup of coffee was steaming.* v.

steel (stēl), an alloy of iron and carbon. Steel has greater hardness and flexibility than cast iron and is used for tools and machinery. n.

stiff (stif), **1** not easily bent; fixed; rigid. **2** hard to move. *adj.*

St. Law·rence Sea·way (sānt′ lôr′əns sē′wā′), waterway that links the Great Lakes to the Atlantic Ocean by means of canals and the St. Lawrence River.

stole (stōl), See **steal**. *They stole my car.* v.

stom·ach (stum′ək), the large muscular bag in the body which receives swallowed food, and digests some of it before passing it on to the intestines. n.

stood (stu̇d), See **stand**. *She stood in the corner for five minutes. I had stood in line all morning to buy tickets to the game.* v.

stop (stop), leave off (moving, acting, doing, being, etc.); come to an end; cease: *The baby stopped crying. The rain is stopping.* v., **stopped, stop·ping.**

storm

a lightning **storm**

storm (stôrm), a strong wind often accompanied by rain, snow, hail, or thunder and lightning. In deserts there are storms of sand. n.

St. Pat·rick's Day (sānt′ pat′riks dā′), a holiday celebrated in honor of St. Patrick, who converted Ireland to Christianity; March 17.

strange (strānj), unusual; odd; peculiar: *a strange accident, a strange experience. adj.,* **strang·er, strang·est.**

strat·e·gy (strat′ə jē), plan based on skillful planning: *We need some strategy to win this game. n., pl.* **strat·e·gies.**

straw·ber·ry (strȯ′ber′ē), the small, juicy, red fruit of a plant that grows close to the ground. Strawberries are good to eat. *n., pl.* **straw·ber·ries.**

street (strēt), place or way for automobiles, wagons, etc., to go. n.

strength (strengkh), **1** quality of being strong; power; force; vigor. **2** something a person is strong in or can do well. n.

strike (strīk), **1** set or be set on fire by hitting or rubbing: *strike a match.* **2** a stopping of work to get better pay, shorter hours, and so on. *The workers were home for six weeks during the strike last year.* **3** baseball pitched through the strike zone and not swung at, any pitch that is swung at and missed, or any pitch that is hit foul. After three strikes, a batter is out. **1** *v.,* **struck** (struk), **struck** or **strick·en** (strik′ən), **strik·ing;** 2,3 *n.*

stroke (strōk), a single complete movement to be made again and again: *He rowed with a strong stroke of the oars. She swims a fast stroke.* n.

stud·y (stud′ē), try to learn: *She studied her spelling lesson for half an hour. I am studying to be a doctor. v.,* **stud·ied, stud·y·ing.**

stuff (stuf), belongings; goods: *What will we do with all this stuff?* n.

suc·cess·ful (sək ses′fəl), having success; ending in success; prosperous; fortunate. *adj.*

sud·den (sud′n), happening without warning or notice; not expected: *a sudden stop, a sudden rainstorm, a sudden rise to power. adj.*

sud·den·ly (sud′n lē), in a sudden manner. *adv.*

suf·fer (suf′ər), **1** have or feel (pain, grief, etc.): *I suffered sunburn from being at the beach all day.* **2** bear with patiently; endure: *I will not suffer such insults.* v.

suf·fix (suf′iks), syllable or syllables put at the end of a word to change its meaning or to make another word, as -*ly* in *badly,* -*ness* in *goodness,* and -*ful* in *spoonful. n., pl.* **suf·fix·es.**

sug·ar (shu̇g′ər), a sweet substance obtained chiefly from sugar cane or sugar beets and used extensively in food products; sucrose. n.

suit (süt), set of clothes to be worn together. A man's suit consists of a coat, pants, and sometimes a vest. A woman's suit consists of a coat and either a skirt or pants. *n.*

Sun., Sunday.

su·pe·ri·or (sə pir′ē ər), above the average; very good; excellent: *superior work in school. adj.*

Su·pe·ri·or (sə pir′ē ər), **Lake,** the largest of the five Great Lakes. These lakes form the largest group of freshwater lakes in the world. *n.*

sup·per (sup′ər), the evening meal; meal eaten early in the evening. *n.*

sup·ply (sə plī′), **1** provide (what is lacking); furnish: *Many cities supply books for children in school.* **2 supplies,** *pl.* the food, equipment, etc., necessary for an army drive, or the like. 1 *v.,* **sup·plied, sup·ply·ing;** 2 *n., pl.* **sup·plies.**

sup·port (sə pôrt′), **1** give strength or courage to; keep up; help. **2** be in favor of; back; second: *She supports the amendment.* **3** help or assistance: *They need our financial support.* 1,2 *v.,* 3 *n.*

sup·pose (sə pōz′), **1** consider as possible; take for granted; assume. **2** believe, think, or imagine: *I suppose he will come at noon.* *v.,* **sup·posed, sup·pos·ing.**

sur·prise (sər prīz′), cause to feel surprised; astonish: *The victory surprised us.* *v.,* **sur·prised, sur·pris·ing.**

sus·pense·ful (sə spens′fəl), characterized by or full of suspense. *adj.*

swarm (swôrm), group of bees settled together in a hive. *n.*

sweat gland (swet′ gland′), gland of the skin that secretes sweat. A sweat gland is connected with the surface of the skin by a tube or duct that ends in a pore. *n.*

swim (swim), move along on or in the water by using arms, legs, fins, etc.: *Fish swim. Most boys and girls like swimming in the lake.* *v.,* **swam** (swam), **swum, swim·ming.**

sword (sôrd), weapon, usually metal, with a long, sharp blade fixed in a handle or hilt. *n.*

swum (swum) See **swim.** *We have swum in that lake many times.* *v.*

T

Taj Ma·hal (täj′ mə häl′), a famous white marble mausoleum in northern India, built in the 1600s.

take (tāk), **1** lay hold of; grasp: *I took her hand when we crossed the street.* **2** indulge in: *take a nap, take a vacation.* *v.,* **took, tak·en** (tā′kən), **tak·ing.**

tax (taks), money paid by people for the support of the government and services; money regularly collected from citizens by the government. *n., pl.* **tax·es.**

teach·er (tē′chər), person who teaches, especially one who teaches in a school: *We entered the teachers' lounge.* *n.*

team·mate (tēm′māt′), a fellow member of a team. *n.*

tear (tir), drop of salty liquid coming from the eye. *n., pl.* **tears.**

tem·per·a·ture (tem′pər ə chər), **1** degree of heat or cold. The temperature of freezing water is 32 degrees Fahrenheit (0 degrees Celsius). **2** a body temperature higher than normal; fever: *A sick person may have a temperature.* *n.*

swim

swimming the backstroke

a	hat	**ī**	ice	**u̇**	put	**ə** *stands for*	
ā	age	**o**	not	**ü**	rule	**a**	in about
ä	far, calm	**ō**	open	**ch**	child	**e**	in taken
âr	care	**ȯ**	saw	**ng**	long	**i**	in pencil
e	let	**ô**	order	**sh**	she	**o**	in lemon
ē	equal	**oi**	oil	**th**	thin	**u**	in circus
ėr	term	**ou**	out	**ᴛʜ**	then		
i	it	**u**	cup	**zh**	measure		

thrill

The roller coaster gave us
a **thrill**.

tiger

The **tiger** is about 9 feet
long with the tail.

tem·ple (tem′pəl), building used for the service or worship of a god or gods. *n.*

ten·sion (ten′shən), **1** a stretching. **2** mental strain: *Tension may be brought on by overwork. n.*

Tex·as (tek′səs), one of the southwestern states of the United States. *Abbreviation:* Tex. or TX *Capital:* Austin. *n.*

than (ᴛᴴan; *unstressed* ᴛᴴən), **1** in comparison with. **2** compared to that which: *You know better than I do.* 1,2 *conj.,* 1 *prep.*

that's (ᴛᴴats), that is: *That's a beautiful picture.*

their (ᴛᴴâr), of them; belonging to them: *I like their house. adj.*

them (ᴛᴴem; *unstressed* ᴛᴴəm), the persons, animals, things, or ideas spoken about: *The books are new; take care of them. pron.*

then (ᴛᴴen), **1** being at that time; existing then: *the then President.* **2** soon afterwards. 1 *adj.,* 2 *adv.*

there (ᴛᴴâr), in or at that place: *Finish reading the page and stop there. adv.*

they (ᴛᴴā), the persons, animals, things, or ideas spoken about: *I had three books yesterday. Do you know where they are? They are on the table. pron. pl.*

they'd (ᴛᴴād), **1** they had: *They'd arrived late.* **2** they would: *They'd come if they could.*

they'll (ᴛᴴāl), they will: *They'll be a few minutes late.*

they're (ᴛᴴâr), they are: *They're going to be leaving soon.*

thirst·y (thėr′stē), **1** feeling thirst; having thirst: *The dog is thirsty; please give it some water.* **2** having a strong desire or craving; eager. *adj.,* **thirst·i·er, thirst·i·est.**

thought·ful (thôt′fəl), full of thought; thinking: *He was thoughtful for a while and then replied, "No." adj.*

thou·sand (thou′znd), ten hundred; 1000. *n., adj.*

threat (thret), sign or cause of possible evil or harm. *n.*

thrill (thril), a shivering, exciting feeling. *n.*

throat (thrōt), the passage from the mouth to the stomach or the lungs. *n.*

throne (thrōn), chair on which a king, queen, bishop, or other person of high rank sits during official ceremonies. *n.*

through (thrü), **1** from end to end of; from side to side of; between the parts of; from beginning to end of: *march through a town, cut a tunnel through a mountain.* **2** here and there in; over; around: *stroll through the streets of a city. prep.*

throw (thrō), **1** send through the air; toss; hurl. **2** bring to the ground: *His horse threw him.* **3** put by force: *throw someone into jail. v.,* **threw** (thrü), **thrown, throw·ing.**

thrown (thrōn), See **throw.** *She has thrown her old toys away. v.*

thumb (thum), the short, thick finger of the hand. It can be moved against any of the other four fingers to grasp things. *n.*

ti·ger (tī′gər), a large, fierce, flesh-eating mammal of Asia, that has dull-yellow fur striped with black. It is related to the cat and the lion. *n., pl.* **ti·gers.**

ti·tle (tī′tl), **1** the name of a book, poem, picture, song, etc. **2** name showing rank, occupation, or condition in life. King, duke, lord, majesty, highness, captain, doctor, and Miss are titles. *n.*

to (tü; *unstressed* tu *or* tə), **1** in the direction of; toward a destination: *She came to school.* **2** *To* is used with verbs. *I like to play the piano.* **3** on against: *Nail the shelf to the wall.* **4** *To* is used to show action toward. *Give the book to me. prep.*

toe (tō), one of the five divisions that end the foot. *n., pl.* **toes.**

tomb (tüm), grave, vault, mausoleum, etc., for a dead body, often above ground. *n.*

to·mor·row (tə mor′ō), **1** the day after today. **2** on the day after today. 1 *n.*, 2 *adv.*

tongue (tung), the movable fleshy organ in the mouth. The tongue is used in tasting and, by people, for talking. *n.*

too (tü), **1** in addition; also; besides. **2** beyond what is desirable, proper, or right; more than enough. *adv.*

took (tůk), See **take.** *She took the car an hour ago. v.*

toot (tüt), sound of a horn or whistle. *n.*

tot (tot), a little child. *n.*

touch·down (tuch′doun′), score of six points made in football by putting the ball on the ground behind the opponent's goal line. *n.*

tough (tuf), **1** hard to cut, tear, or chew. **2** strong; hard: *a tough team. adj.*

track (trak), **1** a double, parallel line of metal rails for cars to run on: *railroad tracks.* **2** a course for running or racing. *n.*

trash (trash), **1** broken or torn bits, such as leaves, twigs, husks, etc.: *Rake up the trash in the yard.* **2** worthless stuff; rubbish: *That magazine is trash. n.*

tread (tred), **1** set the foot down; walk; step: *Don't tread on the flower beds. They trod through the meadow.* **2** move the legs and feet as if walking: *Everyone in swimming class treads water for five minutes.* **3** act or sound of treading: *We heard the tread of marching feet.* 1,2 *v.*, **treads, trod** (trod), **trod·den** (trod′n) or **trod, tread·ing;** 3 *n.*

treat (trēt), **1** entertain with food, drink, or amusement: *treat some friends to ice cream.* **2** anything that gives pleasure. 1 *v.*, 2 *n.*

treat·ment (trēt′mənt), way of treating: *This cat has suffered from bad treatment. n.*

tre·men·dous (tri men′dəs), INFORMAL. very great; enormous: *That is a tremendous house for a family of three. adj.*

tri·an·gle (trī′ang′gəl), a plane figure having three sides and three angles. *n.*

trou·ble (trub′əl), **1** cause trouble to; disturb: *The lack of business troubled the grocer.* **2** extra work; bother; effort: *Take the trouble to work.* 1 *v.*, **trou·bled, trou·bling;** 2 *n.*

truth·ful (trüth′fəl), telling the truth: *He is a truthful boy and will tell exactly what happened. adj.* —**truth′ful·ly,** *adv.*

tun·dra (tun′drə), a vast, level, treeless plain in the arctic regions. The ground beneath its surface is frozen even in summer. Much of Alaska and northern Canada is tundra. *n.*

two (tü), one more than one; 2. *n.*, *pl.* **twos;** *adj.*

track (definition 2)
running on a **track**

U

ug·ly (ug′lē), very unpleasant to look at. *adj.*, **ug·li·er, ug·li·est.**

un·con·test·ed (un′kən tes′tid), undisputed; unopposed: *The referee's decision was uncontested. adj.*

un·for·tu·nate (un fôr′chə nit), not lucky; having bad luck. *adj.* —**un·for′tu·nate·ly,** *adv.*

un·friend·ly (un frend′lē), not friendly; hostile. *adj.*

un·heard (un hėrd′), not listened to; not heard: *unheard melodies. adj.*

a	hat	**ī**	ice	**u̇**	put	**ə** stands for	
ā	age	**o**	not	**ü**	rule	**a**	in about
ä	far, calm	**ō**	open	**ch**	child	**e**	in taken
âr	care	**ȯ**	saw	**ng**	long	**i**	in pencil
e	let	**ô**	order	**sh**	she	**o**	in lemon
ē	equal	**oi**	oil	**th**	thin	**u**	in circus
ėr	term	**ou**	out	**ŦH**	then		
i	it	**u**	cup	**zh**	measure		

u·ni·verse (yü′nə vėrs′), the whole of existing things; everything there is, including all space and matter; the cosmos: *Our world is but a small part of the universe.* n.

un·known (un nōn′), not known; not familiar; strange. *adj.*

un·til (un til′), up to the time when. *conj.*

un·u·su·al (un yü′zhü əl), not usual; not ordinary; not in common use; uncommon; rare. *adj.*

up·on (ə pon′), on. *prep.*

up·set (up′set′), an unexpected defeat: *The hockey team suffered an upset.* n.

up·stairs (up′stârz′), on or to an upper floor: *She lives upstairs (adv.). He is waiting in an upstairs hall (adj.).*

use·less (yüs′lis), of no use; worthless: *A television set would be useless in a house without electricity.* adj.

u·su·al (yü′zhü əl), commonly seen, found, or happening; ordinary; customary. *adj.*

u·su·al·ly (yü′zhü ə lē), according to what is usual; commonly; ordinarily; customarily; often: *We usually eat dinner at 6.* adv.

walrus
The **walrus** has ivory tusks.

V

va·ca·tion (vā kā′shən), **1** freedom from school, business, or other duties: *There is a vacation from school every summer.* **2** take a vacation. 1 *n.,* 2 *v.*

Val·en·tine's Day (val′ən tīnz dā′), a holiday in which cards or small gifts are given to friends and loved ones; February 14.

val·ley (val′ē), low land between hills or mountains. *n., pl.* **val·leys.**

van·ish (van′ish), disappear, especially suddenly: *The sun vanished behind a cloud.* v.

ver·i·fy (ver′ə fī), test the correctness of; check for accuracy: *You can verify the spelling of a word by looking in a dictionary.* v., **ver·i·fied, ver·i·fy·ing.**

ver·tex (vėr′teks), the point where two sides of an angle meet. *n., pl.* **ver·tex·es, ver·ti·ces** (vėr′tə sēz).

vil·lage (vil′ij), group of houses, usually smaller than a town. *n.*

vol·ca·no (vol kā′nō), an opening in the earth's crust through which steam, ashes, and lava are forced out in periods of activity. *n., pl.* **vol·ca·noes** or **vol·ca·nos.**

vol·ume (vol′yəm), space occupied: *The storeroom has a volume of 800 cubic feet.* n.

W

waist (wāst), the part of the human body between the ribs and the hips. *n.*

wal·rus (wȯl′rəs *or* wol′rəs), a large sea mammal of the arctic regions, resembling a seal but having long tusks. It is hunted for its hide, tusks, and blubber oil. *n., pl.* **wal·rus·es** or **wal·rus.**

want (wänt), wish for; wish: *We want a new car. I want to become an engineer.* v.

wash (wäsh), clean with water or other liquid: *wash one's face, wash clothes, wash dishes.* v., **washed, wash·ing.**

wash·a·ble (wäsh′ə bəl), able to be washed without damage: *washable silk.* adj.

wash·cloth (wäsh′klȯth′), a small cloth for washing oneself. *n.*

was·n't (wuz′nt *or* wäz′nt), was not.

waste (wāst), **1** make poor use of; spend uselessly; fail to get full value or benefit from: *Though I had much work to do, I wasted my time doing nothing.* **2** poor use; useless spending; failure to get the most out of something: *Buying that suit was a waste of money.* 1 *v.* **wast·ed, wast·ing;** 2 *n.*

watch (wäch), **1** look attentively or carefully. **2** device for telling time, small enough to be carried in a pocket or worn on the wrist. 1 *v.,* 2 *n., pl.* **watch·es.**

wa·ter foun·tain (wȯ′tər foun′tən), **1** water flowing or rising into the air in a spray. **2** place to get a drink.

wa·ter·way (wȯ′tər wā′), river, canal, or other body of water that ships can go on. *n.*

weak·ness (wēk′nis), a weak point; slight fault: *Putting things off is her weakness. n., pl.* **weak·ness·es.**

weave (wēv), make out of thread, strips, or strands of the same material. *v.,* **wove** (wōv), **wo·ven** (wō′vən) or **wove, weav·ing.**

we'd (wēd), **1** we had: *We'd left the party early.* **2** we would: *We'd love to see you again.*

Wed., Wednesday.

week·end (wēk′end′), Saturday and Sunday as a time for recreation, visiting, etc. *n.*

week·ly (wēk′lē), of a week; for a week; lasting a week: *a weekly wage of $150. adj.*

weight (wāt), how heavy a thing is; the amount a thing weighs. *n.*

weight·less (wāt′lis), being free from the pull of gravity. *adj.*

weird (wird), **1** unearthly or mysterious; wild; strange: *They were awakened by a weird shriek. It was the weirdest noise I had ever heard.* **2** odd; fantastic; queer: *The robin made a weirder sound than the sparrow. adj.,* **weird·er, weird·est.**

wel·come (wel′kəm), **1** greet kindly; give a friendly reception to: *We always welcome guests at our house.* **2** a kind or friendly reception: *You will always have a welcome here.* **1** *v.,* **wel·comed, wel·com·ing;** **2** *n.*

we'll (wēl), we will: *We'll be arriving at about 6:00.*

went (went), See **go.** *I went home promptly after school. v.*

we're (wir), we are: *We're all looking forward to your visit.*

were (wėr), form of the verb **be** used with *you, we, they* or any plural noun to indicate the past tense. *The officer's orders were obeyed. v.*

we've (wēv), we have: *We've had a wonderful time.*

whale (hwāl), mammal shaped like a huge fish and living in the sea. Oil from whales used to be burned in lamps. *n., pl.* **whales** or **whale.**

what·ev·er (hwot ev′ər or hwut ev′ər), anything that: *Do whatever you like. pron.*

what's (hwots or hwuts), **1** what is: *What's the latest news?* **2** what has: *What's been going on here lately?*

wheat (hwēt), the grain of a common cereal grass, used to make flour. *n.*

when (hwen), **1** at what time: *When does school close?* **2** at the time that: *Stand up when your name is called.* **1** *adv.,* **2** *conj.*

when·ev·er (hwen ev′ər), when; at whatever time; at any time that: *Come whenever you wish (conj.). I'll come whenever possible (adv.). conj., adv.*

where (hwâr), in what place; at what place: *Where do you live? Where is he? adv.*

wher·ev·er (hwâr ev′ər), where; to whatever place; in whatever place: *Sit wherever you like (conj.) Wherever are you going? (adv.). conj., adv.*

whirl (hwėrl), **1** turn or swing round and round; spin: *The leaves whirled in the wind.* **2** move round and round: *whirl a lasso. We whirled about the room. v.*

weave

weaving on a large loom

a	hat	**ī**	ice	**u̇**	put	**ə** stands for	
ā	age	**o**	not	**ü**	rule	**a**	in about
ä	far, calm	**ō**	open	**ch**	child	**e**	in taken
âr	care	**ȯ**	saw	**ng**	long	**i**	in pencil
e	let	**ô**	order	**sh**	she	**o**	in lemon
ē	equal	**oi**	oil	**th**	thin	**u**	in circus
ėr	term	**ou**	out	**ᵺ**	then		
i	it	**u**	cup	**zh**	measure		

whole (hōl), 1 having all its proper parts; complete: *whole egg, whole milk.* 2 full; entire: *He ate the whole melon. adj.*

whole milk (hōl′ milk′), milk from which none of the natural elements have been removed.

whole note (hōl′ nōt′), (in music) note to be played four times as long as one quarter note.

whole-wheat (hōl′hwēt′), made from whole-wheat flour: *whole-wheat bread. adj.*

who'll (hül), who will: *Who'll help me wash the dishes?*

who's (hüz), 1 who is: *Who's going with me?* 2 who has: *Who's seen the new wildlife documentary?*

whose (hüz), of whom; of which: *The girl whose work got the prize is very talented. Whose book is this? pron.*

width (width), how wide a thing is; distance across; breadth: *The room is 12 feet in width. n.*

wild (wīld), not in proper control or order: *wild hair. adj.*

will (wil), am going to; is going to; are going to: *We will go to the beach on Saturday. v., past tense* **would.**

win (win), be successful over others; get victory or success in: *We all hope our team will win. v.,* **won** (wun), **win·ning.**

win·dow (win′dō), an opening to let in light or air set into an outer wall or roof of a building or into a vehicle. *n.*

wind sock (wind′ sok′), device somewhat like a large sock, mounted on a pole and open at one end to catch the wind and show its direction.

wind vane (wind′ vān′), a tool that shows wind direction.

wish·y-wash·y (wish′ē wäsh′ē), lacking strength of character; indecisive: *a wishy-washy person. adj.*

wisp (wisp), a flock of birds, especially of marsh birds called snipe. *n.*

wrench
A **wrench** holds and turns bolts and nuts.

with (wiTH *or* with), *With* shows that persons or things are taken together in some way. 1 in the company of: *Come with me.* 2 by means of: *The man cut the meat with a knife. prep.*

with·draw (wiTH drȯ′ *or* with drȯ′), draw back; draw away. *v.,* **with·drew, with·drawn, with·draw·ing.**

with·hold (with hōld′ *or* wiTH hōld′), refrain from giving or granting. *v.,* **with·held, with·hold·ing.**

with·stand (with stand′ *or* wiTH stand′), stand against; hold out against; resist; oppose, especially successfully. *v.,* **with·stood, with·stand·ing.**

wood (wùd), trees or parts of trees cut up for use in building houses, making boats and furniture, etc. *n.*

wor·ry (wėr′ē), 1 feel anxious; be uneasy: *Don't worry about little things. They will worry if we are late.* 2 make anxious; trouble: *The problem worried me. v.,* **wor·ried, wor·ry·ing.**

worth·less (wėrth′lis), without worth; good-for-nothing; useless: *Throw those worthless, broken toys away. adj.*

would (wùd), See **will.** *Would you help us, please? v.*

would·n't (wùd′nt), would not.

would've (wùd′əv), would have.

wow (wou), exclamation of surprise, joy, etc. *interj.*

wreath (rēth), a ring of flowers or leaves twisted together. *n., pl.* **wreaths** (rēTHz).

wreck (rek), 1 what is left of anything that has been destroyed or much injured. 2 cause the wreck of; destroy; ruin: *Raccoons wrecked our campsite looking for food.* 1 *n.,* 2 *v.*

wren (ren), a small songbird with a slender bill and a short tail. Wrens often build their nests near houses. *n.*

wrench (rench), tool for turning nuts, bolts, etc. *n., pl.* **wrench·es.**

wres·tler (res′lər), person who wrestles, especially as a sport. *n.*

wrist (rist), the joint connecting hand and arm. *n.*

write (rīt), make letters or words with pen, pencil, or chalk: *You can read and write. v.,* **wrote** (rōt), **writ·ten, writ·ing.**

writ·ing (rī′ting), literary work; a book or other literary production: *the writings of Benjamin Franklin. n.*

writ·ten (rit′n), See **write.** *He has written a letter. (v.) a written note. (adj.). v., adj.*

Y

yes·ter·day (yes′tər dē), the day before today. *n.*

you'd (yüd; *unstressed* yůd), **1** you had: *You'd already left.* **2** you would: *You'd love this book.*

young (yung), without much experience or practice. *adj.*

your (yůr; *unstressed* yər), belonging to you: *Wash your hands. adj.*

you're (yůr; *unstressed* yər), you are: *Tell me where you're going.*

Z

zin·ni·a (zin′ē ə), a garden plant grown for its showy flowers of many colors. *n.* [The *zinnia* was named in honor of Johann G. *Zinn,* 1727-1759, a German botanist.]

wrestler
wrestlers during
a match

a	hat	ī	ice	ů	put	ə stands for	
ā	age	o	not	ü	rule	a	in about
ä	far, calm	ō	open	ch	child	e	in taken
âr	care	ȯ	saw	ng	long	i	in pencil
e	let	ô	order	sh	she	o	in lemon
ē	equal	oi	oil	th	thin	u	in circus
ėr	term	ou	out	ᴛʜ	then		
i	it	u	cup	zh	measure		

Writer's Thesaurus

Many of your spelling words have synonyms, which are words with same or similar meanings. This thesaurus lists those spelling words alphabetically, defines them, and provides synonyms. For many words, you can also look up antonyms, which are words with opposite meanings. A thesaurus can even introduce you to new words.

Understand a Thesaurus Entry

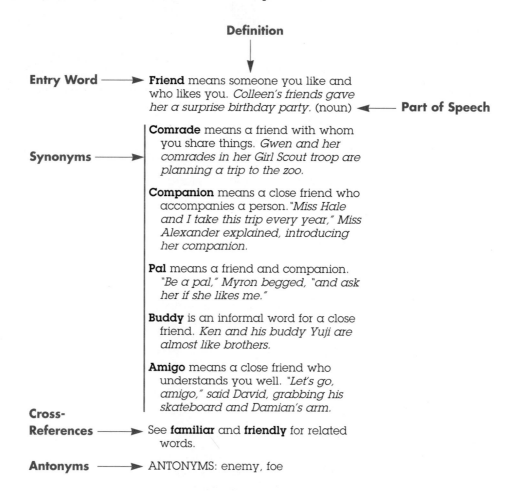

Definition

Entry Word → **Friend** means someone you like and who likes you. *Colleen's friends gave her a surprise birthday party.* (noun) ◄── **Part of Speech**

Synonyms →

Comrade means a friend with whom you share things. *Gwen and her comrades in her Girl Scout troop are planning a trip to the zoo.*

Companion means a close friend who accompanies a person. *"Miss Hale and I take this trip every year," Miss Alexander explained, introducing her companion.*

Pal means a friend and companion. *"Be a pal," Myron begged, "and ask her if she likes me."*

Buddy is an informal word for a close friend. *Ken and his buddy Yuji are almost like brothers.*

Amigo means a close friend who understands you well. *"Let's go, amigo," said David, grabbing his skateboard and Damian's arm.*

Cross-References → See **familiar** and **friendly** for related words.

Antonyms → ANTONYMS: enemy, foe

A a

Ability means the power to do something well. *Renee's ability to make her own clothes has saved her a lot of money.* (noun)

Talent means an inborn ability. *Julio's drumming shows real musical talent.*

Capacity means an inborn ability. *Bob has a great capacity for foreign languages and speaks three.*

Skill means an ability gotten by means of training and practice. *Michiko's skill in cooking has improved.*

Announce means to make something known to the public. *The manager announced that the team had traded two pitchers.* (verb)

Broadcast means to make something widely known by radio or television. *Warnings of the approaching hurricane were broadcast to residents of the coast.*

Advertise means to make something known to the public by paying for it. *The sale was advertised in the local newspaper.*

Publicize means to make something known to as many people as possible. *The kids publicized their car wash by posting signs.*

Ask means to try to get information by using words. *Ask Marcy where she got that great jacket.* (verb)

Inquire means to ask in order to get detailed information. *Yukio inquired about the hours that the video store is open.*

Quiz means to ask questions about what has been learned. *Our science teacher always quizzes us on last night's homework.*

Question means to ask over and over again, in a systematic way. *The police questioned several suspects about the bank robbery.*

ANTONYMS: answer, reply

Attack means to begin fighting someone or something with actions or words. *A mother bear may attack anyone who gets close to her cubs. A group of parents has attacked the plan to close the schools early.* (verb)

Assault means to attack suddenly, usually with weapons. *The enemy assaulted our fort with bombs and cannons.*

Charge can mean to attack by a sudden rush. *An elephant opens its ears wide when it charges.*

ANTONYM: defend

B b

Beat means to hit over and over. *José and his friends spend Saturday mornings beating conga drums at the Caribbean Cultural Center.* (verb)

Winds howled, and waves **pounded** the little ship.

Hammer can mean to beat. *"Why can't I remember?" said Shirley, hammering her head with her fists.*

Pound means to hit hard, over and over. *Winds howled, and waves pounded the little ship.*

Bang can mean to beat noisily. *Liza's little sister loves to bang on pots and pans.*

Beautiful means very pleasing to the senses or the mind. *These beautiful rugs were made by hand in Turkey 100 years ago, but they still look almost like new.* (adjective)

Pretty means pleasing to see or hear. It is often used to describe girls and women. *Mariko looks really pretty in that hat.*

Handsome means pleasing to see. It is often used instead of beautiful or pretty to describe a man or boy. *Candace thinks Mr. Walking Bear, the science teacher, is awfully handsome.*

Lovely means especially beautiful and fine. *The rose garden in the park is so lovely, I could stay there for hours.*

ANTONYMS: ugly, unattractive

Beginning means the time when something first happens or first exists. *The Declaration of Independence marked the beginning of the United States.* (noun)

Start can mean a beginning. *Jason led the sack race from start to finish.*

Creation means the act of making something that did not exist before. *Since the creation of the Cafeteria Committee, we've had better desserts.*

Opening can mean a beginning, especially of a story, music, or other works of art. *The opening of the musical, with its great song and fabulous dancers, really grabbed Mike's attention.*

Introduction can mean a beginning in common use. *Since the introduction of the microwave, cooking habits have changed greatly.*

ANTONYMS: conclusion, end, finish

C c

Care means an unhappy, nervous feeling, with fear of pain or loss. *After weeks of struggle and care, the refugees have escaped from the fighting.* (noun)

Concern can mean an uneasy feeling because something or someone important to you is in trouble. *Marcia's parents feel a lot of concern because she wants to quit school.*

Worry means repeated, nervous thought about possible pain or loss. *Our worry about Billy Don's safety turned to anger when he strolled in two hours late.*

Anxiety means strong worry and fear. *Every time Coach Petrangelis tells us how important this next game is, my anxiety gets worse.*

Tension can mean worry and emotional upset, especially lasting a long time and using up much strength. *After the tension of waiting for the audition, White Bird felt that actually performing was almost easy.*

SEE **worried** for related words.

Careful means paying close attention to what you say and do. *I feel safe in the car with Mrs. Gomez, who is a very careful driver.* (adjective)

Cautious means careful to avoid danger. *Pia has been very cautious about riding her bike in the street after seeing the bike safety movie.*

Wary means very careful and expecting danger. *Mice have to be wary of cats and owls.*

Guarded can mean cautious. It is used especially to describe someone's way of talking. *The scientists are very guarded about their invention, and they say it needs more tests.*

ANTONYMS: careless, negligent, thoughtless

Careless means not paying attention to what you say or do. *Tom was careless, and now his shoes are all wet.* (adjective)

Thoughtless means not thinking before doing or saying something. *Those thoughtless girls talk loudly while everyone else is trying to study.*

Inconsiderate means thoughtless of other people's feelings. *Taking a parking space reserved for the disabled isn't just inconsiderate, it's illegal.*

Reckless means not thinking about possible danger. *Reckless driving frequently causes accidents.*

Rash means dangerously careless, often because of haste. *Maryanne now regrets her rash decision to quit school.*

ANTONYMS: careful, cautious

Change means to make or become different. *Jermayne changes her nail polish every couple of days. Inside its case, the pupa changes to a butterfly.* (verb)

Alter means to change slightly. It suggests limited change of a particular sort. *The pilot altered her flight plan to avoid a bad thunderstorm.*

Vary means to change in a number of ways. It suggests change for the sake of difference, or change according to circumstances. *The form of government varies from country to country.*

Turn can mean to change. It often describes change in color or form. *The sun turned Alan's face red. Water turns to steam when it boils.*

IDIOMS

Change is a key word in several idioms. Here are some of them:

Change hands means to go from one owner to another. *The gas station changed hands twice in one year before Mr. Ortega bought it.*

Change off means to take turns. *Mariolet and I change off doing the dishes and setting the table.*

Change your tune means to say something very different from before. *Cassie thinks she's a better cook than I am, but she'll change her tune when she tastes my barbecue.*

Climb means to move upward, most often by using feet or hands or both. *The squirrels climb the pole to get the birdseed.* (verb)

Ascend means to move upward toward the highest point. *The Japanese mountaineers will try to ascend one of the highest peaks in the Andes.*

Mount means to go up or climb up. *Mrs. Vargas slowly mounted the stairs to her apartment.*

Scramble means to climb where climbing is especially hard and awkward. It may suggest climbing on all fours. *An otter will scramble up a steep, muddy riverbank and slide down again, over and over, just for fun.*

ANTONYM: descend

Clothes means covering for a person's body. *Miguel has grown so much he needs new clothes.* (noun)

Clothing means clothes. It is a slightly more formal word. *New-to-You Fashion Shop sells both women's and men's clothing.*

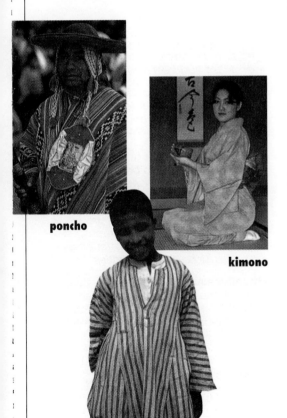

poncho

kimono

caftan

Wardrobe means all the clothes a person has. *Most of Ray's wardrobe came from his older brothers.*

Outfit can mean clothes that go together. *Mom has a plaid skirt and a red blouse that she wears as an outfit with her velvet blazer.*

Uniform means the clothes worn by some special group while at work. *When Aunt Phyllis goes to her Army Reserve training, she looks strong and proud in her uniform.*

Common means happening often or often met with. *"It's just a common cold," Dr. Wu told Jerome.* (adjective)

Ordinary means like most others. *Since the note was written on ordinary paper, the police concentrated on tracing its rare purple ink.*

Average can mean like most others. It is often used with numbers. *On an average day, the store sells two dozen sponges.*

Normal means like most others. It suggests that this is a good way to be. *It is normal for people to want to be liked and respected.*

Popular can mean widespread and done, had, or known by many people. *Grandpa and Grandma like to do popular dances from years ago.*

SEE **usual** for related words.

Confused means unable to think clearly or act correctly. *Alan's directions got us so confused that we arrived more than an hour late.* (adjective)

Bewildered means confused, especially by many parts or items. *On his first day at school, Luis was bewildered by all the long halls, doors, and hurrying students.*

Puzzled means unsure or unable to understand. *The ranger was puzzled by the strange tracks he found.*

Perplexed is a formal word that means very puzzled. *Perplexed by the new disease attacking the sheep, the vet sent for experts from the university.*

Mixed up means confused. *Our waiter got mixed up and brought baked potatoes instead of the rice we had ordered.*

Crazy means senseless and foolish. *Whose crazy idea was it to walk all the way home?* (adjective)

Lunatic means crazy. *It's lunatic to take foolish risks.*

Mad means very crazy and possibly dangerous. *Mr. Brady may look like a mad scientist, but he's actually a lot of fun to talk to.*

Insane means mentally ill and not legally responsible. *The murderer was insane, and he was sent to a mental hospital.*

ANTONYM: sane

Crowd means a large group of people together. *Huge crowds arrived on the day of the big game.* (noun)

Mob means a crowd, especially a noisy and violent one. *The mob made so much noise that the governor returned to her helicopter.*

Flock can mean a crowd. *A flock of preschoolers ran out the door.*

Swarm can mean a crowd moving together. *Every weekday morning and evening, swarms of commuters pour through the train station.*

D d

Danger means a chance of harm or injury. *The approaching tornado brought danger to everything in its path.* (noun)

The house was in great **danger** as the tornado approached.

Risk means a chance of harm or loss. *Lynn wonders if the view would be worth the risk of the climb.*

Hazard means a likely cause of injury or misfortune. *The hazards of mining include cave-ins, explosions, and flooding.*

Threat can mean a possible cause of injury or misfortune. *The weather forecaster warned of the threat of a statewide blizzard.*

ANTONYM: safety

Deal means an arrangement for trade or exchange. This meaning is informal. *Lucy thought that trading three cat's-eye marbles for a circus ticket was a pretty good deal.* (noun)

Bargain means a deal. *William Penn made a fair bargain with the Indians.*

Agreement means an arrangement to act in certain ways. *I thought we had an agreement: you'd vacuum and do the bathroom, and I'd do the laundry and wash the kitchen floor.*

Contract means a legal agreement. *The third baseman has signed a contract for a total of $6,000,000.*

Decide means to make up your mind. *It was such a hot day that we decided to go to the city swimming pool.* (verb)

Determine means to decide firmly, often from several choices. *Jolene is still trying to determine which hairdo looks best on her.*

Conclude can mean to decide after thinking it over. *The police concluded that the driver who caused the accident had been reckless.*

Rule can mean to decide publicly and with authority. *The referee ruled that the ball was out of bounds.*

Different means not alike. *Edgar and Edwin try hard to be different, because they don't want to be known as "the twins."* (adjective)

Various means different. It is used when there are many different things. *The recreation center offers various classes and activities.*

Miscellaneous means of many sorts, not all the same. It may suggest no effort to choose. *My sister collects only clear marbles, but she keeps some miscellaneous ones to trade.*

Mixed means of many kinds combined together. *Connie thinks "Mixed Nuts" would be a good name for our comedy act.*

ANTONYMS: alike, same, similar

Disappear means to go from sight. *Arlene turned off the TV, and the picture disappeared.* (verb)

Vanish means to disappear, usually suddenly and often mysteriously. *The magician will now make her assistant vanish from the stage.*

Evaporate can mean to disappear the way water does when it turns to vapor. *The bad feelings between Lana and Crystal evaporated when Lana broke her arm.*

Fade can mean to disappear slowly. *As the sun rises, stars fade away.*

ANTONYM: appear

Dishonest means willing to lie, cheat, or steal. *A dishonest accountant stole $4,000 from the business.* (adjective)

Crooked can mean dishonest. It expresses contempt. *That man was so crooked his own dog didn't trust him.*

Lying means not telling the truth. *The lying witness tried to mislead the jury.*

Untruthful can mean not telling the truth. *Since she is known to have been untruthful many times in the past, people tend not to believe her.*

ANTONYMS: honest, truthful

Dislike means a feeling of not liking someone or something. *Teresa has a real dislike for long bus rides.* (noun)

Distaste means a strong dislike. *Tanya's distaste for cold weather is even stronger now than when she first came to Chicago.*

Disgust means an extreme dislike of something physically unpleasant. *The smell of the garbage truck filled us with disgust.*

Disapproval means dislike of something because it is bad. *The students showed their disapproval of the movie by protesting outside the theater.*

ANTONYM: fondness

E e

Edge means the line or place where something ends. *Zena planted marigolds around the edges of the class garden.* (noun)

Margin means an area next to an edge. *In the margin of my paper, my teacher wrote a few comments about my work.*

Rim means the edge of something round. *The rims of these plates are decorated with flowers.*

Border means an edge or the area along the edge. *The white linen tablecloth had pink daisies embroidered all around the border.*

Boundary means an edge of a place or the area along the edge. *When the two countries merged, the boundary lines between them were left off the new maps.*

Excellent means having very high quality. *When it was Barry's turn to cook dinner, he made excellent tacos.* (adjective)

First-class means excellent. *"Why, Daniel, this drawing is wonderful!" the art teacher cried. "You're becoming a first-class artist!"*

Superior means having very high quality, especially compared to others. *"Now that you have seen the others," Mr. Bartholomew murmured, "I will show you a truly superior diamond."*

Outstanding means so excellent as to stand out from others. *You have to be an outstanding athlete to be considered for the Olympic team.*

ANTONYMS: bad, poor, terrible

Explain means to make something easier to understand by talking or writing about it. *This book explains the background of the war in Vietnam.* (verb)

Interpret means to explain the meaning of something. *Rob interprets the movie as a comedy, but Tara thinks it was serious.*

Clarify means to make something clearer and easier to understand. *Celia could not understand the diagram and asked her teacher to clarify it.*

Spell out means to give a careful, detailed, and easy-to-understand explanation. *Roger had trouble setting the VCR until Marissa spelled out the process for him, one step at a time.*

ANTONYMS: confuse, misinterpret

WRITING TIP: SLANG

There are lots of slang words that mean "excellent." Here are just a few of them:

bad	icy
boss	keen
chill	neat
cool	nifty
dandy	righteous
dynamite	swell
fab	tough
groovy	

Remember that slang gets old very quickly. Some of the words in this list may already be so out of date that you have never heard them used to mean "excellent." When you see in this book or in your dictionary that a word is slang, be careful about using it in your writing. In dialogue, slang can help suggest a character through conversation, but in description, it can make your story sound old.

HAVE YOU HEARD...?

You may have heard people say that someone has "shed light on the question." This means to provide information about a subject, especially a subject in doubt—as if shining a light into darkness. *"My next witness," said Ms. Ortega, "can shed some light on the question of the defendant's whereabouts at that time."*

Extra means more than usual or more than necessary. *Every student should bring an extra pencil to the exam. Rodney always carries extra batteries for his tape player.* (adjective)

Spare can mean extra. It suggests that something will probably not be needed. *Ms. Healy checks her spare tire every few weeks.*

Surplus means extra. It suggests that there is a lot more of something than necessary. *The bakery sends its surplus bread to the church's shelter for the homeless.*

Additional means added to something else. *"Will you stop now," asked the TV host, "or risk all your prizes for an additional five thousand dollars?"*

F f

Friend means someone you like and who likes you. *Colleen's friends gave her a surprise birthday party.* (noun)

Comrade means a friend with whom you share things. *Gwen and her comrades in her Girl Scout troop are planning a trip to the zoo.*

Companion means a close friend who accompanies a person. *"Miss Hale and I take this trip every year," Miss Alexander explained, introducing her companion.*

Pal means a friend and companion. *"Be a pal," Myron begged, "and ask her if she likes me."*

Buddy is an informal word that means a close friend. *Ken and his buddy Yuji are almost like brothers.*

Amigo means a close friend who understands you well. *"Let's go, amigo," said David, grabbing his skateboard and Damian's arm.*

ANTONYMS: enemy, foe

H h

Hide means to put out of sight. *We quickly hid the birthday present we were making for Mom when we heard her at the front door.* (verb)

Conceal means to hide something on purpose so that it won't be found. *Ugo conceals his comic books, but I always find them.*

Camouflage means to hide something by giving it a false appearance. *This caterpillar's dull colors let it camouflage itself as a twig.*

Stash is an informal word that means to hide something for safekeeping or future use. *Everything the gang stole was stashed in a hiding place under the floor.*

Bury can mean to hide something by covering it. *When Tana saw the teacher coming, she quickly buried Michelle's note under her books.*

ANTONYMS: expose, reveal, show

Hopeless means without any feeling that something good will happen. *Mr. Cho stared at his flooded home and felt more hopeless than ever before in his life.* (adjective)

Desperate means hopeless and reckless. *The mountain climbers made a desperate effort to get back to camp through the raging storm.*

Pessimistic means ready to believe that bad things will happen. *Patrick is too pessimistic even to try out for the swim team.*

ANTONYMS: confident, hopeful

Huge means very big. *A huge oak tree in the park blew down in the storm last night.* (adjective)

Enormous means much larger than normal. *We're celebrating the hundredth anniversary of the founding of the town with an enormous parade and picnic.*

Giant means much larger than other things of the same kind. *That's the Happy Cow Dairy with the giant milk carton on the roof.*

Gigantic means giant. *At the county fair, Richie saw a gigantic pumpkin weighing 150 pounds.*

Colossal means tremendously large. *The colossal head of Washington on Mount Rushmore is as high as a five-story building.*

Mammoth means colossal. *Mammoth Cave has miles of passages and is hundreds of feet deep.*

ANTONYMS: little, small, tiny

I i

Interesting means making you feel like paying attention and knowing more. *To a chameleon, any insect is interesting.* (adjective)

To a chameleon, any insect is **interesting.**

Fascinating means so interesting that it's hard to stop. *Damien finds computer programming so fascinating that he'll sit at his keyboard for hours.*

Spellbinding means so interesting that it is impossible to stop paying attention. *Both pitchers have no-hitters going into the eighth inning of this spellbinding game.*

ANTONYMS: dull, boring, uninteresting

K k

Know means to have knowledge of something or someone. *Marina knows a beautiful spot in the state park.* (verb)

Realize means to understand that something is true. *Watching Mr. Brigano work in his garden, we never realized he was almost 90.*

Recognize can mean to realize. *Matt recognizes now that he was wrong to make fun of his sister's singing.*

Understand means to get the meaning of something. *After years of work, scientists understand something about the writing carved on this stone by an ancient people.*

L l

Loud means having or making a big sound. *The thunder was so loud, it seemed the storm was right over our house.* (adjective)

Noisy means with a lot of loud, harsh sounds. *Elora ran past the noisy street repairs as fast as she could.*

Roaring means making a loud, deep sound. *This is no place for kids to play, with broken glass and roaring traffic.*

Thunderous can mean very loud, like thunder. *"Just listen to that thunderous applause from these hockey fans!" said the announcer.*

Blaring means making a very loud, harsh sound. *The blaring stereo in the upstairs apartment kept Pavel's family awake.*

ANTONYMS: quiet, silent, still

M m

Misfortune means bad luck or an unfortunate happening. *Josleen had the misfortune to race against the city's best sprinter in the first round of the girls' 100-meter dash.* (noun)

Accident means an unfortunate happening, usually a sudden one. *Traffic is backed up because of the auto accident.*

Misadventure means an accident, usually not a serious one. *James and his friends were covered with mud after their misadventure while feeding the pigs.*

Mishap means a misadventure. *"Keep practicing the dance," the director said, "and it will go without any mishap."*

O o

Often means many times. *Casimir often earns a few dollars helping people carry groceries.* (adverb)

Frequently means often and at short intervals. *Rain falls frequently in the tropical forest.*

Repeatedly means many times and the same each time. *Juana must go repeatedly to the stream for her family's water.*

Regularly means often and at the same interval. *"Buses should arrive at this corner regularly," said Mr. Crankshaw, "but I haven't seen one yet."*

ANTONYMS: infrequently, rarely, seldom

IDIOMS

There are many idioms that mean to know something fully and thoroughly. You can **know** something

by heart
like the back of your hand
inside out
backwards and forwards
like a book

There are also many ways to say that someone understands the situation. You can be **in the know,** and you can **know**

the dope   **the score**
the ropes   **what's up**
the scoop   **what's what**

Do you have other ways of saying this?

Most ants have enough **strength** to lift ten times their own weight.

P p

Perfect means having no faults or being the best. *The swimmer made a perfect dive. Vladimir found the perfect gift for his grandmother.* (adjective)

Ideal means perfect, or as wonderful as you could imagine. *When Saturday came, it turned out to be an ideal day for the carnival.*

Flawless means not having any defects. *On the slender fingers of her right hand, the princess wore two flawless diamonds.*

Pure can mean perfect. It suggests that something contains no bad parts. *Ronald prides himself on his homemade candy, made with pure chocolate and fluffy coconut.*

Foolproof means made so that nothing can go wrong. *The prisoners thought that their escape plan was foolproof—until they found the guards waiting in the tunnel.*

SEE **excellent** for related words.

ANTONYM: imperfect

Piece means a small part of something larger, or one thing among others like it. *Della swept the pieces of the broken glass into a pile. The platter was the largest piece of china on the Serra's dinner table.* (noun)

Bit means a small piece of something larger. *Caroline tore the letter into bits.*

Scrap means a little piece, especially a piece left over. *Andrea cut the picture to fit into the frame and then threw away the paper scraps.*

Lump means a small, solid piece of material. *Darryl gave the carnival pony a lump of sugar.*

Slice means a thin, flat, broad piece cut from something. *Franklyn wants a sandwich with one slice of cheese and three slices of ham.*

Power means the ability to do something or to make something happen. *Senator Hughes has the power to get that law changed.* (noun)

Energy can mean power. It often suggests power stored up, ready to be used. *The creative energy of the students really comes out in the school's Festival of Brazil.*

Force means active power. It suggests effort and work. *The force of the blast destroyed the building and took out the side of the mountain.*

Strength means the amount of power that someone or something has. *Most ants have enough strength to lift ten times their own weight.*

Might means great power or strength. *Janek took a deep breath and flung himself at the locked door with all his might.*

ANTONYM: weakness

Proud means pleased with yourself and with what you have done. *Congresswoman Martinez told her election workers that they should all be proud of themselves.* (adjective)

Conceited means having too high an opinion of yourself or your good qualities. *The conceited actor stopped bragging after he forgot his lines.*

Boastful means fond of talking about yourself and how good you are. *The boastful man went on and on about what a great fisherman he was.*

Stuck-up is an informal word that means conceited. *Patricia is so stuck-up that she has no friends at all.*

ANTONYMS: humble, modest

Punish means to cause pain or loss to a person who has done something wrong. *The soldiers were punished for sleeping on duty.* (verb)

Discipline can mean to punish, especially to control people. *Mr. Berman disciplines his students fairly.*

Correct can mean to punish, in order to make someone better. *Mom says she must correct our new puppy so he'll stop chewing furniture and shoes.*

Fine means to make a person pay money for doing something wrong. *Our library fines people five cents a day for late books.*

Ground can mean to punish a young person by not letting him or her go out for fun. This meaning is informal. *When he came home two hours late, Chung-Ho knew his parents would ground him.*

Q q

Quick means moving, happening, or done in a short time. *Graciela made a quick grab and got her purse back from the thief.* (adjective)

Fast means moving with much speed. *Young Raven hurled his fish spear, but the salmon was too fast.*

Swift means very fast. *This train is so swift that we'll be in Los Angeles tomorrow.*

Speedy means very quick. It is often used to describe things that you want to happen or be finished. *The bank robbers could not make a speedy getaway because of the parade.*

Hasty means quick and with not enough time or thought. *Courtney's hasty reply started a quarrel.*

SEE **suddenly** for related words.

ANTONYM: slow

Quiet means to make someone or something less noisy and more peaceful. *Desi quieted his younger brothers when they were frightened by the thunderstorm.* (verb)

Calm means to make someone less excited or nervous. *Following the bomb scare, the police officer calmed the crowd.*

Soothe means to make quiet and comfortable. *Mrs. Benson soothed the crying child.*

Hush means to make someone or something less noisy or silent. *As the mailman approached, the owner hushed his barking dog.*

ANTONYMS: disturb, excite, stir up

R r

Reason means an explanation of why something happened. *Doug says his reason for quitting the job is that he didn't respect the boss.* (noun)

Cause can mean a reason. *The "A" on Jaleel's history final was cause for celebration!*

Motive means a thought or feeling that makes someone do something. *The high cost of city living was Mr. Poole's motive for moving to a small town.*

Rough means having a surface that is not smooth. *Frank snagged his sweater on the rough wall of the basement.* (adjective)

Uneven means not smooth or level. *Our car bounced along the uneven gravel road.*

Bumpy means having a lot of bumps. *The sidewalk was too bumpy for good skateboarding.*

Rugged means having a rough, uneven surface. *The slope looked easy, but the ground became rugged toward the top.*

Coarse can mean rough and heavy. *Silas used coarse sandpaper to smooth the sides of the bookshelf.*

ANTONYMS: even, level, smooth

S s

Separate means to keep things apart or take something apart. *The highway separates these apartment buildings from the neighboring houses. Separate the dark from the light clothes before you wash them.* (verb)

Divide means to separate. It is often used about equal parts or sharing. *Ms. Polanak divided the class into teams for a softball game.*

Split can mean to divide something as if by cutting. *Tom and Dave split the money they got for the empty cans.*

Segregate can mean to separate people of different races. *The people of South Africa were the last in the world to remain officially segregated.*

ANTONYMS: unite, join

Serious means showing deep thought and purpose. *"I am the man of the family now," said Tom in a serious voice.* (adjective)

Earnest means serious and full of strong feeling. *The governor made an earnest appeal for help from the federal government after his state was struck by a hurricane.*

Solemn means serious, formal, and impressive. *The President takes a solemn oath to uphold the Constitution.*

ANTONYMS: lighthearted, cheerful, carefree

Shelter means something that covers or protects from the weather or from danger. *During the rain, the church picnic continued under the shelter of the tents.* (noun)

Cover can mean shelter. *The baby crane took cover between the long legs of its mother.*

Refuge means a shelter or place of safety. It suggests escape from trouble. *The first National Wildlife Refuge was created by Theodore Roosevelt to protect pelicans.*

Sanctuary can mean a refuge or place of protection, especially one where animals are protected from hunters or other dangers. *Behind the zoo is a bird sanctuary, closed to people.*

Preserve can mean a place where animals and plants are protected. *This whole area within the bend of the river is a wildlife preserve.*

Short means taking only a small amount of time. *"This was supposed to be a short assignment, but it's taking forever," Regina sighed.* (adjective)

Brief means taking a small amount of time. *Ken gave a brief talk about collecting beetles.*

Thumbnail means very short. *Dario gave a thumbnail description of the baseball game: "They got the runs; we didn't."*

Summary means brief and limited to main ideas. *Mr. Perrera has his classes hand in summary outlines of each week's reading.*

ANTONYMS: lengthy, long, wordy

Sign means an indication of something that will happen. *The first red and yellow leaves are a sign that summer is over.* (noun)

Symptom means a sign, especially of illness or suffering. *Symptoms of the flu include a fever and nausea.*

Omen means a sign or something believed to be a sign. *Daniel thinks it's an omen of good luck if he sees an all-white pigeon.*

Warning means something that tells of possible trouble or danger to come. *"Let that be a warning to you,"* Alejandro told the sobbing bully.

Soft means easy to bend or push into; not hard or stiff. *After two weeks of sleeping on a hard camp cot, Phil is glad to get back to his own soft bed.* (adjective)

Floppy means easy to bend and hanging or swaying in a loose way. *After a long week in her squad car, Mom spends Saturday morning in her floppy old bathrobe, reading and relaxing.*

Fluffy means as soft as fluff. *The young swan has short, fluffy feathers.*

The young swan has short, **fluffy** feathers.

Limp means so easy to bend that it cannot stay straight. *The noodles were limp when Tessa lifted them from the boiling water.*

ANTONYMS: firm, hard, rigid, stiff

Steal means to take something that belongs to someone else. It suggests secret, usually nonviolent taking. *"I saw the robbers steal the money,"* the witness stated. (verb)

Rob means to take money or property from a person or place. *The convenience store over on 27th Street was robbed twice last weekend.*

Shoplift means to steal things from a store while pretending to be a customer. *Since the Trans installed a lot of mirrors and cameras, nobody shoplifts from that store.*

Hold up means to stop by force and take money or property. *Bandits held up the stagecoach outside Bitterroot Springs.*

Stick up is a slang expression that means to rob. *She stuck up a couple of banks, so she's in jail for fifteen to twenty years.*

WORD STORY

Sanctuary comes from a Latin word meaning "a holy place." In the Middle Ages, people could avoid arrest by staying in a church. Because a church is a holy place, the laws at that time said that a person could be protected there.

WATCH IT !

Steal and *rob* have related meanings, but they are not really synonyms because of the way they are used. The object of *steal* is the thing that is taken. The object of *rob* is the person or place that something is taken from. They *robbed* the store and *stole* the money.

Stiff means not easy to bend or move. *Grandpa prefers a hairbrush with stiff bristles.* (adjective)

Rigid means very stiff. *The wet clothes became rigid overnight in the frosty air.*

Firm means hard. *The butter is still cold and too firm to spread.*

Tense means stretched tight. *Every muscle was tense as the runners waited for the race to start.*

Suddenly means quickly and without being expected. *Suddenly the sky became dark, and a fierce storm began.* (adverb)

Unexpectedly means without any sign that something is going to happen. *The phone rang unexpectedly in the middle of the night.*

Immediately means instantly. *When he missed the bus, Gavin immediately called his mother to let her know he would be late.*

All of a sudden and **all at once** mean suddenly. *All of a sudden, Korinne realized that she was falling. All at once, Tony jumped up and caught her arm.*

SEE **quick** for related words.

ANTONYM: gradually

Surprised means filled with wonder because of something unexpected. *"Marceea, I'm surprised to find you here!" exclaimed Grandpa.* (adjective)

Amazed means greatly surprised. *His parents were amazed when Eldred began composing music at such an early age.*

Startled can mean caused to jump in surprise and fright. *Kazuo is such a light sleeper that once he woke up, startled by a noisy goldfish.*

Shocked means surprised and very upset. *Jamaine was shocked to find her ordinarily quiet dog barking and snapping at the mail carrier.*

T t

Thoughtful means careful of other people's feelings. *"How thoughtful!" said Angelique. "You brought my favorite flowers!"* (adjective)

Considerate means thoughtful. It suggests thinking of people's feelings without having to be told. *They were considerate of the downstairs neighbors by walking quietly in the hallway.*

Sympathetic means thoughtful, kind, and able to understand how someone else feels. *When he saw my braces, Emilio showed his own in a sympathetic smile.*

Caring means attentive. It suggests that someone else's feelings are important to you. *Everyone in class made a fuss when Jacob first broke his leg, but only Amanda was caring enough to visit him often.*

ANTONYMS: inconsiderate, thoughtless

U u

Ugly means unpleasant to look at. *Vandals have covered the wall with ugly spray paint marks.* (adjective)

Homely means not good-looking. It is also not as strong a word as ugly. *Amid the crowds in the railway station, Lise was delighted to see the smiling, homely face of her beloved Uncle Frank.*

Hideous means very ugly and horrible to look at. *Butch loves movies with hideous monsters, but I think they're mostly boring and stupid.*

Monstrous can mean hideous. *The monstrous faces stared at Mr. Williamson and chanted, "Trick or treat!"*

ANTONYMS: beautiful, good-looking

Useless means not worth using or doing, or not able to be used. *It's useless arguing with Bill, because he never admits it when he's wrong.* (adjective)

Worthless means having no use or value. *If the broken leg on that table can't be fixed, the table is really worthless.*

Needless means useless and without purpose. It suggests a waste of time. *Take a safer route to avoid any needless risk.*

Inefficient means not worth using or doing because work is wasted. *Copying whole pages of the textbook is an inefficient way to study the lesson.*

ANTONYM: useful

WORD STORY

Ugly comes from an old Scandinavian word meaning "fear." *Hideous* comes from an old French word meaning "fear." One reason we have synonyms is that sometimes the same idea came into English from different languages.

Usual means most commonly seen, found, or happening. *In Chicago some snow is usual in winter. We'll meet for lunch at the usual time.* (adjective)

Traditional means customary because it has been handed down from generation to generation. *Thanksgiving is a traditional American holiday.*

Regular means usual and according to custom or rule. *Sarah was late and missed her regular bus.*

Ordinary means usual and regular. *Visiting and helping out friends who are sick is an ordinary part of my grandmother's life.*

SEE **common** for related words.

ANTONYMS: peculiar, rare, unusual

W w

Want means to feel an urge to have or do something. *Peter wants a pair of in-line skates for his birthday.* (verb)

Wish means to want or hope for something. *"If you wish to become a ballerina," Madame Claire told Ramona, "you must work as hard as you can."*

Desire is a formal word that means to wish seriously and very much. *Many people desire to conserve the environment but wonder what they personally can do.*

Long means to desire. It suggests thinking about something over and over. *The Navajo children longed to hear more stories about their ancestors.*

Watch means to keep your eyes on something carefully for a period of time. *The burglars tied up the guard, so all he could do was watch as they emptied the warehouse.* (verb)

Look means to turn your eyes to something. *"Look at the sea lions!" Darseea called to her mother.*

Eye means to look. *Mustafa eyed each camel carefully as it approached the starting line.*

Gaze means to watch steadily. It suggests a strong attraction to what is watched. *Mr. Thurman gazed fondly at his newest grandchild.*

Stare means to watch steadily and directly, usually without blinking. *The first time Rachel got a pimple, she felt that everyone in school was staring at her.*

Weird means very strange and mysterious. *From deep in the forest, She Walks Away heard a weird croaking rumble.* (adjective)

Spooky is an informal word that means strange enough to make you nervous. *It's spooky how quiet the street gets at night when traffic stops.*

Creepy can mean weird and frightening. *The heroine of the movie has to save her friend from some creepy villains.*

The heroine of the movie has to save her friend from some **creepy** villains.

Ghostly means like a ghost. *Sometimes, when Obadele walks homeward across the fields at evening, mist rises in ghostly shapes around him.*

ANTONYMS: natural, normal

Welcome means to be glad to let someone or something in. *The Drama Club welcomes new members.* (verb)

Accept can mean to let in with approval. *Raquel's sister has been accepted by a medical school.*

Admit can mean allow to enter. *One hundred lucky contest winners will be admitted early and introduced to the band.*

Take in means to admit, especially as part of business. *The animal shelter takes in stray dogs and cats.*

Whole means with all its parts and with nothing left out. *Adam watched the whole movie, but Bert left when it got scary.* (adjective)

Complete means whole. *Consuela gave complete instructions for making a piñata.*

Entire means whole. *Did Lucy and Calvin eat the entire batch of cookies?*

Total means all added together. *The total bill was $81.16.*

ANTONYM: partial

Wild means extremely excited and out of control. *When Rita scored the goal that won the championship, the fans went wild.* (adjective)

Frantic means wild with rage, fear, pain, or grief. *From the burning building came frantic cries for help.*

Disorderly can mean wild and causing trouble, especially in public. *Ushers asked the disorderly group to be quiet or leave the concert.*

Unruly means hard to control. *Lamar's puppy has so much energy that she is sometimes unruly.*

ANTONYM: calm

Worried means uncertain what will happen and afraid of what may happen. It suggests thinking about something over and over. *Willie Don is worried because his dog won't eat and might be sick.* (adjective)

Uneasy means having a strong feeling that trouble is coming. It suggests not knowing for sure what the trouble will be. *Changes in the Earth's atmosphere make scientists uneasy about possible climate changes.*

Nervous can mean afraid that things will not go well. It suggests restlessness. *Before the race, Emma was nervous and wheeled her chair around the block to calm herself down.*

Anxious means convinced that something bad will happen, and busy thinking about it. It suggests painful excitement. *After an anxious search, Nancy found her contact lens under the seat of the car.*

SEE **care** for related words.

ANTONYMS: calm, relaxed

Y y

Young means in the early part of life. *Some young birds can walk and swim soon after they hatch from eggs.* (adjective)

Youthful means young or like young people. It suggests hope, energy, and imagination. *Grandma Salazar dances with a youthful enthusiasm that makes her seem half her age.*

Immature means not completely grown. It is often used to suggest that feelings or behavior are not grown-up enough. *Justin apologized to the substitute teacher for his immature behavior.*

Teenage means in the years of life from thirteen to nineteen. *With two teenage sons, a job, and night school, Mrs. Chee is always busy.*

ANTONYMS: adult, elderly, mature, old

IDIOMS

There are many idioms meaning *worried* and *nervous*. They describe a restless, uncertain feeling by comparing it to being on top of something that keeps you from being comfortable.

on edge: *It's been two months since Dad had any work, and he's on edge most of the time now.*

on pins and needles: *Afraid of missing the fireworks, the children were on pins and needles until they reached the park.*

like peas on a hot griddle: *When the cat appeared at the window, the birds at the feeder were like peas on a hot griddle.*

The Word List in English and Spanish

A

ability (13)	habilidad
able (13)	capaz, poder
accomplishments (CC)	logros
action (27)	acción
adobe (CC)	adobe
again (19)	otra vez
air mass (CC)	masa de aire
alley (9)	callejón
almost (16)	casi
a lot (16)	mucho, mucha
alphabet (3)	alfabeto
always (16)	siempre
angel (32)	ángel
angle (32, CC)	ángulo
animals (31)	animales
another (32)	otro, otra
anyway (26)	de todos modos
anywhere (7)	dondequiera
appearance (CC)	apariencia
appreciate (CC)	apreciar
April (11)	abril
are (35)	eres, son, somos; estás, están, estamos
area (CC)	área
arrive (11)	llegar
articles (CC)	artículos
artist (CC)	artista
ashes (15)	cenizas
asked (19)	preguntar; pedir *(pasado)*
assign (2)	asignar
assignments (CC)	tareas
Atlantic Ocean (CC)	Océano Atlántico
attack (3)	atacar
August (31)	agosto
aunt's (34)	de la tía
aunts' (34)	de las tías
Ave. (33)	avenida
awhile (7)	un rato

B

babies' (34)	de los bebés
baby's (34)	del bebé
backboard (CC)	tablero
backpack (10)	mochila
backstroke (CC)	brazada de espalda
bacon (11)	tocino
band (10)	banda
barometer (CC)	barómetro
barrel (32)	barril
baseball (26)	béisbol
basketball (26)	baloncesto; balón
beaches (15)	playas
beat (9, 23)	batir; tocar; vencer
beautiful (27)	bello, bella
because (3)	porque
beet (23)	betabel; remolacha
beginning (25)	comenzando
behind (11)	detrás
believe (19)	creer
bicuspid (CC)	primer molar
bicycle (CC)	bicicleta
blanket (10)	manta
block (10)	cuadra
blubber (CC)	grasa
borrow (8)	tomar prestado
bottle (8)	botella
boy's (34)	del muchacho
boys' (34)	de los muchachos
brainstorm (CC)	torrente de ideas
brake (3, 23)	freno; frenar
break (23)	quebrar; faltar
breathe (CC)	respirar
breathless (28)	sin aliento
bridge (14)	puente
brightness (28)	claridad
broadleaf (CC)	hoja ancha
broke (11)	quebrar *(pasado)*
broken (32)	quebrado, quebrada
brook (21)	arroyo
brother's (34)	del hermano
brothers' (34)	de los hermanos

brought (19)   traer *(pasado)*
bruise (22)   magulladura
bubble (8)   burbuja
buffalo (31)   búfalo
build (19)   construir
bunches (15)   montones; racimos
bush (21)   arbusto
business (28)   asunto, negocio
butcher (21)   carnicero
butterfly (CC)   mariposa
button (32)   botón; abrochar
byline (CC)   renglón con nombre de autor

C

cable (11)   cable
cactus (CC)   cacto
cafeteria (CC)   cafetería
camera (25, CC)   cámara
Canada (31)   Canadá
canal (CC)   canal
canoe (31)   canoa; ir en canoa
capacity (CC)   capacidad
care (3)   preocuparse por; preocupación; cuidar
carefully (27)   cuidadosamente
careless (28)   descuidado, descuidada
caribou (CC)   caribú
carnivore (CC)   carnívoro, carnívora
cash (10)   efectivo
catcher (7)   receptor
cathedral (CC)   catedral
caught (25)   agarrar *(pasado)*
celebrated (CC)   célebre
Celsius (CC)   celsius
cement (31)   cemento
ceremony (CC)   ceremonia
certain (20)   seguro, segura
chalkboard (26)   pizarra
change (14)   cambiar
chapter (7)   capítulo
charge (14)   cargar
Chartres (CC)   Chartres
chased (4)   perseguir *(pasado)*
chasing (4)   persiguiendo
cheerful (27)   alegre
childhood (CC)   niñez
children (CC)   niños
Chinese New Year (33)   Año Nuevo Chino

chocolate (7)   chocolate
chop (10)   cortar
chores (CC)   quehaceres
Christmas (33)   Navidad
church (7, CC)   iglesia
circuses (15)   circos
classes (15)   clases
classmate (26)   compañero, compañera
classroom (26)   salón de clases
clear key (CC)   tecla de borrar
climb (2)   escalar
close (23)   cerrar
closer (5)   más cerca
closest (5)   el más íntimo, la más íntima; el más cerca, la más cerca
closet (10)   armario
clothes (23)   ropa
cloud (21)   nube
coal (CC)   carbón
collections (CC)   colecciones
color (32)   color
comb (2)   peinarse; peine
coming (16)   viniendo
common (32)   común
compass (CC)   brújula
compassionate (CC)   compasivo, compasiva
compose (13)   componer
composition (13)   composición
concert (CC)   concierto
conduct (CC)   conducir
confidence (CC)   confianza
confuse (22)   confundir
conifers (CC)   coníferas
Constitution (CC)   constitución
consumers (CC)   consumidores
contest (9)   concurso
cool (22)   fresco, fresca
coordinates (CC)   coordenadas
corn (CC)   maíz
correction (27)   corrección
could've (17)   pudiera haber
counselor (CC)   consejero, consejera
couple (10)   par
course (20)   curso
court (20)   corte
cousin (10)   primo, prima
cover (3)   tapar; cubierta

English	Spanish
crazy (16)	loco, loca
credit (9)	crédito
crosswalks (CC)	cruces de peatones
crowd (21)	multitud
cruise (22)	crucero; hacerun crucero
crumb (13)	migaja
crumble (13)	desmigajar
curfew (22)	toque de queda
current (8, CC)	actual; corriente
curtains (CC)	cortinas
cushion (21)	cojín
cuspid (CC)	colmillo

D

English	Spanish
Dad's (34)	de papá
daily (27)	diario
danced (4)	bailar (*pasado*)
dancing (4)	bailando
danger (11)	peligro
darkness (28)	oscuridad
deadline (CC)	plazo
deal (13)	repartir; tratar con; trato
dealt (13)	repartir; tratar con (*pasado*)
debris (CC)	escombros, desechos
Dec. (33)	dic.
December (25)	diciembre
decide (11)	decidir
decision (CC)	decisión
decomposer (CC)	descomponedor
deeper (5)	más profundo, más profunda
deepest (5)	el más profundo, la más profunda
degrees (CC)	grados
delays (15)	demoras
democratic (CC)	democrático, democrática
demonstrations (CC)	demostraciones
dermis (CC)	dermis
desert (CC)	desierto
design (2)	diseño; diseñar
details (CC)	detalles
determination (CC)	determinación
devastate (CC)	devastar
develops (CC)	desarrolla
didn't (16)	no (*pasado*)
different (8)	diferente
dirty (20)	sucio, sucia
disagree (29, CC)	estar en desacuerdo

English	Spanish
disappear (29)	desaparecer
disappointment (CC)	desilusión
dishonest (29)	deshonesto, deshonesta
dislike (29)	tener aversión a
display (CC)	representación visual
distance (CC)	distancia
distrust (29)	desconfianza
dive (CC)	clavado
divide (CC)	dividir
dividend (CC)	dividendo
divisible (CC)	divisible
division (CC)	división
divisor (CC)	divisor
doctor (32)	doctor, doctora
doesn't (17)	no
dog paddle (CC)	chapotear
dolphin (3)	delfín
donkey (9)	burro
doorbell (26)	timbre
downstairs (26)	piso de abajo
Dr. (33)	Dr.
dribble (CC)	driblear
dried (4)	secar (*pasado*)
driveway (26)	camino de entrada
drove (11)	conducir (*pasado*)
drying (4)	secando
dune (CC)	duna
during (16)	durante

E

English	Spanish
ear canal (CC)	canal auditivo
eardrum (CC)	tímpano
earrings (26)	aretes
earthquake (CC)	terremoto
edge (14)	borde
editors (CC)	editores
elected (CC)	elegido, elegida
electricity (CC)	electricidad
elephant (3)	elefante
eleven (16)	once
emergency (CC)	emergencia
enamel (CC)	enamel
endpoint (CC)	punto final
enemies (15)	enemigos, enemigas
energy (CC)	energía
engine (9)	motor
enough (3)	suficiente
epidermis (CC)	epidermis

equal (14)	igual
equals key (CC)	tecla de resultado
equator (CC)	ecuador
error (CC)	error
especially (31)	especialmente
evening (25)	tarde
evergreens (CC)	árboles de hojas perennes
everybody (25)	todos
everyone (25)	todos
excellent (14)	excelente
except (14)	menos
excited (14)	emocionado, emocionada
excuse (22)	excusa
exhibit (CC)	exhibición
expect (14)	esperar
experiment (CC)	experimento
expert (CC)	experto, experta
explain (14)	explicar
extra (14)	extra
extraordinary (CC)	extraordinario, extraordinaria
eyelashes (15)	pestañas

F

Fahrenheit (CC)	Fahrenheit
fairness (28)	imparcialidad
families' (34)	de las familias
family (CC)	familia
family of facts (CC)	familia de operaciones básicas
family's (34)	de la familia
father (16)	padre
fatter (5)	más gordo, más gorda
fattest (5)	el más gordo, la más gorda
faults (CC)	fallas
favorite (31)	preferido, preferida
Feb. (33)	feb.
February (25)	febrero
federal (CC)	federal
feelings (16)	sentimientos
fence (9)	cerca
ferns (CC)	helechos
fertilize (CC)	fertilizar
few (22)	pocos
field (19)	campo
field goal (CC)	gol de patada
film (CC)	película

finally (25)	finalmente
finger (10)	dedo
first (20)	primero, primera
first aid (CC)	primeros auxilios
flashlight (7)	linterna
floats (CC)	flota
Florida (20)	Florida
flowers (15)	flores
focus (CC)	enfocar
food chain (CC)	cadena alimentaria
food web (CC)	red alimentaria
football (21)	fútbol americano; balón
forecast (CC)	pronóstico
forest (20, CC)	bosque
forgot (10)	olvidar *(pasado)*
form (20)	formulario; formar
foul (CC)	falta
fourteen (20)	catorce
fourth (20)	cuarto
free throw (CC)	tiro libre
freestyle (CC)	estilo libre
friend (19)	amigo, amiga
friend's (34)	del amigo, de la amiga
friends (15)	amigos, amigas
front (CC)	frente
fruit (22, CC)	fruta
fudge (14)	dulce de chocolate
fuel (22)	combustible
fuels (CC)	combustibles
funnier (5)	más gracioso, más graciosa
funniest (5)	el más gracioso, la más graciosa
fur (CC)	piel
furniture (CC)	muebles

G

gallon (32)	galón
gasoline (CC)	gasolina
giant (31)	gigante
giraffe (3)	jirafa
girlfriend (20)	amiga
girl's (34)	de la muchacha
girls' (34)	de las muchachas
glasses (15)	anteojos
goodness (28)	bondad
grandma's (34)	de la abuela
grandpa's (34)	del abuelo
grasshopper (8)	saltamontes

greatness (28)	grandeza		hydroelectric (CC)	hidroeléctrico, hidroeléctrica
grouping (CC)	agrupación			

H

hamster (16)	hámster
hand signal (CC)	señal de mano
Hanukkah (33)	Hanukkah
happened (4)	pasar (pasado)
happening (4)	pasando
happier (5)	más feliz
happiest (5)	el más feliz, la más feliz
headline (CC)	sumario de noticias
heal (13)	sanar
health (13)	salud
heard (19)	oír (pasado)
heart (19)	corazón
he'd (17)	él + (condicional)
height (19, CC)	altura
he'll (17)	él + (futuro)
helmet (CC)	casco
helpless (28)	desamparado, desamparada
hemispheres (CC)	hemisferios
herbivore (CC)	herbívoro
herself (20)	ella misma
hide (11)	esconderse
highway (26)	carretera
hobbies (15)	pasatiempos
hobby (8)	pasatiempo
hockey (9)	hockey
hogans (CC)	hogans
holidays (15)	días de fiesta
home (CC)	hogar
honey (9)	miel
honor (CC)	honor
hopefully (27)	esperanzadamente
hopeless (28)	desesperado, desesperada
hospital (19)	hospital
hotel (16)	hotel
hotter (5)	más caliente
hottest (5)	el más caliente, la más caliente
house (21)	casa
however (21)	como quiera que; sin embargo
huge (22)	enorme
humidity (CC)	humedad
humor (CC)	humor

I

I'd (17)	yo + (condicional)
I'll (17)	yo + (futuro)
I'm (17)	soy, estoy
inactive (29)	inactivo, inactiva
incisor (CC)	incisivo
incomplete (29)	incompleto, incompleta
incorrect (29)	incorrecto, incorrecta
independent (29)	independiente
inner ear (CC)	oído interno
insulation (CC)	insulación
interesting (25)	interesante
intersecting (CC)	cruzando
interview (CC)	entrevista
into (10)	en, por
Inuit (CC)	inuita
invention (27)	invento
invisible (29)	invisible
invite (11)	invitar
iris (CC)	iris
iron (31)	planchar; plancha
island (25)	isla
it's (17)	es

J

January (10)	enero
jaywalking (CC)	cruzar la calle imprudentemente
jewels (CC)	joyas
juice (22)	jugo
July (21)	julio
jump shot (CC)	lanzamiento con salto
June (33)	junio

K

Kansas (3)	Kansas
kayak (CC)	kayac
key sequence (CC)	secuencia de teclas
kicks (CC)	patadas
kitchen (7)	cocina
kneel (2)	arrodillarse
knit (2)	tejer
knob (2)	tirador
knot (2)	nudo
know (2)	saber
known (25)	conocido, conocida
Kwanzaa (33)	Kwanzaa

L

ladies' (34)	de las damas
lady's (34)	de la dama
Lake Erie (CC)	lago Erie
Lake Huron (CC)	lago Huron
Lake Michigan (CC)	lago Michigan
Lake Ontario (CC)	lago Ontario
Lake Superior (CC)	lago Superior
lamb (2)	cordero
landforms (CC)	accidentes geográficos
larger (5)	más grande
largest (5)	el más grande, la más grande
lately (27)	últimamente
latitude (CC)	latitud
laughed (3)	reír (pasado)
lay-up (CC)	(en baloncesto) lanzamiento desde abajo del aro
lazy (16)	perezoso, perezosa
lead (CC)	párrafo introductor
leaders (CC)	líderes
least (9)	el menos, lo menos
length (CC)	largo
lens (CC)	cristalino; lente
let's (17)	vamos a
lettuce (8)	lechuga
librarian (CC)	bibliotecario, bibliotecaria
library (CC)	biblioteca
limb (2)	rama
line (CC)	recta
lion (11)	león
liquid (14)	líquido
local (CC)	local
location (27, CC)	localidad
lock (CC)	esclusa
longitude (CC)	longitud
loose (35)	suelto, suelta
lose (35)	perder
loud (21)	fuerte
love (CC)	amar

M

machine (31)	máquina
magnet (CC)	imán
magnetic field (CC)	campo magnético
magnetism (CC)	magnetismo
marble (CC)	mármol
March (7)	marzo

matter (8)	importar
May (33)	mayo
mean (13)	tener la intención; malo, mala; querer decir
meant (13)	tener la intención (pasado)
Memorial Day (33)	Día de conmemoración de los caídos
memories (15, CC)	recuerdos
memory minus (CC)	tecla de memoria para el signo menos
memory plus (CC)	tecla de memoria para el signo más
memory recall (CC)	tecla de llamada de la memoria
menu (22)	menú
meridians (CC)	meridianos
meteorologist (CC)	meteorólogo, meteoróloga
meter (13)	metro
metric (13)	métrico, métrica
middle ear (CC)	oído medio
might (25)	poder
misbehave (29)	portarse mal
misled (29)	engañar (pasado)
misplace (29)	extraviar
missed (16)	perder; echar de menos (pasado)
misspell (29)	deletrear mal
mistreat (29)	maltratar
model (32)	ejemplo; modelo
moisture (CC)	humedad
molar (CC)	muela
moment (31)	momento
money (9)	dinero
monkey (9)	mono, mona
monkeys (15)	monos, monas
mood (22)	humor
morning (20)	mañana
motor (32)	motor
motorcycle (26)	motocicleta
mountain (21)	montaña
mountains (CC)	montañas
movement (28)	movimiento
Mr. (33)	Sr.
Mrs. (33)	Sra.
Ms. (33)	Srta., Sra.
muffin (3)	panecillo
myself (26)	yo mismo, yo misma
mysteries (15)	misterios

N

natural gas (CC)	gas natural
Navajo (CC)	návajo
needleleaf (CC)	hoja de aguja
negative (CC)	negativo
neighbor (19)	vecino, vecina
nephew (22)	sobrino
nerve (20)	nervio
newspaper (26)	periódico
nighttime (26)	noche
November (33)	noviembre
number (32)	número
number keys (CC)	teclas de números
number sentence (CC)	expresión numérica

O

oak (CC)	roble
October (32)	octubre
odd (8)	raro, rara
of (35)	de
off (35)	apagado, apagada; de
offer (8)	ofrecer
office (CC)	oficina
often (25)	a menudo
oil (CC)	petróleo
oil gland (CC)	glándula sebácea
omnivore (CC)	omnívoro
only (19)	sólo
opened (4)	abrir *(pasado)*
opening (4)	abriendo
operation key (CC)	tecla de operación
optic nerve (CC)	nervio óptico
orchestra (CC)	orquesta
other (32)	otro, otra
our (35)	nuestro, nuestra
outer ear (CC)	oído externo
outside (21)	afuera
oven (32)	horno

P

paddle (8)	remar; canalete
painful (27)	doloroso, dolorosa
panic (CC)	dejarse llevar por el pánico
parallel (CC)	paralelo, paralela
parallel circuit (CC)	circuito paralelo
parallels (CC)	paralelos
parents (CC)	padres
Parthenon (CC)	Partenón

participate (CC)	participar
pavement (28)	pavimento
payment (28)	pago
peace (23)	paz
peaceful (27)	pacífico
pedestrians (CC)	peatones
people (32)	gente; personas
perfect (20)	perfecto, perfecta
perimeter (CC)	perímetro
perpendicular (CC)	perpendicular
photo (3)	foto
pickle (19)	pepino
piece (19, 23)	trozo; pedazo
pint (11)	pinta
pistil (CC)	pistilo
pitcher (7)	lanzador, lanzadora
plains (CC)	praderas
plateau (CC)	meseta
plates (CC)	placas
pocket (3)	bolsillo
point (CC)	punto
polar bear (CC)	oso polar
poles (CC)	polos
pollen (CC)	polen
pollution (27)	contaminación
pond (10)	charco
pore (CC)	poro
portrait (CC)	retrato
pottery (CC)	loza
pour (20)	verter
power (21)	poder; fuerza
powerful (27)	poderoso, poderosa
predator (CC)	depredador, depredadora
pressure (CC)	presión
prey (CC)	presa
prime meridian (CC)	línea de Greenwich
print (CC)	impresión
probably (31)	probablemente
producers (CC)	productores, productoras
products (CC)	productos
proud (21)	orgulloso, orgullosa
psychologist (CC)	sicólogo, sicóloga
pudding (21)	pudín, budín
pueblo (CC)	pueblo
punish (7)	castigar
punishment (28)	castigo

pupil (22, CC)	alumno, alumna; pupilo, pupila

Q

quart (14)	cuarto
queen (14)	reina
quick (14)	rápido, rápida
quiet (35)	silencio; quieto, quieta
quilt (14)	colcha de retazos
quit (35)	abandonar
quite (35)	muy
quotient (CC)	cociente

R

rain gauge (CC)	pluviómetro
rattle (19)	sonaja
ray (CC)	rayo
Rd. (33)	ruta
react (29)	reaccionar
really (25)	verdaderamente
reason (9)	razón
rebound (CC)	rebote
rebuild (29)	reconstruir
recall (29)	recordar
record (3)	disco
recover (CC)	recobrar
reflector (CC)	reflector
relate (13)	relacionarse; contar
relative (13)	pariente
relatives (31)	parientes
relax (14)	relajar
remainder (CC)	residuo
remember (25)	recordar
remote (11)	remoto, remota
replace (29)	reemplazar
represent (CC)	representar
reproduce (CC)	reproducir
republic (CC)	república
rescue (CC)	rescatar
research (CC)	investigar
reservation (CC)	reservación
result (CC)	resultado
retina (CC)	retina
reuse (29)	reusar
Richter scale (CC)	Escala Richter
ridden (8)	montado
rim (CC)	aro
river (10)	río
robbed (4)	robar (pasado)
robbing (4)	robando

rough (3)	desigual; difícil; áspero, áspera

S

sadder (5)	más triste
saddest (5)	el más triste, la más triste
safely (27)	con toda seguridad
sagebrush (CC)	artemisa
said (19)	decir (pasado)
scarier (5)	más espantoso, más espantosa
scariest (5)	el más espantoso, la más espantosa
school (22)	escuela
scrapbook (CC)	libro de recuerdos
scratch (1)	rascar; arañazo
scream (1)	grito; gritar
screen (1)	biombo
scrub (1)	fregar
seal (CC)	foca
season (9)	estación
seed (CC)	semilla
segment (CC)	segmento
seismograph (CC)	sismógrafo
September (33)	septiembre
series circuit (CC)	circuito de series
serve (20)	servir
set (35)	poner
several (25)	varios, varias
shampoo (22)	champú
shared (CC)	compartir
she'll (17)	ella + (futuro)
shelter (7)	refugio
shoot (22)	tirar; sacar una foto
short (7)	corto, corta
shouldn't (17)	no deber
shower (21)	ducha
shown (7)	mostrado
shudder (8)	estremecerse
shutter (CC)	obturador
sign (2, 13)	señal; letrero; seña
signal (13)	señalar; señal
silver (CC)	plata
simple (32)	sencillo, sencilla
siren (CC)	sirena
sit (35)	sentarse
skateboarding (CC)	patinaje
skirt (20)	falda
skyscraper (1)	rascacielos

slam-dunk | they'll

slam-dunk (CC)	(en baloncesto) lanzamiento desde arriba del aro	**strange** (1)	raro, rara
		strategy (CC)	estrategia
slipped (4)	resbalarse *(pasado)*	**strawberry** (1)	fresa
slippers (8)	zapatillas	**street** (1)	calle
slipping (4)	resbalándose	**strength** (1)	fuerza
slowly (27)	despacio	**strengths** (CC)	fuerzas
smaller (5)	más pequeño, más pequeña	**strike** (1)	golpe; golpear; prender un cerillo
smallest (5)	el más pequeño, la más pequeña	**stroke** (CC)	brazada
smoke (11)	humo	**studied** (4)	estudiar *(pasado)*
snack (3)	bocadillo	**studying** (4)	estudiando
snapshot (CC)	fotografía instantánea	**successful** (CC)	exitoso, exitosa
soft (13)	suave; blando, blanda	**sudden** (32)	imprevisto, imprevista
softball (26)	sóftbol	**suddenly** (27)	de repente
soften (13)	suavizar; ablandar	**suffer** (8)	sufrir
softness (28)	suavidad	**suffixes** (15)	sufijos
something (26)	algo	**suit** (22)	traje
sometimes (26)	a veces	**Sun.** (33)	dom.
somewhere (7)	en alguna parte	**supper** (8)	cena
sources (CC)	fuentes	**supplies** (15)	provisiones; materiales para escuela
speak (9)	hablar	**support** (31)	apoyo
special (CC)	especial	**suppose** (31)	suponer
spider web (CC)	telaraña	**surprised** (25)	sorprendido, sorprendida
spores (CC)	esporas	**sweat gland** (CC)	glándula sudorífera
spotless (28)	inmaculado, inmaculada	**swimming** (25)	nadando
square (1)	cuadrado		
squeal (1)	chillido; chillar	**T**	
squeeze (1)	exprimir	**Taj Mahal** (CC)	Taj Mahal
squirm (1)	retorcerse	**taxes** (15)	impuestos
squirt (1)	dejar salir a chorros	**teacher's** (34)	del maestro, de la maestra
stamen (CC)	estambre	**teachers'** (34)	de los maestros, de las maestras
state (CC)	estado	**tears** (CC)	lágrimas
statement (28)	declaración	**temperature** (CC)	temperatura
station (11)	estación	**temple** (CC)	templo
steal (9)	robar; marcharse furtivamente *(pasado)*	**Texas** (14)	Texas, Tejas
steel (CC)	acero	**than** (35)	que
stiff (3)	tieso, tiesa	**that's** (17)	eso es
St. Lawrence Seaway (CC)	Ruta marítima de San Laurencio	**their** (23)	su (de ellos, de ellas), sus (de ellos, de ellas)
stole (11)	robar	**them** (9)	ellos, ellas, los, las, les
stomach (31)	estómago	**then** (35)	entonces; luego
stood (21)	pararse *(pasado)*	**there** (23)	ahí, allí
stopped (4)	cesar; parar; detenerse *(pasado)*	**they** (25)	ellos, ellas
		they'd (17)	ellos + *(condicional)*, ellas + *(condicional)*
stopping (4)	deteniéndose; parando	**they'll** (17)	ellos + *(futuro)*, ellas + *(futuro)*
storm (20)	tormenta		

they're (23)	ellos (ellas) son, ellos (ellas) están
thirsty (20)	tener sed
thoughtful (27)	considerado, considerada
threat (1)	amenaza
thrill (1)	emoción
throat (1)	garganta
throne (23)	trono
through (1)	por, a través de
thrown (1, 23)	tirado, tirada
thumb (2)	pulgar
tigers (15)	tigres
title (32)	título
to (23)	a, hacia
toes (19)	dedos de los pies
tomb (CC)	tumba
tomorrow (8)	mañana
too (23)	también; demasiado, demasiada
took (21)	tomar; llevar (pasado)
tough (10)	duro, dura
track (3)	vía; pista
trash (7)	basura
treads (CC)	pedalea en agua
treat (9)	convidar; tratar; gusto
treatment (28)	tratamiento
tremendous (CC)	tremendo
trouble (10)	preocupar; dificultad
truthfully (27)	verdaderamente
tundra (CC)	tundra
two (23)	dos

U

ugly (16)	feo, fea
unknown (2)	desconocido, desconocida
until (16)	hasta
upon (16)	sobre
upstairs (26)	arriba
useless (28)	inútil
usual (22)	usual
usually (31)	usualmente

V

vacation (11)	vacación
Valentine's Day (33)	día de San Valentín
valley (9)	valle
verify (CC)	verificar
vertex (CC)	vértice
village (14)	pueblo
volcano (CC)	volcán
volume (CC)	volumen

W

walrus (CC)	morsa
want (16)	querer
washed (16)	lavar (pasado)
wasn't (16)	no era, no ser, no estar (pasado)
watch (7)	observar; reloj
water fountain (CC)	fuente de agua
waterway (CC)	vía fluvial
weaknesses (CC)	debilidades
weaving (CC)	tejido
Wed. (33)	miér.
weekend (26)	fin de semana
weekly (27)	semanal
weight (19, CC)	peso
weird (19)	raro, rara
welcome (31)	bienvenido, bienvenida
we'll (17)	nosotros + (futuro), nosotras + (futuro)
went (9)	ir (pasado)
were (35)	ser; estar (pasado, subjunctivo)
we're (35)	somos, estamos
we've (17)	hemos
whale (CC)	ballena
what's (17)	qué es
whatever (7)	todo lo que
wheat (7)	trigo
when (35)	cuando, cuándo
whenever (7)	cuando sea
where (35)	donde, dónde
wherever (7)	donde sea
who's (35)	quien es, quien está
whole (11)	entero, entera
whose (35)	de quien
width (CC)	anchura
wild (11)	salvaje
win (35)	ganar
wind vane (CC)	veleta
window (10)	ventana
with (10)	con
wood (21, 23)	madera
worried (4)	preocupado, preocupada; preocuparse (pasado)

worry | your

worry (8)	preocuparse
worrying (4)	preocupándose
worthless (28)	sin valor
would (23)	*(condicional)*
would've (17)	*(condicional)* + haber
wouldn't (17)	no + *(condicional)*
wreath (2)	guirnalda
wreck (2)	restos (de un auto); accidente
wren (2)	reyezuelo
wrench (2)	llave inglesa
wrist (2)	muñeca
writing (2)	escribiendo
written (8)	escrito, escrita

Y

yesterday (31)	ayer
you'd (17)	tú + *(condicional)*, usted + *(condicional)*
you're (23)	eres, estás
young (10)	joven
your (23)	tu, tus, su, sus